Web Security Basics

Web Security Basics

Shweta Bhasin

WITH NIIT

Premier
Press

The Premier Press logo and related trade dress are trademarks of Premier Press, Inc. and may not be used without written permission. All other trademarks are the property of their respective owners.

Microsoft, Windows, Internet Explorer, Notepad, VBScript, and ActiveX are either registered trademarks or trademarks of Microsoft Corporation in the United States and/or other countries. Netscape is a registered trademark of Netscape Communications Corporation in the U.S. and other countries.

All other trademarks are the property of their respective owners.

Important: Premier Press cannot provide software support. Please contact the appropriate software manufacturer's technical support line or Web site for assistance.

Premier Press and the author have attempted throughout this book to distinguish proprietary trademarks from descriptive terms by following the capitalization style used by the manufacturer.

Information contained in this book has been obtained by Premier Press from sources believed to be reliable. However, because of the possibility of human or mechanical error by our sources, Premier Press, or others, the Publisher does not guarantee the accuracy, adequacy, or completeness of any information and is not responsible for any errors or omissions or the results obtained from use of such information. Readers should be particularly aware of the fact that the Internet is an ever-changing entity. Some facts may have changed since this book went to press.

ISBN: 1-59200-006-1

Library of Congress Catalog Card Number: 2002106531

Printed in the United States of America

03 04 05 06 07 BH 10 9 8 7 6 5 4 3 2 1

Premier Press, a division of Course Technology
2645 Erie Avenue, Suite 41
Cincinnati, Ohio 45208

Publisher:
Stacy L. Hiquet

Marketing Manager:
Heather Hurley

Development Editor:
Vikram Bhatia

Managing Editor:
Heather Talbot

Project Editor:
Kim V. Benbow

Technical Reviewers:
Subramani A and Russ Smith

Interior Layout:
LJ Graphics, Susan Honeywell

Cover Design:
Phil Velikan

Indexer:
Katherine Stimson

Acknowledgements

From Shweta Bhasin:

First and foremost, thanks to my family who has been my strength, driving force and support, tirelessly encouraging me to carry out this project. A special thanks to my father and mother, Jitender and Sudha Bhasin, who spent several sleepless nights just to ensure that I was awake and writing this book. It is their trust and confidence that helped me to work tirelessly and complete this book. A special heart felt thanks to the newest member of my family, my niece Sumedha, whose smile revived me all through this journey.

I would also like to thank our project manager at NIIT, Anita Sastry for all her support and guidance. A special thanks to Vikram Bhatia, for being a wonderful development manager and for his valuable input, without which this book would not have been in its present form. Both Anita and Vikram managed the project meticulously and made sailing so smooth for us.

Thanks to the technical reviewers Subramani A and Russ Smith for their valuable input, and to my colleague Deepshikha Bhatia, whose input has added much value. Thanks are also due to Priyanka Verma for the great illustrations.

Thanks to my editor Kim Benbow for editing our book so well. I would also like to thank Stacy Hiquet for her active support in all development stages of the book.

From Vikram Bhatia:

I would first like to acknowledge Shweta for tirelessly working day and night on this book. Next, I would like to thank Anita Sastry, our project manager at NIIT, for being a constant source of inspiration and guidance.

Our technical reviewers Subramani A and Russ Smith deserve special mention. Without their valuable input, we would not have come out with such a good book. Thanks are also due to Priyanka Verma for the wonderful illustrations.

A special thanks to our wonderful editor Kim Benbow for making our book read so well. And to Stacy Hiquet, for her ever-availability and active support throughout the development of the book.

Last but not the least, a warm thanks to my family, who has endured the late nights and smiled through innumerable lost weekends that I spent writing and getting the book out. I owe a tremendous debt of gratitude to my mom and dad for having faith in me throughout the development of this book. I owe a lot of appreciation to my sister, Deepshikha, for being a constant source of inspiration. And finally, hearty thanks to my fiancée, Monika, for all her support in these months.

About the Author

Shweta Bhasin holds an Advanced Diploma in Software Engineering. She has been with NIIT for the past 2.5 years as a development executive, working in the Knowledge Solutions Business (KSB) division. Her responsibilities include designing, developing, testing, and implementing Instructor Led Training (ILT) courses. She has also authored a book on JavaScript that used a task-based approach to explain concepts typical to the language. In addition, she has also scripted for ILT courses on technologies such as Advanced Java, WAP, and Macromedia Freehand 9. Shweta has also authored an advanced-level textbook on RMI and Corba. She also is an active technical contributor of various articles appearing on the NIIT Web site.

Other than writing, Shweta loves to spend time with her parents and friends. In her free time, she takes a keen interest in needlework and interior designing.

Vikram Bhatia was the development manager for this project. Vikram holds Master's degrees in Computer Applications and Business Administration. In addition, he has completed the GNX diploma in software exports. He is also a Microsoft Certified Professional.

Vikram has authored several ILT courses and books, which include Excel XP VBA, Windows Programming, and Visual Basic 6.0. At NIIT, Vikram has led numerous projects, including the Office XP series, Windows 2000 Security, and a series of textbooks on scripting languages.

When Vikram is not working, you can catch him watching cricket or chatting about cricket.

Contents at a Glance

Contents

Part III   Security Countermeasures 229

Chapter 6   Secure Authentication and Messaging 231

Chapter 7 Understanding Public Key Infrastructure. . . 269

Introduction

The past couple of years have seen a tremendous growth in the World Wide Web. The growth and viability of the IT industry today depends on the Internet becoming a profitable institution. Therefore, more and more Web sites today are offering paid services. With the success online services have enjoyed in the last few years, more and more organizations are looking to use the Internet to expand their business opportunities.

As Web sites opt for commercial viability, the threat of hackers, viruses, or annoyance attacks becomes more pronounced. Organizations face several security-related challenges. The moment you install a Web server at your site, you've opened a window into your local network that the entire Internet can peer through. Most visitors are content to window shop, but a few will try to peek at things that aren't intended for public consumption. Others, not content with looking without touching, will attempt to force the window open and crawl in. The results may differ—for instance, your site's home page may be replaced, or your entire database of customer information may be stolen.

A virus or hacker attack can cost companies and Web site owners millions of dollars. It is because of this that Web security is a major concern for most Web developers. A single break-in that successfully compromises a key e-commerce server can leave an e-business out of business for hours.

This book on Web security is an endeavor to launch a book that offers in-depth knowledge in the simplest way. The book will start by covering basics and then move on to cover the intricacies of securing the data and knowledgebase of an organization.

PART I

Overview of Web Security

Chapter 1

In the past, the primary purpose of computers was to store information that was required by the organization for its daily functioning. Computers were used as mere data center devices, limited to an organization's internal use only. Therefore, computer security threats were uncommon and basically related to the staff of the organization (for example, misuse of accounts, theft, or data manipulation by authorized users). Tackling these threats was easy for organizations as there were almost no chances of an external threat. These threats were generally dealt with by keeping computers with critical information in locked rooms and manually verifying that the data on the computer had not been tampered with.

However, the use of computers since those early days has radically changed. Now organizations use computers to store data that can be accessed from anywhere in the world. In addition, computers are no longer used just in organizations. Computers are widely used by individuals and households to communicate faster across the globe. Due to such extensive use, naturally computer security threats have increased. Many security threats occur in the form of virtual thefts on the Internet. Within seconds, a virtual thief can access a system and steal important information, such as passwords and credit card numbers. Damage can also be done by infiltrating the system and the information on it by passing viruses and worms.

This chapter introduces you to the basic concepts of security. The chapter has been divided into two sections. The first section deals with the need for security and the components themselves that need to be secured on the Web. The second section deals with basic requirements that must be fulfilled for implementing security measures.

Why Do You Need Web Security?

Today, the Internet has become a medium on which people can connect. It is a platform where millions of computers, all over the world, share and access information. E-commerce business transactions, such as online markets, are now a reality. However, with the evolution of the Web and its increased use in every aspect of life, the need for Web security has become imperative (see Figure 1.1).

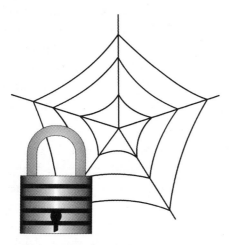

FIGURE 1.1 *Web security*

There are several key concerns related to Web security: How secure are the systems that control the exchange of information on the Web? How secure is the information stored on the numerous computers across the Web? It is a known fact that what can be used can also be misused. For example, e-commerce has made our lives easier, but there are some risks attached. Following this line of thought, we need to plan Web security in an organization at both the system and data levels. Security at the *system* level ensures that your system is not hacked to the extent that it is crashed. Security at the *data* level ensures that information on your system is not tampered with.

You should always remember that if organizational information is hacked either through the network or through other means, it could incur a heavy cost to the company. A failure in network security could also cost the organization in terms of its goodwill and reputation. No other organization would be interested in doing business with an organization that cannot protect its information and security system.

Today, our lives and organizations revolve around computerized systems, such as payroll accounting, inventory control, and transaction-processing systems (for example, airline and railway reservation systems). Can you imagine what would happen if these computerized systems stopped functioning? Life across the world would come to a halt because computerized systems store volumes of information in databases: hospitals store patient histories, banks and credit card companies store personal as well as account details of their customers, and organizations store information about employees, customers, business partners, and future financial and expansion plans. What would happen if a person with malicious intentions accessed this information? This information could be used against these organizations in any manner. A common example of misuse of information can be seen when personal details are used in terrorist attacks. If an attackers were able gain access to the database that manages social security numbers, the personal details of people would be available to them, and they could use this information to impersonate anyone.

Another reason that highlights the need for Web security is the rate at which new technologies (such as languages used to write programs on the Web, or software applications used to provide support and security) are emerging. The complexity of these technologies handling the Web is increasing, while the number of people who really understand how they function is decreasing. Breaches of Internet security are becoming more and more sophisticated, whereas the availability of people who can detect these attacks is scarce. The hacking tools, which are easy to access and use, are highly devastating and hard to detect, increasing the rate of intrusion attempts. There is a common myth that "the more complex a system, the more difficult it is to hack." This myth has not only created an impact on the users of these technologies but has also created an attitude of complacency in the inventors of the complex technologies. However, the more complex a system, the more loopholes and bugs it might have.

Finally, let me summarize the discussion:

- ◆ As use of the Internet spreads, the potential for misusing it has increased. The chances of a security breach are very high if the organizational network is not properly secured.
- ◆ It is important to plan security at the organization level.
- ◆ A security breach incurs a cost for the organization in terms of money as well as goodwill.
- ◆ Databases store confidential and sensitive information. Therefore, it is important to safeguard crucial information from being misused.
- ◆ The more complex a system, the more prone it is to loopholes and bugs. The attitude of security by obscurity should be avoided.

What Is a Breach of Web Security?

A breach of security can be defined as illegal access to information that can result in disclosure, obliteration, or alteration of information (see Figure 1.2). In other words, a security breach occurs when information or systems are used or accessed for illegal purposes or for purposes that they are not supposed to be used for.

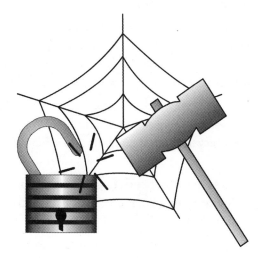

FIGURE 1.2 *A breach of Web security*

A Web security breach can take place in several forms, such as infringement on the network of an organization, hacking into systems or networks, alteration of organizational or individual information, virus attacks, interruption or refutation of services, defacement, and theft. The following are a few common types of security breaches:

◆ **Accessing subscriber details to send spam e-mail.** To promote new offers, a credit card company accesses subscriber details from the database of an e-mail service provider. This pursuit takes place without the knowledge of the service provider.

◆ **Unauthorized access of confidential data to create fraudulent identities.** An individual accesses details, such as residential address, contact numbers, the social security number, and account number details from the database of a bank to create a false identity.

◆ **Eavesdropping.** An intelligence agency of a country connects to the network of another country to access sensitive and confidential defense information.

◆ **Promoting your organization on somebody else's Web site.** An organization sets up a server to host its site on the Web. Another similar organization accesses this Web server by illegal means and hosts a few Web pages on the site to promote its organization.

◆ **Using an automated script to try to log in to a computer system.** A hacker uses an automated script to make various attempts to log in to a computer system. As a result, the authorized users are denied logon services by the computer because the computer is busy in denying the requests of the hacker.

◆ **Gaining unauthorized access to a mail server.** An individual gains unauthorized access to the mail server of an organization to send and receive e-mail messages.

◆ **Gaining unauthorized access to the network to gain information.** Individuals breaking into the network of a bank or a finance firm to transfer a large sum of money to a fictitious account.

◆ **Virus attacks.** Viruses usually spread via e-mail messages. A virus attack can also occur in an organization's network, and through that network it spreads over the Internet.

◆ **DNS hijacking.** *Domain Name System (DNS)* is a database that maps domain names to IP addresses. Computers that are connected to the Internet use DNS to resolve URLs to the IP addresses of the sites that need to be accessed. In DNS hijacking, the hacker gains access to DNS services and makes changes in the information that maps a domain name to an IP address. Due to this, users are directed to a different site than the one they want to access.

◆ **DoS attacks.** *Denial-of-service (DoS)* attacks are network-based attacks in which authorized users are denied the use of network services. DoS attacks occur because of various reasons, such as the unauthorized use of resources. A common example of a DoS attack is an unauthorized user using your ftp location to upload large volumes of data. This causes unnecessary blockage of disk space and generates network traffic.

◆ **DDoS attacks**. *Distributed denial-of-service (DDoS)* attacks are a sophisticated form of DoS attacks. In a DDoS attack, the target system is attacked from several computers across the Internet. Without the owner's knowledge, the hacker creates an application and places the application in multiple locations across the Internet. Such applications go undetected, as they do not harm the system on which they reside. When the attack is launched, the target system is compromised from all the different computers that have this application installed.

DDoS attacks are extremely difficult to detect, as the attack is not coming from one source. Without the knowledge of its owner, if a computer is being used to launch attacks on other networks, the owner of the used computer should treat this as a compromise.

The owners of the target system can take legal action against the compromised system. This is because it is expected out of every system on the network to safeguard its resources from being used by unfair means. If a system fails to do so, it is also held responsible for the attack even though it is not a known party to the attack.

 NOTE

In the preceding explanation, the target system is the system that is attacked. The compromised system is the system that is used in the distributed DoS attack.

◆ **Breaking into the physical boundaries of an organization**. The office of an organization is broken into and the hard disks of the database server are physically removed and stolen.

What Needs to Be Secure on the Web?

To ensure Web security, you need to understand exactly what needs to be secured. However, from the previous discussion, you must have gotten a fair idea of what is insecure on the Web. The Web is an ocean of information where individuals and organizations connect to each other through different networks. Therefore, whether it is an individual or an organization, security on the Web mostly implies security of information. However, from the perspective of the Web, three areas need to be secured:

◆ A *client*

◆ A *server*

◆ A *network*

Before identifying the various security threats for each of these components of the Web, I'll briefly discuss how these components interact in the Web architecture. The client sends a request to the server by entering a URL in a Web browser. By default, the request is first directed to the DNS server. The DNS server translates the domain name in the URL to the IP address of the Web site that the client has requested. Using the IP address, a connection is established with the server that hosts the Web site and a request is sent to the Web server for the Web page. The Web server sends the requested Web page to the client. The browser then displays the Web page on the screen. This interaction between the client and the server is facilitated by several networks that link all the computers on the net.

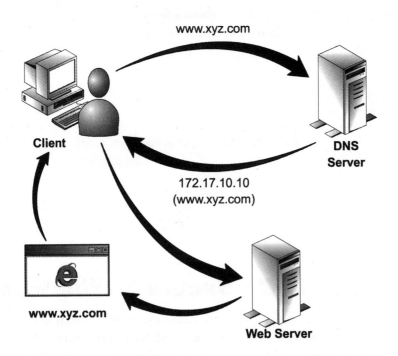

FIGURE 1.3 *The Web architecture*

Figure 1.3 displays the various components of the Web that need to be secured from revelation, obliteration, or alteration of information.

The following are the security threats that each of the above components face in the Web environment:

♦ **Threats on the client side**. The computer at the client end is vulnerable to virus attacks by hackers, crackers, or malicious codes. In addition, a client on the Web is prone to infringement of personal information or identification.

♦ **Threats on the server side**. Data on Web servers is exposed to unauthorized access. There might be an intrusion of the server that could lead to a reduction in speed or, in the worst cases, the server could crash. In addition, server resources might be used for purposes other than those for which it was intended.

♦ **Network threats**. A network on the Web, if not secured properly, can become the root cause for infringement of information. This is because the network is the entry point to computer systems. A weak network can cause the data being transferred from the source computer to the destination computer to be easily modified and tampered with. Hackers can also use your computer resources by breaking into the network. Most cases of fraudulent identities and eavesdropping occur mostly because of a loophole in network security.

Can the Web Be Secure?

Absolute security on the Web is impossible. However, it is not a futile endeavor. You can enforce the maximum possible security in a cost- and time-effective manner. Security is not only a goal but an absolute requirement that is proactive. To enforce the maximum possible security, some serious changes need to be made, including improving public awareness about this problem. We need to change the attitude that "security of the Internet will be taken care of by experts." The saying, "Prevention is a key to security" is also applicable to the Web. A classic comparison is the precautions that we take while crossing a road: To avoid accidents, we always look both ways before crossing. Similarly, if we apply the same approach toward Web security, many problems can be easily avoided. The Computer Emergency Response Team/Coordination Center (CERT/CC) at Carnegie-Mellon University (CMU) has estimated that 80 percent or more of the problems reported are due to poorly chosen passwords.

Another aspect of human nature that promotes security threats on the Web is that organizations are fearful to share information on any security attack. A security breach on a Web site becomes front-page news for the media. However, if an internal system of an organization is cracked, it is somehow avoided in the media. Organizations simply deny any security breach incident to save their reputation and goodwill in the eyes of prospective partners or customers. However, this attitude deprives the security community of much needed statistics and data.

Lastly, Web security must be a collective effort. Everyone needs to be security-conscious. Security is possible only if individuals from all sections—from users to administrators to top management—take it seriously. No one individual can solve security problems. The bright side is that many users are security-conscious, and this number is growing with each passing day. As public awareness increases, reports related to security problems will decrease.

In the previous sections, stress was laid on the importance and relevance of Web security. You also identified the various security threats that an individual or an organization can face while accessing the Internet. The next section discusses the aspects of security that help in planning and implementing security measures in the Web environment.

Aspects of Web Security

While implementing Web security, you need to consider two important aspects. The first includes defining the purpose of security. The second aspect includes establishing a *security equation*. A security equation involves identifying the critical information that needs to be secured and the level to which it should be secured.

Purpose of Web Security

Though I have already discussed the need for Web security, this section will throw light on the purpose of Web security (see Figure 1.4). Web security is essential in order to implement

- ◆ Confidentiality
- ◆ Integrity
- ◆ Availability
- ◆ Authentication

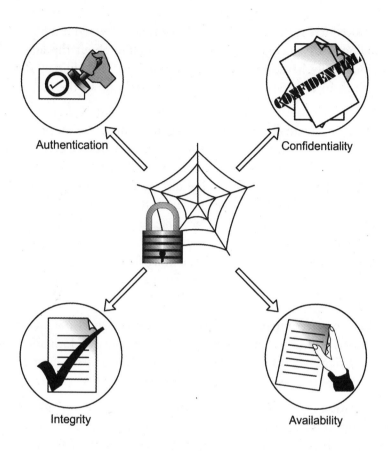

FIGURE 1.4 *Ensuring confidentiality, integrity, availability, and authentication*

Confidentiality

The term *confidentiality* refers to securing critical information from disclosure to unauthorized users. The extent to which confidentiality should be maintained depends upon the type of information you are trying to secure. For instance, there is a high level of confidentiality required when the annual report of an organization (which is not yet released to the public) is transmitted on the Web. Conversely, the confidentiality level required is comparatively low when a previous quarterly earnings report (which has already been released to the public) is transmitted.

The type of information an organization shares with its employees, and conversely with people outside the organization, is another example that illustrates the difference in levels of confidentiality maintained. An organization would share all policies and procedures with its employees. In contrast, it would not like to share such information with outsiders. Similarly, information about the appraisal of employees would only be accessible to supervisors and the Human Resources department. Such information would not be accessible to all the employees of the company.

Infringement in confidentiality can have a negative impact on an organization. However, the impact of such damage depends on the importance of the information that is disclosed. Therefore, different levels of confidentiality should be maintained for different types of information. For instance, if the details of prospective customers and the offers made by an organization to the customers are disclosed to a competitor, the organization could incur heavy business losses. Also, if the appraisal information of all employees is somehow leaked to all employees of the company, it would cause distrust and unrest among them.

Integrity

The term *data integrity* implies ensuring that information is not modified by unauthorized users. It is essential to maintain the integrity of information on the Web if you don't want that information to be misinterpreted by the intended audience. The following are a few common ways that data integrity is often breached:

◆ **Modification of an audit report**. An audit report of an organization is important to the stockholders, the clients, the management, and the employees. If there is any unauthorized modification of data and figures, they would not reflect the correct picture of the organization.

◆ **Modifications in bank accounts**. If modifications are made to reflect higher figures in the existing cash balance of a savings account, a bank may incur heavy losses.

◆ **Modifications to the content of a news site**. If the content of a news site is modified and fictitious news is published, it could create havoc and confusion in the minds of the readers.

A breach of data integrity may not always be an intentional act. Mistakes can occur at the time data is entered and stored in databases. For example, a data entry operator could type in incorrect figures that might reflect the losses of the company as profits. Data integrity might be lost if the files or systems become corrupt or are completely destroyed.

The impact of the damage caused by data integrity infringement depends on the criticality of the information that is modified.

Availability

Ensuring the availability of data or information implies that the data or information is available for use whenever the need arises. In the context of Web security, it essentially means placing the security systems at such points that it prevents any unauthorized activity resulting in the nonavailability of information. The term *availability* is not limited to the availability of information; it includes the availability of systems and the other resources required to access the information.

In addition, ensuring the availability of information includes ensuring that users are not deprived of services when they are required. A denial of service occurs when the system is swamped with requests from unauthorized users and, as a result, authorized users are unable to access the system.

Authentication

If you want to avoid hackers infiltrating your system or network, it is essential to check the authenticity of users. *Authentication* is a mechanism for ensuring that an individual who is trying to access a resource on the Web is who he or she actually claims to be. It is also implies ensuring that only authorized individuals are permitted to access information.

A Security Equation

Establishing a security equation is another important aspect of planning and implementing Web security measures. It is basically a part of the risk management process. Risk management primarily involves determining what is to be secured along with the corresponding security measures that need to be implemented in a cost-effective manner. Determining a security equation entails rigorous analysis in context of the cost involved in implementing the security measures and the expected benefits of those measures.

The aim of establishing a security equation should be to maintain a balance between the cost incurred and the benefits reaped. This implies that extra care should be taken while incurring a cost on implementing security measures. Organizations should reap equal (if not more) benefits from that cost.

The following factors should be considered while determining a security equation:

◆ The tangible value of the information

◆ The perceived value of the information

◆ The cost of securing the information

◆ The cost if security is breached

The Tangible Value of Information

Tangible value refers to the actual value of the information that an organization wants to secure. Determining the actual value of information is not an easy task because, unlike physical assets, it is not always possible to determine a fixed monetary value for information (see Figure 1.5). The value of information for an organization is always relative and depends on various factors. The following are a few factors that determine the value of information:

◆ The market value of information, or the price at which the information can be sold in the market.

◆ The cost involved in attaining the information.

◆ The cost incurred to restore the information (in case the information is lost)

◆ The cost of operations, including the cost of all operations affected due to the information loss.

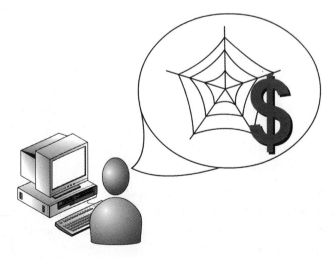

FIGURE 1.5 *The tangible value of information*

The Perceived Value of Information

The *perceived value of information* refers to the gain that a user would derive upon attaining the information through unfair means (see Figure 1.6). For example, consider that an employee sells important information about an organization to a rival organization. In this case, the perceived value of information would be the dollar amount the employee gets after selling the information.

Like tangible value, the perceived value of information also depends on various factors. One of these is the manner in which the information sold is used. In other words, the perceived value may be different for different users. Consider another example: Someone steals software that has been custom-developed for an organization for a transaction processing system. If the stolen software were sold to a similar organization, its perceived value would be high, as the rival organization could save the money that it would otherwise need to develop the software. On the other hand, the perceived value of information would not be very high if the software were sold to an organization that did not use it.

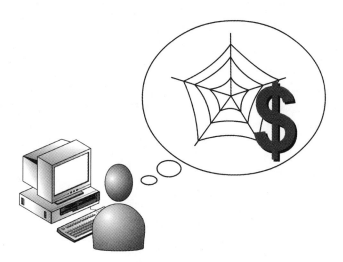

FIGURE 1.6 *The perceived value of information*

The Cost of Securing Information

The *cost of securing information* includes the total resources, monetary or nonmonetary, invested in deploying measures to secure information. The nonmonetary resources include the time and effort spent in deploying, maintaining, and monitoring security systems. The cost of deploying and maintaining security controls should be less than or equal to the value of information that it is protecting (see Figure 1.7).

FIGURE 1.7 *The cost of securing information*

The Cost of Breaching Security

The *cost of breaching security* includes the cost that an intruder would have to incur to break into a system and access the information. For instance, to gain access to some important information, an organization may employ people to hack into the security system of another organization. The cost of breaching security would thus include the salary that the organization pays to these people, the tools deployed to hack the system, and the cost of the time spent in hacking (see Figure 1.8).

FIGURE 1.8 *The cost of breaching security*

Defining a Security Equation

While defining a security equation, organizations need to consider the following factors:

◆ An organization must evaluate the value of assets (both perceived and tangible). Then it should evaluate the costs of existing security controls compared to the new controls (in case it plans to deploy any). This can be accomplished by appointing a risk management team.

◆ An organization should ensure that the cost of securing information is less than or equal to the tangible value of information. This implies that the value of the resources spent on securing information should not exceed the loss that an organization may suffer if the security of information is breached (see Figure 1.9).

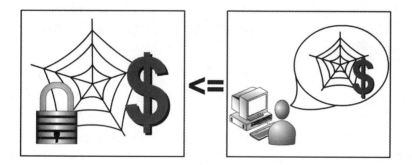

FIGURE 1.9 *The cost of securing information should be less than the tangible value of information.*

◆ The cost of breaching information should be greater than the perceived value of information. This implies that the cost an intruder would incur to hack into a security system should be greater than the benefits the intruder would derive upon selling that information (see Figure 1.10).

FIGURE 1.10 *The cost of breaching information should be greater than the perceived value of information.*

◆ If you can ensure that the security controls deployed incur a certain amount of costs to penetrate, the value of the information gained by breaching these controls should be lower. This would maintain security. For example, why would a hacker spend $100 to get information worth only $10?

Summary

This chapter dealt with the basic concepts of Web security. The first section defined the need for Web security. It also defined a breach of security and listed the common types of breaches. The second section discussed two aspects of security: the goals of security and the security equation.

Check Your Understanding

Short Questions

1. What do you understand by breach of Web security? Briefly list five instances that reflect a breach of Web security.

2. Identify the components that need to be secured on the Web. Also, briefly state the threats that each one of these components confront?

3. What are the two aspects that need to be considered while implementing Web security?

4. What is the purpose of Web security?

5. Define *security equation* and list the factors that need to be considered while determining a security equation.

Answers

Short Answers

1 A breach of Web security takes place when information or systems are used or accessed for illegal purposes. The following are instances of security breaches:

   • Accessing subscriber details to send spam e-mail.

   • Unauthorized access of confidential data to create fraudulent identities.

   • Gaining unauthorized access to a mail server.

   • Using automated script to try to log in to a computer system.

   • DoS and DDoS attacks.

2. The components that need to be secured on the Web are the client, server, and network. Threats on the client side include virus attacks by hackers, malicious code, and infringement of personnel information or identification. Threats on the server side include unauthorized access on the server that may result in reduction in speed. Network threats include utilizing network resources for purposes other than those they are intended for.

3. The two aspects that need to be considered while implementing Web security are the purpose of that security and how a security equation is established.

4. It is essential to implement Web security because of the following reasons:

   • Confidentiality

   • Integrity

   • Availability

   • Authentication

5. A security equation implies maintaining a balance between the cost incurred on implementing security and the benefits derived from it. The following factors should be considered while determining a security equation:

- The tangible value of information
- The perceived value of information
- The cost of securing information
- The cost if security is breached

Chapter 2

*Common Threats
on the Web*

The previous chapter introduced you to the basic concepts of Web security. This chapter goes a step further and identifies common threats on the Web, classifying them into various categories.

Threats and Vulnerabilities

In the context of IT security, you may define threats as acts or events, internal or external, that can cause harm to systems, associated applications, or information. Internal or external means a threat may occur from either inside or outside an organization. A threat may cause an unauthorized disclosure, maneuvering, disruption, or destruction of information and systems. Computer Emergency Response Team (CERT 1993) defines a threat as "any circumstances or event that has the potential to cause harm to a system or network."

You can classify threats as physical or electronic. Physical threats damage machines and links (destruction of communication equipment). Electronic threats can be done by hackers through malicious applications, which may take the form of viruses, worms, Trojan horses, or attack scripts. Electronic threats have the ability to cause greater harm than physical threats. Consider an example: A computer program whose only function is to steal secrets from organizations' computers can cause greater harm to an organization compared to a small theft caused by an employee of that organization.

A threat occurs when vulnerability exists in a system or a network. At times, vulnerability may not exist, but a system is always open to threats.

Vulnerability is a flaw or loophole in a system or program that facilitates an attacker to enter a security system. Computer Emergency Response Team (CERT 1993) defines vulnerability as "an aspect of a system or network that leaves it open to attack."

Vulnerabilities can be known or unknown. *Known vulnerabilities* are those that are known at the time of manufacturing. For example, suppose the operating systems that an organization is using have known flaws in them. However, the organization is not aware of these flaws and continues to use the operating systems without taking preventive action. Due to this ignorance, the organization faces several threats. Intruders, who are aware of the loopholes in the operating system, try to take maximum advantage and thus cause damage to the information and the systems. This is a typical case of known vulnerability. Most known vulnerabilities lead to security threats because organizations don't abide by accepted security practices.

Unknown vulnerabilities are those that exist in systems but remain undetected by manufacturers. Consider another example: Suppose an organization is using operating systems that have flaws. However, these flaws are neither known to the organization nor to the manufacturer. An intruder, who is trying to hack into the organization's network, comes across the bugs and through them finds a way to access organization's information. In this case, if the intruder is a white hat hacker, he may inform the organization about the flaw in the system. However, if the intruder is a person with malicious intent, he may try to take maximum advantage of the flaw to jeopardize the information system of the organization.

 NOTE

White hat hackers are computer professionals who use their skills and knowledge to find and report new security vulnerabilities in the systems and networks of organizations. The intent of the explorations and experiments done by these professionals is to find how things work. If they find any bugs, they report them to the people concerned and, if possible, also provide solutions.

I would like to recapitulate the preceding discussion by saying that all vulnerabilities whether in the form of bugs, loopholes, flaws, or ignorance, act as an entry point for intruders.

Types of Threats

The Web is prone to a variety of threats, including computer fraud, espionage, vandalism, defacement, computer viruses, and other hacking attempts. As the world's reliance on the Web continues to increase, these threats are becoming pervasive and increasingly sophisticated. Based on their nature and source, I have classified attacks on the Web under the following broad categories:

- Accidental threats
- Malicious threats
- Authorization threats
- Application threats
- Privacy threats
- Access control threats

Each preceding category, in turn, comprises several subgroups, which are examined below.

Accidental Threats

As the name suggests, *accidental threats* encompass unplanned and unintentional threats. These threats cover problems that generally arise from human error, such as poor password choices, accidental or mistaken business transactions, an accidental disclosure of information, and the use of erroneous or obsolete software. Accidental threats generally arise due to a lack of awareness about online security systems, the inappropriate configuration of security devices, and information leakage resulting from insecure information transfer.

Malicious Threats

Malicious threats include attacks that are specially intended to cause harm to people, systems, and the networks of organizations. Malicious attacks can be subgrouped into the following two categories:

- Malicious software
- Social engineering threats

Malicious Software

Malicious software is a set of code purposely written to cause harm to a system or network. Viruses, worms, and Trojans are typical examples of malicious software programs.

The term *virus* is often used as a common reference to any malicious code. However, this is not correct. There is some degree of difference between viruses, worms, and Trojans. However, when it comes to quoting examples of viruses, the three terms are used interchangeably.

Virus

A virus is a small program that infects computers by replicating and attaching itself to other files. When an infected file is opened, the virus executes in the background without the user's knowledge. For a more detailed account, see the section, "Viruses," later in this chapter.

Trojan

A Trojan is a destructive program that masquerades as a useful or benign program. The main aim of a Trojan is to gather information from the computer. An example of a Trojan can be a program that masquerades as a signon screen and grabs the user's password when it is typed. However, unlike viruses, Trojans don't replicate themselves.

Trojans generally appear as games or valid programs; therefore, users install Trojans thinking they are legitimate programs. For example, a user might receive an e-mail message from an unknown sender. The message has a game attached. When the user executes the game, the Trojan is executed. Trojans can be hidden in any software.

Worm

Worms are programs that replicate themselves from computer to computer but do not infect other programs. The basic damage caused by worms is in terms of lost CPU time and the hours spent trying to eliminate them from the system.

Unlike viruses, worms do not use a host file to spread themselves. But worms generally exist inside documents only. The difference between viruses and worms is in the manner in which both use the host file. Worms usually release the document to which they are attached. This document then travels from one computer to another across networks. This implies that if a document has a worm attached, then that document, as a whole, should be considered a worm. However, a virus spreads from one document to other.

An example of a worm is the code red worm, which was one of the most destructive worms that affected Microsoft Internet Information Servers (IIS) across the globe. It defaced Web sites with a message, "Hacked By Chinese," and it spread at an alarming rate. Some 90,000 computers running IIS on the Internet were affected in only about 4 hours. The effect was so intense that many organizations involved in Internet security, such as SANS, CERT, Microsoft, and even the FBI, issued alert bulletins to people all over the world.

Social Engineering Threats

Securing computers on the Web is similar to creating a shield around networks to protect them from the outside world. Unfortunately, regardless of how much money and time is spent on securing networks, one factor that is always neglected—human psychology. By employing a technique known as *social engineering*, many attackers and hackers use this factor to bypass the most stern defense systems.

Social engineering may be defined as the art of using interpersonal skills for extracting confidential information. It basically involves an outsider fooling an organization's personnel into providing proprietary information or allowing unauthorized access to resources.

Social engineering has been defined by various authors. One of these definitions is as follows:

> Social engineering can be regarded as 'people hacking,' basically hacker jargon for soliciting unwitting participation from a person inside a company rather than breaking into the system independently.
>
> —VIGILANTe. http://www.vigilante.com/inetsecurity/socialengineering.htm.

Harl in *People Hacking: The Psychology of Social Engineering* has very appropriately defined social engineering as "the art and science of getting people to comply to your wishes." For further reference, you can refer to the article written by Harl at http://packetstorm.decepticons.org/docs/social-engineering/aaatalk.html.

Common Techniques Used in Social Engineering

A social engineer can deploy a variety of techniques, their impact depending upon the engineer's skill and the ability to convince people. A good social engineer may begin by researching the target organization to obtain an idea of its basic structure and names of the employees. The information obtained from such research may not immediately help the intruder, but it may help him later to obtain further information. The intruder may then use different techniques to achieve his objective.

Each technique deployed in social engineering may be classified into two categories: human-based attacks and computer-based attacks. The human-based attack uses interpersonal skills, relationships, and deception to obtain information. This type of attack is a test for the engineer in terms of how well he can flatter, intimidate, or lie. For instance, an intruder impersonating a bank customer makes a phone call to a bank employee. The intruder cooks up a story and eventually asks for the relevant account number and password. The employee innocently gives away the information thinking the intruder is a real customer. The employee realizes his or her mistake only when the authentic customer reports a misappropriation of funds in the account.

The computer-based attack is based on technology and tricks people into supplying information. For example, a Web user may encounter a window displaying the message "Network connection lost. Please reenter your user name and password to reconnect." Once the user supplies the password, the information is e-mailed back to the intruder.

Following are the most common techniques used in social engineering:

- ◆ **Direct approach**. The social engineer may directly ask the target about some information. Calling the receptionist of an organization and asking for user names and passwords is an example of the direct approach. In most cases, this approach does not succeed, as people today are security-conscious and wary of providing such information.

- ◆ **Significant employee**. Another technique of social engineering is pretending to be a senior official of an organization. Usually, subordinates or the employees in lower ranks obey the orders of senior officials in the organization. Taking advantage of this, the intruder pressures subordinates by imposing important deadlines, thereby managing to extract important information about the type of remote access software used in the organization, how to configure it, telephone numbers of the RAS (Remote Access Server) server, and the user name and password used to log in to the server. After obtaining this information, the intruder might set up remote access to the organization's network.

- ◆ **New and helpless employee**. In this technique, the intruder pretends to be an employee who needs help to access an organization's resources. This type of attack is simple. An attacker calls the secretary of an organization, pretending to be a new temporary employee who is having trouble accessing the organization's network. The secretary, not wanting to offend or appear incompetent, may tend to help out by giving away the user name and password of an active account or even her own account.

◆ **Help desk.** The intruder pretends to belong to an organization's technical support team and extracts information from innocent and ignorant employees by pretending to be a system administrator trying to solve a network problem. To solve the problem, he asks for user names and passwords.

◆ **Reverse Social Engineering (RSE).** With RSE, the user is manipulated into asking the intruder questions that, in turn, reveal information about the organization. In this approach, the intruder usually impersonates a senior official. A typical RSE attack consists of three parts: sabotage, advertising, and assisting. The intruder sabotages the workstation of the user or gives it the appearance of being corrupted. Seeing this, the user looks for help. In order to ensure that the user calls the intruder (rather than authentic technical support staff), the intruder advertises his presence either by leaving his business card on the workstation or displaying his contact number on the error message itself. Finally, the intruder assists the target in solving the problem, thereby obtaining the information he requires.

◆ **E-mail cons.** An e-mail con involves the use of contemporary subjects to elicit emotions that may lead to unconscious participation from the user. For example, a user might receive an e-mail message from a reputable Web site that discusses sensitive issues about child labor. The site promises to pay prize money if the user answers a few questions. It also asks the user to fill out a form, attached in the e-mail message, so that it can ensure the prize money goes only to the intended recipient. Such e-mails could be a hoax, their only intended purpose being to gather information about the user or his organization.

◆ **Web site scams.** A common type of Web site scam is frame-spoofing. *Frame-spoofing* takes advantage of the vulnerabilities existing in Web sites. For example, an intruder might want to obtain information about credit card numbers. To obtain this information, the intruder inserts a fake frame into the Web site of a famous e-commerce site. The insertion of the page is done so well that there is no mark of infringement on the site. The customers who visit the site, unaware of such intrusions, provide their credit card numbers and other details during the course of transactions. In this manner, the intruder is able to obtain the required information.

Another common Web site scam works by embedding illegal content, such as pornographic ads in seemingly legitimate Web pages. For example, a perpetrator might host a legitimate news site but embeds the pages with JavaScript content that pops up porn ads. When a user does a search on such news sites, he sees a page listed with a valid name, but when he opens the page it reveals something illegal.

Another similar Web site scam is related to maligning ISPs. A user may receive e-mail from his ISP with the following message: "According to our records, payment for your Internet access account is late. Perhaps you overlooked it? It is important that you contact us as soon as possible. To update your account information, please go to http://www.newpqrxyz. com. When the user clicks on the link, it takes the user to an illegal site.

Authorization Threats

Authorization threats are an outcome of hackers posing as authorized users. A common authorization attack is when an intruder cracks the network password of a user and logs in to the system. Intruders use various methods (such as a dictionary attack or password-cracking utilities, covered in more detail below) to crack passwords.

Password Cracking

Cracking passwords is a pursuit undertaken by both intruders and system administrators of organizations. While intruders crack passwords to gain unauthorized entry, system administrators crack passwords for security reasons. System administrators need to ensure that the network passwords used are not easily decipherable to maintain security. Therefore, they frequently hack passwords to qualify the passwords' rigidity.

To understand password-cracking techniques, you need know the concept of *hashing*. When an account is created, the user is given a login ID and a password, and the details are stored in a database. However, password information is not stored in the database in its original form. Instead, the password is encrypted and stored in the form of a *hash*.

A hash is an encryption algorithm. Usually, in databases, hashing is done by adding or replacing a random set of characters to the original set of characters. For example, suppose the password you use is Maria and you have entered the house number in the address field as 497. The hashed password may be encrypted as 45M64a8ri12a.

However, a core cryptographic hash function takes an input of any length and generates an output, known as the *hash value*, of fixed length. The function is known, and it is impossible to compute the original input from the hash value. For example, if you take a hash function F and give it input x, the resulting output h, which is calculated as F(x)=h is a one-way transformation. This implies that even if you know the function F and the output h you cannot calculate x from F and h.

To crack passwords or hashes, intruders use *password cracker* utilities. There are several of these utilities (sold by different vendors) available in the market. Most utilities operate by encrypting thousands of passwords into hashes. They then compare the resultant hashes with the hashes stored in the database. While comparing the hashes, the utility either uses a particular logic or tries all possible combinations until all the passwords are cracked.

Another technique used by an intruder for hacking passwords is the *dictionary attack*. Initially, the term dictionary attack was limited to finding the passwords in a specific list, such as a dictionary, and then checking the validity of each by trial and error. If the password of the system being attacked matched a word present in the dictionary, the intruder was successful in getting into the system. Dictionary attacks are successful only if common words are used for passwords.

The following are some common dictionary attacks:

- ◆ **Short attacks.** Unlike normal dictionary attacks, where a set of passwords is tried on one system, in the short dictionary attack, a small dictionary is tried against several systems.

- ◆ **Brute force attacks.** This is a sophisticated form of a traditional dictionary attack performed by internal intruders who want additional privileges and permissions on a network. In a brute force attack, the intruder first obtains a list of used passwords from bona fide sources. He then hashes these passwords using encryption schemes supported by the system being attacked. The resultant encrypted hash values are then compared with the hash passwords stored in the database. The comparison is successful whenever the hash value from the dictionary matches the hash value in the database.

Application Threats

In the early days of the Internet, Web sites only displayed static pages. Altering the code of these Web sites was easy because most of it could be viewed. However, it was not possible to compromise the security of the applications or platforms on which the Web sites were running. Sound network, platform, and physical security were enough to protect these applications against any security threat.

Today, many Web sites are used for e-commerce purposes and are dynamic. Most of these consist of applications that can interact with each other, with database servers, and with other computers. These applications also contain several objects that can be easily compromised. Several security mechanisms—such as firewalls that permit only certain ports to be accessed by the outside world and operating system security safeguarding systems and networks from within—protect against most vulnerability on the Web. However, situations may arise where a hacker may access system resources by entering through the very port that is open for the Web site to operate. Through this port, hackers can attack the applications running on a Web site.

 NOTE

A port is an interface that enables you to connect devices to computers, such as disk drives, monitors, keyboards, modems, printers, and other peripheral devices.

In the context of TCP/IP, a port is a logical connection place. For example, for connecting a client to the server using TCP/IP, the server application will accept a TCP/IP connection from the client only to a specified port. Applications that use Hypertext Transfer Protocol as the Web protocol typically use port 80 to connect to a Web server as, by default, most Web servers run on port 80.

Having identified the importance of securing applications, let me now acquaint you with some of the more common application threats, listed below:

◆ Privilege elevation
◆ Third-party and customized software vulnerabilities

◆ Denial of Service (DoS)

◆ Distributed Denial of Service (DoS)

◆ DNS hijacking

◆ Web server vulnerabilities

◆ Session hijacking

◆ E-mail attacks

NOTE

In this section, the focus will be on discussing application threats apart from a denial-of-service attack, a distributed denial-of-service attack, and DNS hijacking. For a detailed discussion of these threats, please refer to Chapter 1, "Security: An Overview."

Privilege Elevation

Privilege elevation occurs when an intruder is able to increase his or her system rights and permissions to a level higher than what they should be. If this type of attack is successful, then the intruder may be able to gain privileges and access levels as high as the root directory of a UNIX system or administrative rights on a Windows 2000 machine.

Third-Party and Customized Software Vulnerabilities

Service providers often use software developed by third-party vendors and customize the software according their own needs. However, third-party and customized software programs contain several loopholes, providing opportunities to penetrate systems on a network. Therefore, looking at the vulnerabilities, it is essential to create, use, and maintain secure HTTP (Hypertext Transfer Protocol) applications. As the name suggests, HTTP is a protocol that manages the transfer of hypertext between computers over the Internet. Hypertext is text in the form of graphical or textual links that, when clicked, takes the user to other resources, such as HTML documents, text files, graphics, animations, or sound.

Web Server Vulnerabilities

Many instances of vulnerabilities discovered in Web servers exist because servers provide more than one service at a time, even if those services are not required.

From a security perspective, a server should be dedicated to provide only one service at a time. For instance, if a server's primary purpose is to host Web sites, then it should close all other services that are not in use. If the other services are not closed, then they may cause a security compromise, as the attacker might use the other services to launch an attack.

Another loophole reported in Web servers is that they allow intruders to bypass access restrictions for files with long names. In addition, some Web servers provide root-level access that may pose a major threat. Providing root-level access is similar to providing administrative-level access. If an administrator does not restrict access levels in a server and gives administrative privileges to all users, it is, indeed, a cause for grave security concern, as all users have unrestricted rights to information on the server.

Web servers also face threats from poorly written CGI scripts. CGI is a server-side scripting language that enables Web pages to be interactive and dynamic. Most Web servers use CGI as its default server-side scripting language. CGI by itself is a secure scripting language. However, poorly written CGI scripts have certain loopholes due to which Web servers have become prone to vulnerabilities. For example, CGI scripts reflect features of Web servers and if these are not written well, they invite the attention of intruders. Poorly written CGI scripts can give attackers the opportunity to check on server capabilities and thus manipulate it.

Session Hijacking

HTTP protocol is a stateless protocol. This means that once the initial communication exchange between the server and the client is completed, the connection is dropped. In other words, HTTP protocol does not maintain the state of a session.

As HTTP is by default stateless, session IDs are a kind of workaround to maintain session states. Cookies implement session IDs. On the Web, each communication session between the client and the server is assigned a session ID, a part of the authentication process that keeps a track of session activity and the link to the user. The link is maintained by assigning an authentication number to the user. This session ID and the user authentication number are stored in a transaction database on the server.

Upon subsequent access to the site, the user's session ID and authentication information travel with the URL and the actual content of the site. All this information is collectively known as the extended URL. In session hijacking, the intruder hijacks the session IDs by accessing the data on servers and networks. The intruder modifies the details of the extended URL using a text editor, then reconnects to the Web site using the extended URL.

E-mail Attacks

Attackers exploit the vulnerabilities of e-mail to disrupt network services and systems on the Web. The following are a few e-mail attacks used by intruders on the Web:

◆ E-mail bombing

◆ E-mail spamming

◆ E-mail sniffing and spoofing

E-mail Bombing

E-mail bombing is a method in which an intruder sends identical e-mail messages to a target user one after the other, locking up the user's Inbox with unwanted mail.

An e-mail bomb attack could be costly in terms of the access limit and misuse of network resources. For people who access e-mail through accounts in which a particular space is provided, an e-mail bomb attack could result in important e-mail bouncing back, as the Inbox could be flooded. In other words, e-mail bombing can bring an e-mail server down, which results in legitimate e-mail being missed or delayed. Also, it may clog network resources, which can affect other systems on the same network.

Mail Bomber and Doomsday are a couple of popular utilities used by attackers for e-mail bombing.

E-mail Spamming

E-mail spamming is a method in which attackers send e-mail to hundreds or thousands of users. In this method, the attacker subscribes to a mailing list or gets lists of e-mail addresses from companies that maintain them. He then sends unwanted e-mail to these users on a continuous basis.

 NOTE

Mailing lists are groups on the Internet that exchange information through e-mail.

E-mail spamming cannot really be controlled because anyone with a valid e-mail address can send messages to any other e-mail address, newsgroup, or bulletin board. Due to spamming, a large amount of e-mail is sent to or through a single Web site. This may result in a denial-of-service attack as transmission of excessive e-mail messages consumes high bandwidth on the network, slows down the e-mail server, and uses all the available system resources.

E-mail Sniffing and Spoofing

Another form of attack is e-mail sniffing and spoofing. In e-mail sniffing, attackers capture e-mails over the network before they are delivered to the destination address.

Attackers use packet sniffer software to sniff out information. These applications have the ability to capturing information traveling from one computer to another. Once the e-mail is captured, attackers retrieve confidential information such as credit card numbers, user names and passwords, or important information about organizations.

In e-mail spoofing, the attacker captures e-mail messages over a network and then tampers with the information in the message for malicious purposes. In cases of e-mail spoofing, attackers generally operate by forwarding captured messages under a changed identity.

Privacy Threats

Privacy threats include various types of eavesdropping attacks. The following are a couple of common eavesdropping attacks:

◆ Network eavesdropping
◆ Radio signal eavesdropping

Network Eavesdropping

Network eavesdropping involves monitoring data being transmitted on local networks and then extracting the data that is required. An interface controller is a network device used to monitor data on the network. It is used often used by hackers to intercept data for eavesdropping.

Network sniffing is a common method of eavesdropping in a network. It involves capturing data packets traveling over a network and deciphering them to obtain critical information, such as user names and passwords. Due to the existence of such methods, it is always recommended to transfer data in encrypted form.

Radio Signal Eavesdropping

Radio signal eavesdropping involves capturing radio signals emitted from computers and mobile phones. This type of attack is not commonly used, as it requires expensive equipment (such as antennae and tuning equipment) to intercept data on a network. Nowadays, there is software available that enable computers to tune into radio signals of computers and mobile phones on all wavebands. An example of radio signal eavesdropping would be intercepting the signals passed by monitors, viewing the documents on his interceptor receiver.

I'll now brief you on how attackers use mobile phones to capture information. You cannot use a mobile phone to intercept signals of other mobile phones. You need special decoding equipment to listen to mobile phone conversation. However, such equipment is banned in most countries and only available to intelligence agents or police. However, through illegal means, modified versions of such equipment is available.

Access Control Threats

As the name suggests, *access control threats* include attacks made to gain access to systems on the Internet. The most common method is password cracking. Other attacks include accessing password files and communication points such as modems or using software that allows access to internal and external systems through visible and invisible backdoors, thereby exploiting network flaws.

Intruders commonly use the backdoor attack to gain access to systems. After gaining access, the intruder usually leaves an entry point (also called the backdoor) open by manipulating program code so that he can access the system from the same point again. The intruder leaves a backdoor open so that the system remains accessible even if the intrusion is detected. Backdoors also help intruders avoid being traced through log entries. In other words, backdoor entry bypasses the detection mechanism of the system.

Having discussed threats, I'll now come back to viruses. The next section gives you detailed information about the history of viruses, how they spread, and the different types of viruses. It also discusses the measures that should be taken to prevent, detect, and recover systems from virus attacks.

Viruses

Computer viruses were first introduced to the IT industry in the 1980s. Over the years, viruses have not only spread mysteriously but also have captured our attention. Every time a new virus hits the world, it makes the news.

On one hand, viruses have proved how naively susceptible we are. They have proved that well-written viruses can have devastating effects on the whole world. On the other hand, viruses have also shown how sophisticated and intelligent computer professionals have become. For example, the Melissa virus introduced in 1990 became world-renowned. It was so accurately engineered and powerful that it forced big organizations, such as Microsoft, to shut down their e-mail systems until the virus was controlled. The ILOVEYOU virus also had a similar impressive effect. Another noticeable point about these viruses was that they were written in VBScript, a scripting language that is extremely simple. Almost any developer who knows HTML knows VBScript. Therefore, these viruses were simple to make but had a devastating effect. Does it not impress you when you realize how simple the Melissa and ILOVEYOU viruses are in reality!

Traditionally, viruses spread through detachable media, like floppy disks. However, now that we live in a networked environment, viruses don't solely rely on floppies or any other detachable media to spread themselves. Viruses may easily spread through e-mail or other documents that you download from the Internet. In this section, I'll take you through a detailed tour of computer viruses—both traditional and new computer-to-computer e-mail viruses—so that you can understand how viruses operate, detect them, and protect yourself against them. I'll also talk about various antivirus programs that help to fend off viruses and propose the best methods to solve the troubles caused by viruses.

What Is a Virus?

By definition, a computer *virus* is a small program that copies itself to other programs or files. For example, a virus might attach itself to an executable program, such as a spreadsheet. Each time the spreadsheet program is executed, the virus is also executed. Computer viruses are so called because they share some of the characteristics of biological viruses. A computer virus passes from computer to computer like a biological virus passes from person to person. As a biological virus uses existing cells to reproduce itself, a computer virus needs an executable program to replicate itself.

Viruses may not immediately go on a rampage as soon as they infect a system. A virus may lie dormant for some time, and then get triggered on some specific date. But even while the virus is dormant, the machine is still infected.

The effect of a virus can vary from simply displaying irritating messages (for example, the WM97/Class-D virus, which repeatedly displays messages such as "I think 'username' is a big stupid jerk") to deleting specific files or formatting your hard drive (for example, the CIH virus, which tries to overwrite the Flash BIOS, can cause permanent damage).

Most computer viruses are written in an assembly language. A few viruses are also written in higher-level languages, such as C or Pascal. However, this does not imply that a person who does not know assembly language or C and Pascal cannot write a virus program. Anybody with minimal programming skills can create a virus program. The level of skill required to create a virus program depends entirely upon the degree of damage you want the virus to cause. For example, to write a virus program that just displays annoying messages does not require extensive programming skill. However, to create a virus that causes serious damage to the network of an entire organization, a person needs to have considerable knowledge about vulnerabilities that exists in the network.

 NOTE

An *assembly language* is a low-level language that involves direct interaction with a system. It has a similar structure and set of commands as a machine language that uses numbers to interact with a system. The difference between the two is that machine language consists of numbers and is difficult to understand, whereas assembly language uses names instead of numbers. For example, consider cars that require drivers to change gears manually and cars that have an automatic transmission. The former can be equated to an assembly language because it requires the driver to interact more with the car; whereas the automatic car can be equated with a high-level language where the gear is changed by the car automatically and the driver does not have to manually change gears. Similarly, in assembly and other low-level languages, a programmer has to interact more with the system (computer). Whereas, high-level languages do not require you to know the intricacies of your system.

An example of an assembly language is Cobol.

Carriers of Viruses

As stated earlier, a virus usually goes into action when the program or file to which it is attached is executed. In addition, the manner in which a virus replicates and spreads from one computer to another may vary because each virus is programmed to perform in a different manner.

The most common media through which viruses can spread have been classified into the following categories:

◆ Floppy disks and CDs
◆ Files downloaded from the Internet
◆ E-mail attachments

Floppy Disks and CDs

The most common carriers of viruses are physical storage devices such as floppy disks and CDs. Many times, the floppy disks and CDs that you use are infected with a virus. Whenever you use the infected floppy disk or CD in your system, the virus is transferred to your hard disk (see Figure 2.1). Sometimes the boot sector of the floppy disk is also infected. If you start a computer with the infected boot floppy disk, the virus may corrupt the boot sector of the hard disk also. The next time the computer is rebooted, the virus infects the booting process of the system.

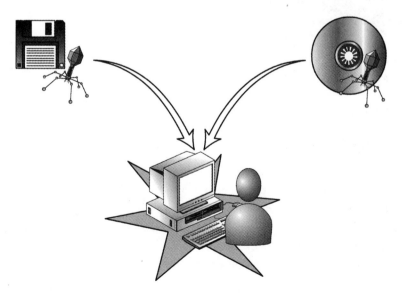

FIGURE 2.1 *How a virus spreads through floppy disks and CDs.*

Files Downloaded from the Internet

The Internet is another medium through which a virus is transferred to computers due to the wide availability of downloadable freeware, shareware, software, games, MP3 files, tools, and images. Most sites ensure that the downloadable material they offer is virus-free. However, there is always a possibility that such material is infected. If you download virus-infected material from the Internet, your computer will also get infected (see Figure 2.2). In turn, if you are on a network and share such infected files with other users, the virus may spread across the entire network.

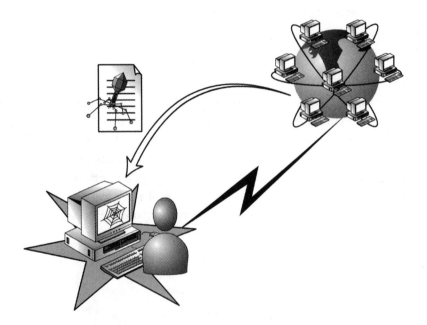

FIGURE 2.2 *How a virus spreads through material downloaded from the Internet.*

E-mail Attachments

E-mail is another popular medium of spreading a virus through the Internet. A virus-infected document is sent as an e-mail attachment. When the receiver opens the attached document, the virus residing in the document is activated. Consequently, the virus replicates itself as several executable copies, attaches itself to other e-mail messages, and eventually sends infected messages to all e-mail addresses listed in the mailing list or address book of the user.

For example, a user might receive a game as an attachment from an unknown source. When the user executes the game, the virus residing in the game software automatically executes without the user's knowledge. In such a case, the virus may not only damage computer files but may also send copies of the attachment to every person in the user's e-mail address book. The user would not even realize that the message and virus have been sent from his or her account. The recipient might not even realize that it's a potentially destructive e-mail because it was sent by a known person (see Figure 2.3).

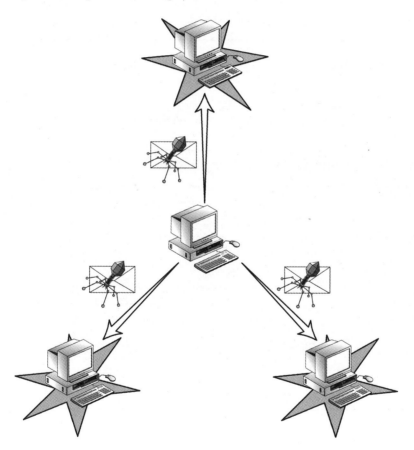

FIGURE 2.3 *How a virus spreads through e-mail.*

Table 2.1 shows the trend in virus attacks through various media over five years (1996-2000).

Table 2.1 Trends in Virus Encounters

Source	1996	1997	1998	1999	2000
Floppy Disk	74%	88%	67%	39%	7%
E-mail	9%	26%	32%	56%	87%
Internet	12%	18%	12%	13%	2%

Source: ICSA Labs 6th Annual Computer Virus Prevalence Survey 2000

Figure 2.4 shows a line chart representation of these trends.

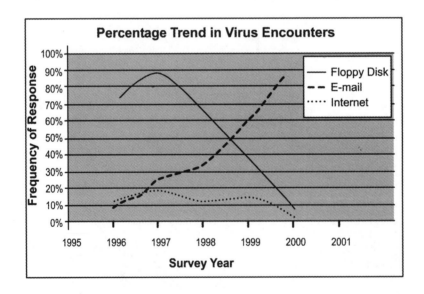

FIGURE 2.4 *Trends in virus encounters from 1996 to 2000.*

Most Likely Targets of a Virus Attack

These days, anybody with a computer and an e-mail account can be the target of a virus attack. However, the most likely targets of virus attacks are professionals who work in IT organizations, the employees of an organization (apart from

IT) who use information technology to perform organizational work, or individuals who use information technology to perform routine operations. This is because these people tend to interact more on the Internet compared to people who use their computers at home.

However, in an organization there are certain employee roles more vulnerable to virus attacks than others. For example, personnel who access the organization's network while they are on the move are likely targets of an attack. This is because they access client networks that may contain viruses. In this process, these people might unknowingly transfer a virus to their own organization. The other role is of supervisors and team leaders who may have access rights to the computers of their subordinates. A subordinate's computer may already be infected with a virus, and as a result, the supervisor's or team leader's computer may become infected. People who share computers on networks or exchange floppy disks to transfer files are also prone to virus attacks.

Following is a list of computer components that may be affected by a virus:

◆ Software components, such as the operating system, used during computer startup. A virus can make the operating system fail to use hardware devices, which may give the impression that the hardware has also failed.

◆ DOS program files, such as .COM, .EXE, and .SYS format files.

◆ Document files with macro capabilities, such as Microsoft Word.

Virus Types

Based on a virus's behavior and also the area of the computer that it will attack, you can classify viruses into two categories: boot sector and file virus. The following types of virus can, in turn, be subclassified as either boot sector or file viruses.

◆ Macro virus

◆ Script virus

◆ Parasitic virus

◆ Stealth virus

◆ Polymorphic virus

Boot Sector Viruses

Boot sector viruses are generally passed when an infected boot floppy disk is left unattended in the drive and the system is rebooted. The virus is read from the infected boot sector of the floppy disk and written to the master boot record (MBR) of the system's hard drive. The master boot record (MBR) is the first sector from where the system reads when the booting process starts. Now, whenever the computer is booted, the virus is loaded into the system's memory. The virus replaces and modifies operating system files in the boot sector. Examples of boot sector viruses are Disk Killer, Stoned, and Michelangelo.

 NOTE

Every hard disk has a starting point where key information about the disk is stored, such as how many partitions it has, what kind of partitions these are, and information about the BIOS that loads the initial boot program. The place on the hard disk where this information is stored is called the *master boot record* or the *master boot sector* or just the boot sector, as shown in Figure 2.5.

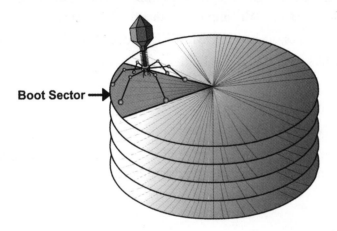

Boot Sector →

FIGURE 2.5 *A boot sector virus*

File or Program Viruses

File viruses, also called *program* viruses, infect executable files, such as files with .EXE, .COM, and .DLL extensions (although in some cases they also infect executable files with .SYS, .DRV, .BIN, .OVL, and other less common extensions).

These viruses overwrite or modify the contents of infected files. Most file viruses are easy to detect because they change the size of the file to which they attach. File viruses can spread through floppy disks, CDs, or the Internet. Examples of file viruses are Dark Avenger and Cascade.

There are a few file viruses that also change the extension of an executable file. For example, they may change the original .COM file to .EXE, and then create a new file with the same name and a .COM extension. It is difficult to detect such an infected file as, in this case, the file size of the new file created by the virus is the same as the original file.

The most successful file viruses are resident viruses that load into memory the first time an infected file is run, and then take complete control of the computer. Such viruses generally infect additional programs each time an infected file is executed or even when new directories are made. However, there are also many nonresident viruses that simply infect one or more files each time an infected file is run. In the traditional .EXE and .COM file viruses, nonresident viruses have not been very successful in terms of pervasiveness of infection worldwide.

 NOTE

The advent of Windows has slowed the growth of both the boot and .EXE viruses. This is because most boot viruses are incompatible with the 32-bit file system extensions that were first introduced as an option in Windows 3.1. Then this file system, by default, came installed with Windows for WorkGroups 3.11, and finally came standard in Windows 95 and its later versions. The 32-bit NT and Windows 2000 systems also display incompatibility with boot viruses. New, 16-bit Windows 'New Executable' (or NE) and 32-bit Windows 'Portable Executable' (PE) .EXE file formats have also discouraged the efforts of virus programmers in view of the introduction of these newer platforms.

Macro Viruses

Macro viruses are basically instructions for applications written in languages such as WordBasic or Visual Basic. These viruses generally reside in application document files, such as Word documents, Excel workbooks, or the templates of these file types. Initially, documents were just considered data files and were the least expected to be infected by viruses. However, with the advent of macro viruses, any application that supports macros, which are embedded (or can be included in some way) in a document file, has the potential of being infected with a macro virus (see Figure 2.6). Examples of macro viruses are W97M.Melissa, WM.NiceDay, and W97M.Groov.

 NOTE

A *macro* is a set of instructions that perform specific tasks automatically.

Macros need not necessarily be embedded in document files for the host application to be infected with the virus. For example, in early 1999, the first virus, named CSC/CSV.A, for applications supporting CorelScript macro language was discovered. However, CorelScript is based on several macro code files. Therefore, this virus was not much of a threat to the users of other applications with CorelScript support. This is a case of application compatibility, which implies that you can't write a single macro code that will work with all applications supporting CorelScript. In the case of CSC/CSV.A, because of compatibility issues with CorelScript, the virus failed to replicate fast enough because it was only compatible with the application type for which it was created.

Macro viruses pose greater threats as compared to traditional boot sector or file viruses. The rate at which macro viruses affect systems is very high because they are simple to create. However they can't affect the complete system because they are application-specific. A macro virus that corrupts Word documents will not affect documents created with Lotus Notes or Star Office. However, macro viruses are more popular because it's easy to infect applications that support macros. Another factor that makes macro viruses more dominant is the widespread use of the macro language VBA. VBA is both a powerful language and an easy one to learn; therefore, it is very popular among professional programmers and hackers. It also allows access to complex Windows API programs. Accessing Windows APIs is difficult through low-level languages. Therefore, many people who could not previously create a virus due to the complexity in low-level languages can now easily program viruses.

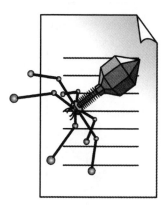

FIGURE 2.6 *A macro virus infecting an application that supports macros.*

Script Viruses

Script viruses infect applications written in scripting languages, such as JavaScript (JS) and Visual Basic Script (VBS)(see Figure 2.7). JS and VBS languages are hosted under the Windows Scripting Host (WSH), which is an active scripting component, provided in Windows 98 and Windows 2000 operating systems. Script viruses are becoming widespread because a large number of computers use WSH to run script-based applications.

Another reason that script viruses are becoming more common is that writing the code is easy. JS and VBS, which are high-level scripting languages, can be so easily understood that even someone without a programming background can write script using these languages. You do not need advanced programming skills to write code for a script virus. For example, string manipulation operators have made many tasks, which were practically not possible in lower-level languages, trivial in JS and VBS scripts.

Like macro viruses, script viruses can spread through sharing floppy disks or CDs, while accessing e-mail, or while sharing directories over a network. Script viruses can also spread through ActiveX applications. ActiveX is a Microsoft application that enables Web pages to download components. This implies that while accessing the Internet, script virus–infected modules can be downloaded to the machine through ActiveX. In addition, script viruses can spread through applications such as Windows Help, Windows installation files, and Windows registry files. Unlike macro viruses, script viruses can also spread through Internet Relay Chat (IRC), a system that enables online chat on the Internet.

FIGURE 2.7 *How a script virus infects JavaScript and VBScript applications.*

Parasitic Viruses

Parasitic viruses infect executables, also known as programs. When an infected executable program is launched, a parasitic virus is activated first. However, to hide its presence, the virus then starts the original program to which it is attached. Since the operating system understands the virus to be a part of the program, the parasitic virus is given the same rights as the program to which it is attached. This in turn, enables the virus to replicate, install itself into memory, and destroy files and other applications. Jerusalem is a well-known parasitic virus, which slows down the computer and deletes every program that the user tries to start.

Stealth Viruses

A *stealth* virus is a type of boot sector virus that infects the files and boot record of the hard disk. This type of virus monitors the system functions used by programs to read files or the physical block from the disk and modifies the results of such functions so that programs trying to read these areas see the original uninfected form of the file instead of the actual infected form. Therefore, the damage or modifications caused by the virus go undetected by antivirus programs. However, if you want the virus to be detected by antivirus programs, the virus must reside in memory.

Polymorphic Viruses

A *polymorphic* virus produces diverse (yet fully operational) copies of itself in the hope that virus scanners will not be able to detect all instances of the virus. These viruses masquerade and change their appearance with every infection. Some polymorphic viruses are also known as *encrypted* viruses because they use an encryption technique to hide from antivirus software. These viruses encrypt their main code and use a random set of commands to decrypt the code.

As stated earlier, polymorphic viruses are difficult to detect; therefore, you must use antivirus software that performs algorithm scanning. Algorithm scanning is more complicated and sophisticated compared to the normal string-based scanning used to detect simple viruses. An example of a polymorphic virus is MtE, which stands for Mutation Engine.

Table 2.2 shows the trend in reported encounters of various types of viruses over three years (1999–2000).

Figure 2.8 shows a bar chart representation of these trends.

Table 2.2 Trends in Reported Encounters of Various Virus Types

Virus Type	Early 2000	Early 1999	Early 1998
Boot	277	14, 58	196
File	3, 114	73, 488	779
Macro	51, 374	112, 423	351, 623
Script	35, 226	21, 112	188

Source: ICSA Labs 6th Annual Computer Virus Prevalence Survey 2000

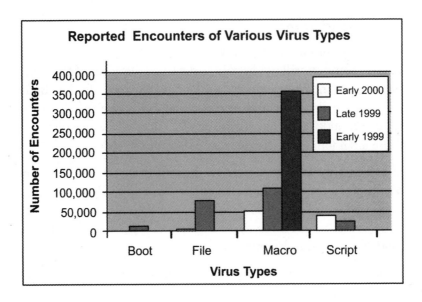

FIGURE 2.8 *Trend in reported encounters of various virus types*

Preventing, Detecting, and Recovering from Virus Attacks

Today, threats from viruses are a known vulnerability on the Internet. To prevent these threats from infecting computers worldwide, there a few prevention, detection, and recovery measures that organizations need to take.

Security Measures to Prevent Virus Attacks

The best way for individuals and network administrators of organizations to protect network and stand-alone computers against viruses is to apply the following antivirus measures:

◆ First and foremost, anyone associated with computers should have a basic knowledge about the various types of viruses and how they function. This awareness would help individuals evade general threats that arise from viruses. For instance, Word or Excel documents contain macros and, therefore, are more prone to macro virus threats. When sending documents via e-mail, you should ensure that any attachment being sent is saved in Rich Text Format (RTF). RTF files do not contain macros and, therefore, the possibility of a virus infecting such files is bleak.

◆ If you want to protect your computer against traditional viruses, such as boot sector viruses, you can install a secure operating system such as UNIX. Virus attacks on UNIX operating systems are not very common, as this operating system has security features that keep unauthorized visitors away from the hard disk. Also, there are almost no viruses created that can infect UNIX platforms because of their secure features.

◆ Avoid downloading software and other material from unknown sources on the Web directly to your hard disk. To prevent virus infection from such sources, download the material onto a floppy disk, and then scan the floppy for viruses before transferring the content to the hard disk. To avoid these hassles and the lengthy procedure, it is best to buy software from trusted authorized dealers.

◆ Avoid purchasing pirated and illegal software, as they are not purchased from reliable sources and may also contain viruses. As mentioned earlier, it is best to purchase software from trusted authorized dealers.

◆ Nowadays, most systems disable booting from a floppy disk. Some systems include booting from floppies as the last option. However, many tech savvy users still include booting through floppies in the boot sequence. If you have ever allowed your computer to boot through a floppy disk, you should disable floppy-disk booting by changing the CMOS boot sequence stored in the CMOS memory—most computers now allow you to do this. This eliminates the risk of a boot sector virus getting transferred from a floppy disk, which may be left unattended in the drive accidentally.

◆ Ensure that Macro Virus Protection is enabled in all Microsoft applications. Also, avoid running the macros in a document if you are not sure what their function is. To ensure virus protection against macros, Word and Excel 2000 define the three security levels as shown in Figure 2.9. To open the Security dialog box, you need to go to Tools, Macros, Security.

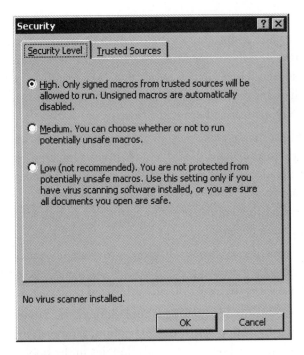

FIGURE 2.9 *Security dialog box*

- ◆ Avoid opening attachments in e-mail messages if the sender is unknown to you. Before opening e-mail messages, it is always advised to scan them for viruses using antivirus software.

- ◆ If you share floppy disks and CDs with other users, scan the floppy disks and CDs using antivirus software before you transfer any data from these onto your computer.

- ◆ Another security measure that can minimize the consequences of a personal computer virus infection is making regular backups of your hard drive. In an organization, you can set up backup servers on the network where users can make regular backups. Organizations can also make backups on multiple computers on the network and also on floppy disks or tapes. However, after making backups on floppy disks, you should ensure that the disks are write-protected. Viruses cannot infect write-protected disks.

- ◆ Ensure that antivirus software is installed on your computer and updated regularly to detect, report, and disinfect viruses.

◆ To prevent attacks from script viruses, disable Windows Scripting Host when it is not required. You can disable Windows Scripting Host in Windows 98 by clicking on Add/Remove Programs in the Windows Control Panel. Click on the Windows Setup tab, select Accessories, and then click on the Details button. In the Accessories dialog box, clear the Windows Scripting Host checkbox and click on the OK button.

Figure 2.10 shows the Accessories dialog box with the Windows Scripting Host option disabled in Windows 98.

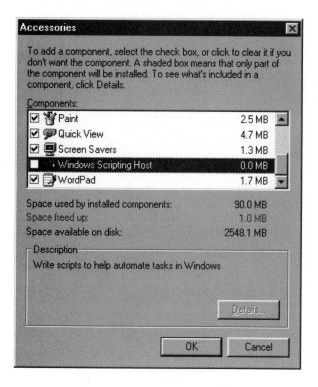

FIGURE 2.10 *Accessories dialog box*

To prevent scripts with a .VBS extension from executing in Windows 2000 and Windows Me, perform the following steps:

1. Log on as an Administrator.
2. From the Tools menu in My Computer, select Folder Options. The Folder Options dialog box will open, as shown in Figure 2.11.

3. Click the File Types tab.

4. In the list of file types, select VBScript Script File. (If you can't find this file type, it implies that your system does not have Windows Scripting Host installed. Therefore, your system is safe, and you need not do anything.)

5. Click the Delete button.

6. If you see a dialog box asking for confirmation to remove this option, click Yes.

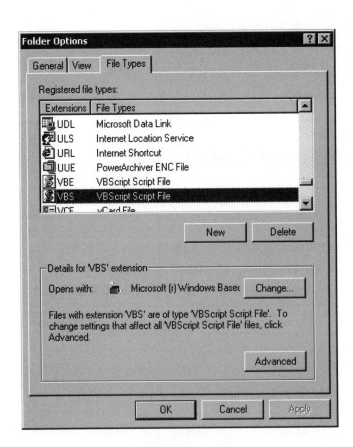

FIGURE 2.11 *The Folder Options dialog box*

In addition to the preceding measures, organizations should take the following precautions to ensure that networks are completely secure:

◆ The network should be set up such that only authorized users can access network resources. To implement this, various tools are available that prevent unauthorized access.

◆ Organizations should set up dedicated machines whose sole purpose is to test new software, files, and disks. Files that need to be shared across the network should be scanned on these machines before anyone can access them.

◆ Transferring executable files to and from external sources should be blocked. As you already know, many viruses spread as executable files through e-mail messages. Blocking executable files from being exchanged in this manner will ensure and maintain overall security against virus attacks.

◆ For added protection, organizations can also use diskless computers, which have a hard disk drive but not have a floppy disk drive. This prevents computers from using infected floppy disks, thus ensuring a virus is not passed to the network.

Detecting Virus Attacks

To facilitate the detection of a virus attack on a network, organizations should observe the network for signs of unusual behavior or activities. Virus-infected computer systems show a number of common symptoms. If you are aware of these symptoms, you may help the organization prevent a virus from spreading across the entire network. The following are some common symptoms of a virus attack:

◆ The network slows down, and data may frequently get blocked.

◆ A computer may run slower than usual or may even stop responding.

◆ There may be an unusual number of memory-related or program errors.

◆ The sizes and last-changed dates of objects that are infected may change.

◆ There may be unexplained data loss or modification.

◆ The hard disk of a computer may appear occupied even though there is enough free space.

◆ The CHKDSK command does not show the correct number of bytes.

◆ The computer may not respond when trying to boot from a boot floppy disk.

◆ Applications may take longer than usual to start or open.

◆ There may be a sudden appearance of unrecognized file types in the system.

◆ Documents may display junk characters though the documents were saved properly.

◆ The keyboard may make sounds even when it is not responding.

◆ The screen becomes distorted, or characters might start falling from the screen.

◆ Programs may mysteriously execute under apparently secure user profiles.

Recovering from Virus Attacks

Personal computers may not perform in the expected manner for a variety of reasons. In most cases, the cause of unexpected behavior is not a virus attack but rather common network problems. However, most office users are not aware of this. Tech support personnel should educate office users on how to prevent or rectify such small problems at their end. For instance, if a user suspects that his computer is behaving in an unusual manner, he should get in touch with the tech support coordinator of his organization. In addition to this, he should facilitate the trouble shooting process by taking careful notes of the problem, the error messages that might be appearing, the task being performed at the time of the error's occurrence, the history of the problem, and any changes made to the system hardware or software that existed prior to the problem's occurrence.

After a careful examination of the problem, if tech support still suspects that a virus has infected the computer, they should then isolate the computer from the network. However, first and foremost, they should consider recovering and backing up all data in the infected computer. As part of this exercise, they should use virus-scanning software to check if the computer has a virus. They also need to ensure that the virus is removed from every segment of the network because there may be hidden viruses that go undetected by antivirus software and that may activate and spread later.

To ensure that a computer has successfully recovered from virus attacks, a system administrator should perform the following steps:

♦ **Assess the extent of damage caused.** Once you are sure that a virus has infected your computer, the first step should be to assess the extent of the damage. If the computer is part of a network, tech support needs to identify how many other computers are affected as well as other locations that might be affected. Infected computers should then be isolated from the network so that the virus does not spread further. To prevent any further attacks, you also need to identify the source from which the virus originated, which can be done by monitoring the log files on both the computer and servers.

♦ **Check backup servers for virus infection.** After removing infected computers from the network, you need to check backup servers for virus infection. To eliminate the remote possibility of the virus attacking the backup servers, you should remove the servers from the network. Then, clean the servers using antivirus software. However, before doing this, it is preferable to backup the data stored on this server so that if, while cleaning, there is data loss, you can still recover data from the backup.

♦ **Disinfect all computers on the network.** The next step is to disinfect all other computers on the network. Then, identify the data and programs that are infected by using antivirus software.

Summary

This chapter identified common threats on the Web and classified these threats into various categories, such as accidental, malicious, authorization, application, privacy, and access control threats. The first section of the chapter discussed various categories of threats in general. The second section discussed viruses in detail.

Check Your Understanding

Multiple Choice Questions

1. Which of the following is a reverse social engineering technique?

    a. A phone call to a receptionist of an organization asking for user names and passwords.

    b. The intruder pretends to belong to the organization's technical support team and extracts information from employees.

    c. The computer of the user is corrupted and displays the contact number of the intruder on the error message itself.

2. Which of the following is a destructive program that masquerades as a useful or benign program.

    a. Virus

    b. Trojan

    c. Worm

3. Consider the following two statements:

    Statement A: Social engineering may be defined as the art of using interpersonal skills for extracting confidential information.

    Statement B: With RSE, the user is manipulated into asking the intruder questions that, in turn, reveal information about the organization.

    Which one is TRUE about the statements written above?

    a. Statement A is TRUE but statement B is FALSE.

    b. Statement B is TRUE but statement A is FALSE.

    c. Both the statements are TRUE.

    d. Both the statements are FALSE.

4. State whether the following statement is TRUE or FALSE:

    Polymorphic viruses masquerade and change their appearance with every infection.

5. Which one of the following is a macro virus?

    a. A virus that resides in application document files, such as Word documents and Excel workbooks or the templates of these file types.

    b. A virus infecting applications written in scripting languages, such as JavaScript and Visual Basic Script.

    c. A virus infecting executables.

    d. A virus infecting files and boot records of the hard disk.

Short Questions

1. What is the difference between viruses and worms?

2. What is a brute force attack?

3. What are the two main categories of viruses?

4. How can you disable the Windows Scripting Host option in Windows 2000?

5. Briefly list the steps that a system administrator will perform to ensure that the system has successfully recovered from a virus attack.

Answers

Multiple Choice Answers

1. c.

2. c. A Trojan is a destructive program that masquerades as a useful or benign program.

3. c.

4. TRUE.

5. a.

Short Answers

1. The difference between viruses and worms is in the manner in which both use the host file. Worms usually release the document to which they are attached. This document then travels from one computer to another across networks. This implies that if a document has a worm attached, then that document, as a whole, should be considered a worm. However, a virus spreads from one document to other.

2. In a brute force attack, the intruder first obtains a list of used passwords from bona fide sources. He then hashes these passwords using encryption schemes supported by the system being attacked. The resultant encrypted hash values are then compared with the hash passwords stored in the database. The comparison is successful whenever the hash value from the dictionary matches the hash value in the database.

3. The two main categories of viruses are boot sector viruses and file viruses.

4. In Windows 2000, to prevent scripts with a .VBS extension from executing, perform the following steps:

   1. Log on as an Administrator.
   2. From the Tools menu in My Computer, select Folder Options. The Folder Options dialog box will open, as shown in Figure 2.11.
   3. Click the File Types tab.
   4. In the list of file types, select VBScript Script File.
   5. Click the Delete button.

5. The following are steps that a system administrator should perform to ensure that the system has completely recovered from a virus attack:

   1. Assess the extent of damage caused.
   2. Check backup servers for virus infection.

PART II

Network and Application Security

Chapter 3

etwork security is an intricate topic that is a domain of well-trained and experienced network engineers. However, as the span of computer networks has extended from within organizations to the world outside, anyone using a computer needs to understand the basics of network security so that they can protect information exchange from various threats on the network. This chapter has been written with the people in mind who understand the basics of network communication, including the system and Web administrators. A basic knowledge of TCP/IP networking is also assumed, but not essential, to understand the contents of this chapter.

This chapter has been divided into three sections. The first section covers general introduction to the history of networking and various types of networks. The second section gives an introduction to TCP/IP and internetworking. The knowledge of these concepts is necessary to understand the various weaknesses on a TCP/IP network. The third section discusses various weaknesses and vulnerabilities on a TCP/IP network. People who are comfortable with basic concepts of networking and TCP/IP can skip the first two sections and jump straight to the third section of the chapter.

The chapter is not intended as a handbook on setting up a secure network. The purpose is to acquaint you with various attacks that may occur on a network.

Networking Basics

As stated earlier, to understand the principles of network security, a basic knowledge of computer networks is necessary. However, in this section, as a refresher course, I will quickly browse through the fundamental concepts of computer networks and give an overview of some popular networks.

What Is a Network?

A *network*, as defined by the New Lexicon Webster's Encyclopedia Dictionary of the English Language, is "any set of interlinking lines resembling a net, a network of roads, an interconnected system, or a network of alliances."

This definition is appropriate for computer networks also. In terms of information technology, a network may be defined as a group of devices linked together to facilitate communication. These devices may include computers, printers, and routers that may be placed within one room, in different rooms of a building, or span a vast geographical area.

Types of Networks

There is no fixed formal classification for computer networks. However, there are two prominent classifications, which include transmission technology used and area covered by the networks. Broadly speaking, these are

◆ Broadcast networks

◆ Point-to-point networks

Broadcast Networks

On a *broadcast network*, all computers share a single communication channel. If a computer wants to communicate with another computer, a message (in the form of packets) is sent to all the computers on the network. The packets contain the address of the computer to which the message is to be sent. When any computer on the network receives a packet, it checks the address attached with the packet. If the address in the packet matches the computer's address, the computer processes the packet. However, if the packet is not intended for that computer, it is simply ignored and passed on to the next computer on the network so that it finally reaches the destination computer.

You can compare the communication on a broadcast network to a teacher taking roll call in a class. During roll, a teacher calls the name of each student in the class and only the student whose name is called responds. For example, for a student named Marie, the teacher calls, "Marie, are you present?" Although all the students in the class hear this message, only Marie responds and the other students ignore the message.

On a broadcast network, a packet can either be sent to all computers on the network or delivered to just a particular group of computers. When the packets are delivered to all computers on the network, it is termed as *broadcasting*. When the packets are delivered to a particular subset of computers on the network, it is called *multicasting*.

Broadcast technology is generally implemented in small networks that have a small number of computers spanning across a small geographical area.

Point-to-Point Networks

Unlike broadcast networks, *point-to-point networks* consist of several communication channels among computers on the same network. The data packets may travel through different routes of varying length to reach the destination computer. A routing algorithm is used to determine the path taken by a packet to reach its destination.

Point-to-point communication technology is generally implemented on large networks that may contain subnetworks in them.

As stated earlier, networks can also be classified based on the area they cover, such as in the following network categories:

◆ Local area networks (LAN)

◆ Metropolitan area networks (MAN)

◆ Wide area networks (WAN)

Figure 3.1 displays the organization of networks based on computers arranged by their size and the area in which they operate. The figure places the data flow computers on the top. These computers are highly parallel computers with several units working on the same program and covering a distance of 0.1 meters. Multicomputers are placed at the second level of the hierarchy. These computers communicate over a distance of 1 meter. Local, metropolitan, and wide area networks are placed under multicomputers. Computers placed in local area networks can communicate across rooms, buildings, and campuses. The network of these computers can span across an area in the range of 10 to 1,000 meters. Computers placed on metropolitan area networks can communicate across a city and cover an area of 10 kilometers. Wide area networks operate across countries and continents, and their coverage may range from 100 to 1,000 kilometers. Finally, at the last level is the Internet, which is simply the connection of several networks (also called an internetwork) that span across the globe.

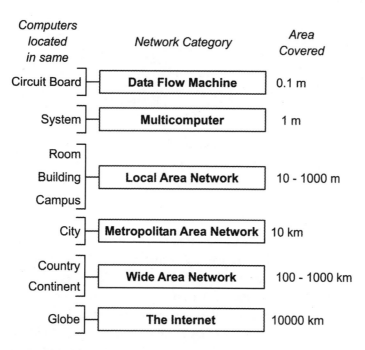

FIGURE 3.1 *Classification of networks based on area*

Before going into details of local, metropolitan, and wide area networks, it is essential to brush up on the various topologies that exist. Local, metropolitan, and wide area networks can be further classified into one of the following topologies.

Topologies

Topology refers to the arrangement of devices on a network. In other words, topology determines how various devices are connected to each other and how they communicate. Topologies can either be physical or logical. *Physical topology* is the manner in which devices are physically connected to each other through cables on a network. On the other hand, *logical topology* is the manner in which data moves from one device to another on a network, irrespective of the manner in which devices are laid out.

The following are the five most common topologies:

◆ **Bus topology.** In a bus topology, all devices are connected to a central cable, referred to as the *bus* or the *backbone*. Networks that use the bus topology are also referred to as *bus networks*. Figure 3.2 depicts the arrangement of computers in a network based on bus topology.

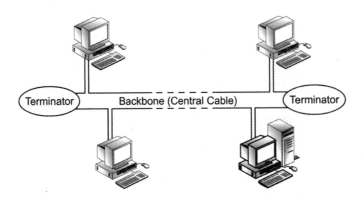

FIGURE 3.2 *A network based on bus topology*

On a bus network, data is transmitted using the broadcast transmission technology method. The device that wants to transmit data first checks if the bus is free for transmission. If no other device is sending data, the device sends the data to each device on the network. Upon receiving the data, each device checks the address attached with the data packet. If the address in the data packet matches the destination device's address, the data packet is delivered. If the data packet is not intended for that device, it is ignored.

There may be a case when two or more computers want to transmit data simultaneously. In such a situation, an arbitration mechanism is needed to resolve the conflict. In arbitration method, each device may have to wait and try again later.

◆ **Ring topology.** In a ring topology, all devices are connected to each other in such a manner that each device is directly connected to two other devices (see Figure 3.3).

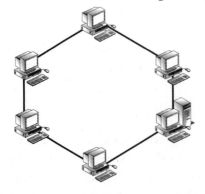

FIGURE 3.3 *A network based on ring topology*

A ring topology is also based on broadcast transmission technology. However, in a ring topology, devices use the *token passing method* to transmit data across the network. An empty token is passed around the ring and the device that wants to send data captures the token. The data along with the token then pass through the ring and reach the destination computer. Upon receipt of the data, the destination computer sends back the token to the sender computer as an acknowledgment signal. After the token reaches the sender computer again, it is emptied back into the network so that other devices can use it to pass data.

◆ **Star topology**. On a network that is based on a star topology, all devices communicate across the network by passing data through a central device (see Figure 3.4).

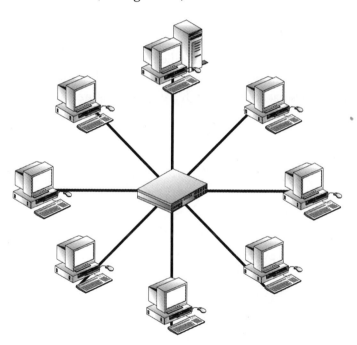

FIGURE 3.4 *A network based on star topology*

◆ **Mesh topology**. In a mesh topology, devices are connected with several interconnections between each other. In a typical mesh topology, every device is connected to every other device on the network (see Figure 3.5).

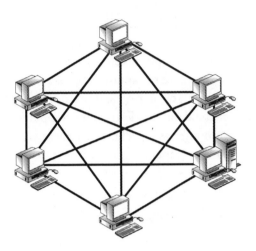

FIGURE 3.5 *A network based on mesh topology*

◆ **Tree topology**. A tree topology, also called a *hybrid* topology, is a mixture of bus and star topologies. In a tree topology, several star networks are connected to a bus backbone through a hub (see Figure 3.6).

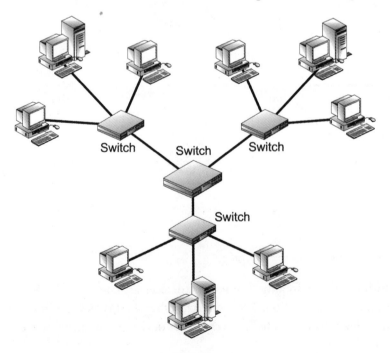

FIGURE 3.6 *A network based on tree topology*

A network topology may have different physical and logical topologies at the same time. For example, twisted pair Ethernet operates in a logical bus topology and has a physical star topology layout. Similarly, IBM's Token Ring is a logical ring topology but has the physical set up of a star topology.

Having discussed various topologies, let me come back to our discussion on local, metropolitan, and wide area networks. In the next section, I'll take you through a tour of these networks.

Local Area Networks

Local area networks (LAN) connect devices that are placed in a single building or on a campus that may spread across a few kilometers. The main purpose of LANs is to connect computers and other devices, such as printers, in offices to facilitate sharing resources and information. LANs may be differentiated from each other on the basis of their size, transmission technology, and the topology used.

Most LANs use broadcast technology to transmit data. There are several topologies possible for broadcast LANs. An example of a broadcast LAN based on a bus topology is Ethernet. Examples of broadcast LANs based on a ring topology are Attached Resource Computer Network (ARCNET) and Fiber Distributed Data Interface (FDDI).

Depending on the channel allocation method used, LAN broadcast networks may further be categorized as *static* and *dynamic*. On a static broadcast network, time is divided into distinct intervals and allotted to computers in a round robin algorithm. Each computer is allowed to broadcast only during its allotted time slot. Static time allocation results in wastage of channel capacity when a computer has no message to broadcast in the allocated time.

A dynamic LAN broadcast network may be centralized or decentralized. In a centralized network, a central entity determines the order in which the computers can send messages. This entity may determine the order by some internal algorithm. In a decentralized network, there is no central entity. Based on an internal algorithm, each computer decides for itself whether or not to transmit.

Some LANs also use point-to-point transmission technology. In this type of network, individual lines connect one computer to the other. Point-to-point based LANs are another form of miniature wide area networks.

Metropolitan Area Networks

Metropolitan area networks, also called MANs, are basically bigger versions of LANs and generally use similar technology. MANs connect devices that may be laid out over an area ranging 5 to 50 kilometers. The communication links and equipment used in MANs are generally owned by an association of users or by Internet service providers.

MANs have a key aspect called Distributed Queue Dual Bus (DQDB) on which they operate. DQDB is an IEEE (Institute of Electrical and Electronics Engineers) standard that consists of two unidirectional buses to which all computers are connected.

Wide Area Networks

Wide Area Networks, also called WANs, extend to large geographical areas. A WAN is an amalgamation of two or more LANs connected to each other through different networking technologies.

In the case of a WAN, the error rate in data transmission is the highest compared to the other types of networks. In addition, the cost of equipment needed (such as communication circuits taken on lease from telephone companies or communication carriers) to set up a WAN is very high. Moreover, the speed of data transmission in a WAN network is much slower than on a LAN network.

A WAN has mainly two aspects, network and application. The network aspect deals with transmission lines and switching elements. The application aspect deals with all computers that participate in the WAN, referred to as *hosts*.

Now that we have discussed different types of networks, let me now brief you on certain terms that are commonly used in today's world: intranet, extranet, and the Internet.

Intranet

An intranet is a private network of an organization that may span across various countries. The networks can be based on different topologies; however, they share a common connection medium. The main purpose of an intranet is to share organizational information and resources among employees.

Extranet

An extranet is part of an organization's intranet that can be accessed by users (including other organizations) from outside the organization. The need for an extranet is highlighted when two organizations want to share resources for business development. Organizations use an extranet to exchange volumes of data, share news of common interest, and for other developmental efforts.

Because users from outside the organization can access an organization's network, it becomes necessary to secure that organization's intranet to avoid any security breaches. The security measures may include installing firewalls, user authentication systems, or use of Virtual Private Networks (VPN).

Internet

The Internet is a worldwide system of computer networks—a network of networks—which enable computers of all types to directly and transparently communicate and share information throughout the world. You may refer to the Internet as a large public network that is open to all users.

In the previous discussion, the terms private and public network were used in the context of intranet and Internet. The next section clearly defines public and private networks.

Public and Private Networks

Hosts (computers) on a network can be divided into the following three categories:

- ◆ Hosts that do not need to access remote resources and services provided by hosts on other networks or on the Internet.
- ◆ Hosts that need to access limited resources or services provided by secure networks or hosts outside their own network. These services might include e-mail, FTP, and remote login.
- ◆ Hosts that provide services, such as DNS, Web, and e-mail that can be accessed via the Internet. These hosts are typically the Web, DNS, and mail servers.

The hosts defined in the first and second categories are part of a private network. An example of a private network would be that of a travel agency organization whose operations spread across the world. To support the operations of the organization, its branches need to be interconnected. The network of such an organization may be termed a private network. LAN is also a form of a private network.

The hosts defined in the third category belong to a public network. As stated earlier, the Internet is one of the best-known examples.

Certain hosts in a private network need to use services available through public networks. This is mostly enabled by using a host that is a part of the private network as well as the public network. The remaining hosts on the private network that need access to services on the Internet would then connect to the public network through this host. Also note that it is not necessary that all computers of a private network need to use the Web, FTP, or e-mail services. Many organizations only allow e-mail access to their employees (and nothing else). This access is also through an internal network, as the hosts would connect to the organization's mail server (which would be on a private network as well as public). The mail server then forwards the e-mail to the destination through the public network or the Internet.

Now, if your private network is connected to the public network, the users on the public network can access all your organization's crucial information. The thought itself is very scary, isn't it? Indeed. Hosts on a private network need to access services of a public network in such a way that the users in a private network can access the public network but not vice versa. Organizations use security measures, such as firewalls and Intrusion Detection Systems (IDS), to protect their private network from unauthorized access by the users of the public network.

The Role of Firewalls in Securing Private Networks

A *firewall* is a combination of hardware and software that protects a network from another network. The most basic use of a firewall is to protect internal networks from public networks, which may be an organization's private network or a public network such as the Internet. A firewall acts as a line of defense against external threats to an organization's network from a public network.

To strengthen security on a private network, a firewall is installed or attached to a computer that is separate from the rest of the private network. This ensures that no data is transmitted directly to the network (see Figure 3.7). A firewall, before allowing outside traffic to access the private network, checks the data packets based on rules that are defined in it.

Another popular implementation of firewalls is to restrict access to a Web server. In this case, the firewall is configured to allow external connections only to the TCP/IP port 80 of the Web server. Defining firewall rules, which are mostly on an "allow" or "deny" basis, can also be used to enforce further restrictions.

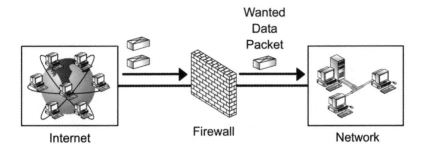

FIGURE 3.7 *A firewall separating a private network from a public network.*

 NOTE

To understand the role of firewalls in securing networks, refer to Chapter 8, "Firewall Solutions," which covers firewalls as a security measure against the attacks discussed in this chapter.

Devices Connecting Networks

At this point, you may be asking exactly how are networks connected to each other? Broadly speaking, networks are connected by devices called bridges, routers, and gateways.

A *bridge* connects two or more devices on two similar or dissimilar networks. Bridges allow communication between devices attached to different networks in such a manner that it appears as if they were on the same network.

A *router* is an intelligent bridge device used to interconnect large networks. A router has additional capabilities, such as filtering data packets and routing them to destinations through the best network paths. Networks (similar or dissimilar) that are connected to each other using routers are known as *subnets*.

A large network (such as WAN) may contain two or more routers. Cables or telephone lines connect two routers on such networks. However, if two routers are placed distantly and do not share a common cable, how will they communicate?

If two routers do not share a common cable and they wish to communicate, they do so through other routers. When a packet is sent from one router to another via more than one intermediate router, the packet is received at each intermediary router in its entirety, stored until another output line is available, and then forwarded (see Figure 3.8). Remember, a network based on this principal is called a *point-to-point network*.

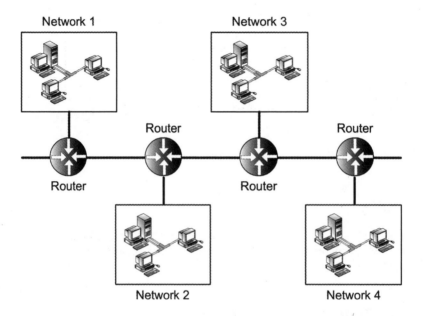

FIGURE 3.8 *The role of routers in a point-to-point network*

To enable communication over networks or the Internet, a network protocol is necessary. The following section discusses the most commonly used protocol over the Internet, TCP/IP.

TCP/IP

Before the advent of TCP/IP, there were several protocols that facilitated communication between computers across networks. These protocols mainly catered to small networks with computers that had similar hardware and software specifications. They were not designed for large networks with heavy traffic. Consequently, the protocols were volatile and frequently crashed systems when used for communication across large and heterogeneous networks. To counter the short-comings of these protocols, the evolution of Transmission Control Protocol/Internet Protocol (TCP/IP) took place. TCP/IP enabled communication among large and heterogeneous networks.

TCP/IP is a result of investigative research into networking protocols initiated by the U.S. Department of Defense (DoD) in 1969. In 1968, the DoD's Advanced Research Projects Agency (ARPA) started a research project to develop network technologies. This project created a packet switching network, also called Advanced Research Projects Agency Network (ARPANET).

The early ARPANET used protocols that were quite slow. In 1974, Vinton G. Cerf and Robert E. Kahn developed a new set of protocols. In the 1980s, based on the design of these protocols, the DoD developed TCP/IP protocols. To increase acceptance and recognition of TC/IP as a standard protocol, the DoD provided a low-cost implementation of TCP/IP in the user community. The DoD introduced the protocol at the U. C. Berkeley's BSD UNIX implementation by sponsoring the company Bolt, Beranek, and Newman, Inc. (BBN). At this point, several sites were implementing local area network technologies. By 1983, all the computers con-nected to ARPANET were using TCP/IP for communication. In addition, many sites that were initially not using TCP/IP also adopted this protocol.

The recognition of TCP/IP as a standard protocol has created a large market for the technology. The protocol can be implemented on numerous network topolo-gies and across different architectural networks. The acceptance of TCP/IP is so widespread that even network operating systems that have their own protocols, such as Novell Netware, also provide support for TCP/IP.

Features of TCP/IP

TCP/IP refers to the suite of protocols used to connect heterogeneous networks to form the Internet. The name, TCP/IP, comes from the two most important protocols in the suite, the Transmission Control Protocol (TCP) and the Internet Protocol (IP). TCP is responsible for ensuring that data is not lost during deliv-ery of data packets between the client and the server. Additionally, it provides sup-port for detecting any errors that may occur during transmission of data. It also provides a mechanism for retransmission of data until the data reaches its desti-nation completely. IP is responsible for transferring data from source to destina-tion by attaching the destination address to each data packet that needs to be transferred.

The following are a few important features of TCP/IP:

◆ **Industry standard suite of protocols.** TCP/IP is a set of protocols established on the basis of a predefined model called the OSI model. The details of the OSI model are discussed a little later in this section.

◆ **Routable enterprise networking protocol.** TCP/IP can send data by using routers. Routers improve network efficiency by using routing protocols, such as RIP (Routing Information Protocol), OSPF (Open Shortest Path First), and BGP-4 (Border Gateway Protocol).

◆ **Technology for connecting dissimilar systems.** Computers across the world that have different hardware configuration and operating systems are able to communicate through the Internet because it uses TCP/IP.

◆ **Robust and scalable protocol.** TCP/IP is a robust protocol because it can endure high network error rates. Unlike earlier protocols, which crashed and generated errors in large networks, TCP/IP does not crash in a large, heterogeneous environment and can also sustain errors.

◆ **Supports peer-to-peer communication.** In peer-to-peer communication, computers using the same networking software can communicate directly with each other. This implies that each computer can directly access data from another computer on the same network. This saves time and the cost of maintaining a central server through which data communication takes place.

◆ **Three-way handshake mechanism.** TCP/IP hosts establish a *three-way handshake* mechanism to ensure reliable transport services. This method ensures that data packets are transmitted only when both hosts are ready to send and receive data packets. Details about the three-way handshake mechanism are explained a little later in this chapter.

◆ **Uses checksums.** Before data is transferred, an algorithm is run on the data that generates a unique number for each data packet. When the data reaches its destination, the algorithm is again run on the data and a number is generated. This number is matched with the number generated at the time of transmission. If the numbers match, it implies that the data has been transmitted completely and is free of errors. The TCP checksum is not an optional feature; the sender always generates a checksum and the receiver always checks it.

TCP/IP Protocol Architecture

The TCP/IP protocol architecture maps to a four-layer reference model, also known as the DARPA model or the TCP/IP reference model. The four layers of the TCP/IP reference model are Application, Transport, Internet, and Network Interface. Each layer in this model corresponds to one or more layers of the seven-layer Open Systems Interconnection (OSI) model. Figure 3.9 shows a comparison between the layers of the TCP/IP reference model and the layers of the OSI model from which the TCP/IP reference model is derived.

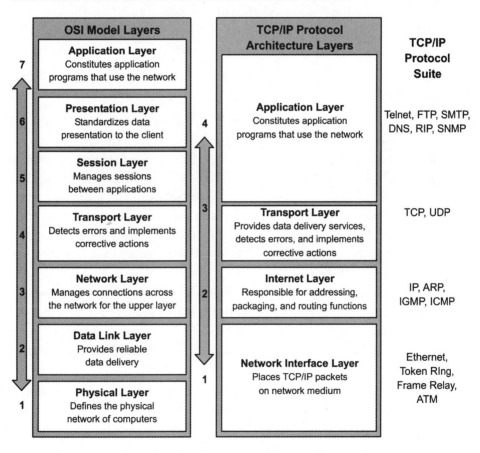

FIGURE 3.9 *The TCP/IP reference model versus the OSI model*

In the preceding figure, notice that the Application layer of the TCP/IP reference model corresponds to the Application, Presentation, and Session layers of the OSI model. The Transport layer corresponds to the Transport layer and the Internet layer corresponds to the Network layer of the OSI model. The Network Interface layer corresponds to the Data Link and Physical layers of the OSI model.

In Figure 3.9, also notice that each layer of the TCP/IP reference model contains a group of protocols (that actually form the protocol suite of the TCP/IP reference model). Each protocol in the layers performs a set of functions and also communicates with its peer protocols. The protocol layers are designed in such a manner that the upper layers depend upon the lower layers to transfer data from the applications on one host to another host. Data is passed down the protocol suite from one layer to the other until the data is transferred to the destination computer through the physical layer. On reaching the destination, the data is again transferred from the physical layer to the remote application.

The following list gives a brief description about each layer of the TCP/IP protocol suite:

◆ **The Network Interface layer.** The Network Interface layer (also called the Network Access layer) is the lowest layer in the Internet reference model. This layer provides an interface for the hardware of the network. The primary purpose of this layer is to deliver data packets on the physical medium (such as a network interface card) and receive data packets off the physical medium. This layer minimizes the need to write to the higher layers of the TCP/IP suite when new network technologies are introduced that use different network mediums, frame formats, and access methods.

◆ **The Internet layer.** The Internet layer is responsible for addressing, packaging, and routing data to the higher layer. It contains several protocols, such as the Internet Protocol (IP), Address Resolution Protocol (ARP), Internet Control Message Protocol (ICMP), and Internet Group Management Protocol (IGMP).

The protocols of the Internet layer are responsible for fragmenting and reassembling datagrams. Datagrams are data packets that consist of a header, data, and trailer. The header contains information, such as the destination address, source address, and security labels. The trailer contains a checksum value that is used to maintain integrity of data in transit.

The datagram service does not maintain the connection state of a session. This implies that once the message is sent or received, the service does not maintain the information about the entity with which it was communicating. If such information is required, the service relies on the protocols of the Transport layer. In addition, the datagram service does not also have the ability to retransmit data or check it for errors. Using checksum values, if the datagram service detects an error during data transmission, it simply drops the datagram packet without notifying the receiving higher layer.

The above explanation is a general list of protocol functionality in the Internet layer. Following are one-line explanations of each of these protocols:

- The Internet Protocol (IP) is a routable protocol that is responsible for attaching destination IP addresses to the packets as well as fragmenting and reassembling packets.
- The Address Resolution Protocol (ARP) is responsible for the resolution of an Internet layer address to a Network Interface layer address.
- The Internet Control Message Protocol (ICMP) is responsible for reporting errors that may occur while data is in transit.
- The Internet Group Management Protocol (IGMP) is responsible for managing IP multicast groups.

◆ **The Transport layer**. The Transport layer is responsible for maintaining reliable data transmission. The two most important protocols in this layer are the Transmission Control Protocol (TCP) and the User Datagram Protocol (UDP).

TCP (also called the connection-oriented protocol) provides a reliable two-way connection by sending the data again when the transmission results in an error. To sum up, the primary function of TCP is to establish a TCP connection, sequence and acknowledge data packets sent, and to recover packets in case data is lost during transit. In addition, TCP also facilitates multiple connections with a host.

Compared to TCP, UDP provides a connectionless, unreliable communication service. UDP is used when the amount of data to be transferred is small, when overheads of a TCP connection are not required, or when the applications or upper layer protocols provide reliable delivery.

◆ **The Application layer**. The Application layer provides applications with the ability to access the services of other layers. It defines protocols that applications use to exchange data over the network. Other protocols that process user data, such as data encryption and decryption and compression and decompression, can also reside at the Application layer.

The most widely known Application layer protocols are those used for the exchange of user information. The following are a few Application layer protocols: HyperText Transfer Protocol (HTTP), File Transfer Protocol (FTP), Simple Mail Transfer Protocol (SMTP), and Telnet.

In the previous discussion, whenever I talked about TCP, IP, or UDP, the terms *connection-oriented*, *connectionless*, or *connection state of sessions* were used. To clarify these terms, let me brief you on the difference between connection-oriented and connectionless services in a layered protocol model. To highlight the difference, I'll use simple examples that you can relate to daily life.

Connection-Oriented and Connectionless Services/Protocols

Layers in a protocol suite provide two services to the layers above them: connection-oriented and connectionless.

A connection-oriented service is similar to a telephone conversation—a connection is set up when you pick up the phone and dial the number, the connection is used when you talk, and the connection is released when you hang up. Similarly, in a connection-oriented service, a connection is set up, used, and then released. The connection can be checked for errors, and some form of error recovery can be attempted.

The best example for a connectionless service is the postal system—each letter bears the full destination address and is sent to the destination independent of the other letters in the system. Here, no formal connection is established. If the letter is lost in the transit, the postal system does not take responsibility for delivery or recovery of the letter. Similarly, in a connectionless service, there is no overhead of establishing a connection. As a result, the connectionless transmission does not guarantee delivery of data packets across networks.

The following section takes a tour of how TCP establishes a connection-oriented session with its hosts.

The TCP Three-Way Handshake Mechanism

To use the reliable services on the Transport layer, TCP hosts must establish a connection-oriented session with each other. TCP establishes this with the three-way handshake mechanism.

A three-way handshake mechanism synchronizes both ends of a connection by allotting an initial sequence number to the hosts, which ensures that both ends agree that the connection has been established successfully and the data packets can be transmitted reliably. The initial sequence number also ensures that data packets are not transmitted or retransmitted before the session is established or after the session is terminated.

Connection Setup

Following are the steps used to set up a connection between two hosts (for example, Host A and Host B):

1. Host A commences a connection by sending a SYN packet with the initial sequence number (X) to Host B. SYN refers to the synchronization packet.

2. When Host B receives the SYN packet, it records the initial sequence number X and acknowledges receipt by sending the SYN with an ACK= X + 1. ACK refers to acknowledgment. Host B also sends its own initial sequence number (Y).

3. In response to the acknowledgment sent by Host B, Host A then acknowledges all bytes by sending a forward acknowledgement indicating the next byte (ACK=Y+1) that Host B expects to receive (see Figure 3.10).

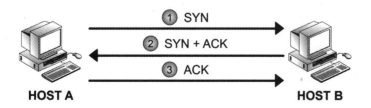

FIGURE 3.10 *The three-way handshake process*

Connection Release

Following are the steps used to release a connection between two hosts (Host A and Host B):

1. Host A sends a FIN packet to Host B. FIN refers to finish.

2. When Host B receives the FIN packet, it acknowledges the receipt by sending back a FIN along with an ACK.

3. In response to the acknowledgment sent by Host B, Host A then acknowledges and finally ends the connection by sending an ACK to Host B (see Figure 3.11).

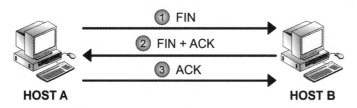

HOST A   **HOST B**

FIGURE 3.11 *The three-way handshake release process*

Threats and Vulnerabilities on TCP/IP Networks

TCP/IP has raised many issues of security because, originally, it was not designed to keep in mind the different aspects of security. Rather, it was intended to support applications and provide interconnectivity and interoperability between networks. In addition, controlling networks on such a large scale is difficult. In recent years, weaknesses in the TCP/IP protocol suite have opened major security holes, making networks prone to several vulnerabilities.

Classification of Security Threats on Networks

There are several methods used to exploit the vulnerabilities of TCP/IP networks. These vulnerabilities can be classified into the following three categories:

◆ Denial-of-service (DoS) attacks

◆ Distributed denial-of-service (DoS) attacks

◆ Data diddling attacks

Denial-of-Service (DoS) Attacks

One common form of a network-based attack is denial of service (DoS). In DoS attacks, authorized users are denied the use of network services. Usually, the main targets of a DoS attack are Web servers, application servers, and communication links. Hackers swamp the servers and communication links with useless data, disrupt data access, and crash the computers. A common example of a DoS attack is an unauthorized user using an FTP location to upload large volumes of data. This causes unnecessary blockage of disk space and generates network traffic. As a result, the FTP location is no longer usable.

It is easy to implement a DoS attack because they do not require any specialized technical skills or access to data on a network. In fact, DoS attacks are different from other network attacks because they strike at network services, eventually making them unavailable to authorized users. Other attacks usually target data on a network; they do not disrupt network services. In addition, compared to other attacks, tracing the identity of the attackers in a DoS attack is difficult because the attackers are placed at different locations on the network and often spoof their identity.

DoS attacks can come from any point on the network. Figure 3.12 displays the entry points in networks from where a DoS attack may be executed.

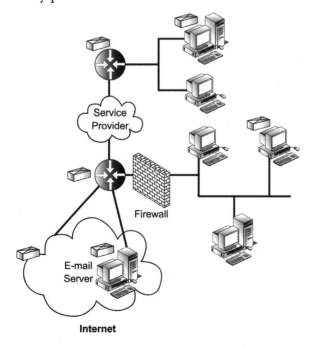

FIGURE 3.12 *Vulnerable DoS entry points on a network*

DoS attacks may occur in various forms, such as the following:

◆ Disruption of network traffic

◆ Disruption of the network connection between two computers

◆ Denial of server services to a client

Let me give you an example of a DoS attack where services of a network component are disrupted temporarily, in this case, on the printer server. In an organization, there are three floors, and the network of each floor has a printer installed. Employees have been using the printer services smoothly for a long time. Then, the users accessing the printer on the first floor inform the network administrator that they are not able to print documents using this printer. On investigating the printer server, the network administrator finds that a large number of print jobs are queued. These jobs have taken up the available printer space on the printer server, denying access to other users.

You can classify DoS attacks into two categories: flood attacks and software attacks. The following section briefs you on these two types of attacks.

Flood Attacks

A flood attack swamps a computer's resources and the network with numerous false requests. Network devices, such as routers and NICs, have limited capacity to process packets. Taking advantage of this, attackers send numerous small packets at a fast rate in order to overload the network. Due to the overflow, routers start dropping legitimate packets as they try to keep pace with both fake packets and legitimate packets. The router becomes so busy that the network slows down. It is difficult to detect a flood attack because the attack traffic appears to be the same as legitimate user traffic.

SYN Flood Attacks

SYN flood attacks exploit the three-way handshake process of TCP. This attack is aimed at using up the network TCP connections to a site, thus preventing legitimate users from connecting to that site. As you already know, to establish a connection with a server, the client sends a SYN packet (containing the initial sequence number and host ID) to the server. The server acknowledges receipt by returning a SYN + ACK packet back to the client. The connection is established completely when the client acknowledges by sending an ACK packet to the server.

The problem starts if a fake ID is sent in the SYN packet. Because of this, the acknowledgement (SYN + ACK) sent by the server never actually reaches the legitimate client. Eventually, the connection times out, and the incoming channel on the server is made available for another request. In a SYN attack, the attacker sends numerous fake SYN requests (in other words, fake IDs) that result in a server sending the acknowledgement (SYN + ACK) to nonexistent clients. Consequently, the server awaits acknowledgement for 75 seconds per connection request. Because the server is already busy waiting, it does not respond to the requests of legitimate users. Therefore, the server is flooded with SYN requests because the incoming channel is free (see Figure 3.13).

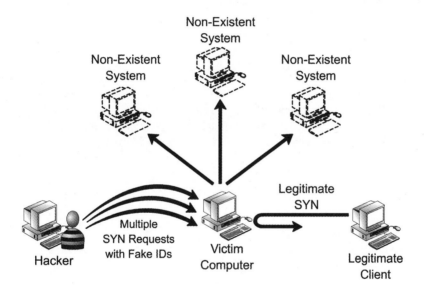

FIGURE 3.13 *SYN flooding attack*

SMURF or ICMP_ECHOREPLY Flooding Attacks

SMURF attacks are based on ICMP echo request and reply packets. But before I explain SMURF attacks, let us recap ICMP. ICMP stands for Internet Control Message Protocol, which is responsible for troubleshooting and reporting errors regarding the delivery of IP packets. Through the *ping* utility (see following Note), ICMP reports the state of a network or host on a network. If all goes well, then an ICMP reply is received from the host that you pinged. If the host is unreachable, ICMP gives a "destination unreachable" message (see Table 3.1).

Table 3.1 ICMP Unreachable Destination Messages

ICMP Message	Description
Echo Request	Message that verifies IP connectivity to a desired host
Echo Reply	Response to an ICMP echo request
Redirect	Message sent by a router to inform a sending host of a better route to a destination IP address
Source Quench	Message sent by a router that its IP datagrams are being dropped because of congestion
Destination Unreachable	Message sent by a router or the destination host to inform the sending host that the datagram cannot be delivered

 NOTE

Ping is a TCP/IP utility that allows you to check the existence of a computer on the network. The function ICMP_ECHO sends an ICMP echo request to the specified host, waits for the corresponding echo reply, and returns the ICMP message trip time (in milliseconds). It can be used by networking monitoring tools to test whether an IP device can be reached.

When a ping command is given, an ICMP_ECHO_REQUEST is sent to the computer whose existence has to be verified. If the computer is present on the network, an ICMP_ECHOREPLY is returned from the other end (see Figure 3.14).

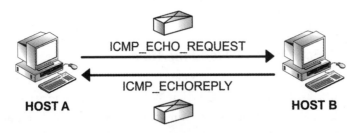

FIGURE 3.14 *Implementation of ICMP in a ping command*

In a SMURF attack, there are three components involved: the hacker's computer, the packet amplifier, and the target (victim) computer. The SMURF attacks begin when a hacker forges the source address of an echo request packet to the source address of a selected victim host. He then sends the packet to a broadcast address of a third-party network, which is also known as the amplifier network. Now all hosts on the amplifier network send an echo reply packet to the victim computer. This not only affects the victim computer but also the amplifier network.

As stated earlier, the ICMP request packets are passed through the intermediary packet amplifier network. Ideally, if the computer is present on the network, this device passes the ICMP reply packets back to the device that has sent the request. However, in a SMURF attack, the ICMP reply packets are not returned to the hacker's computer because ICMP request packets contain the spoofed IP address of the victim computer. Therefore, the victim computer is flooded with several ICMP reply packets (see Figure 3.15).

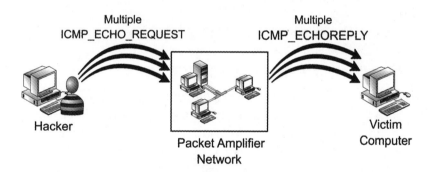

FIGURE 3.15 *SMURF attack on a computer on a network*

To summarize, SMURF attacks exhaust the bandwidth available to the target (victim) computer and deny its services to legitimate users because the computer is busy with the ICMP echo reply messages.

Fraggle or UDP Flood Attacks

Fraggle or UDP flood attacks are similar to SMURF attacks. Just like the SMURF attack broadcasts ICMP echo request packets on a network, the fraggle attack broadcasts UDP packets on a network. These packets contain spoofed IP address of some other computer on the network. All the hosts to which a UDP echo request has been sent reply to the other computer on the network.

Software Attacks

Software attacks take advantage of inherent vulnerabilities of software. In this type of attack, hackers create packets with spurious information to exploit known software weaknesses. Consider a few examples. A computer on a network may not be configured properly. A hacker who knows about this may try to alter or destroy the configuration information of this computer. As a result, other computers on the network may not be able to access this computer. In the same manner, due to weaknesses in a router's firmware, a hacker may be able to change the route entries in the routing table. As a result, the network may stop functioning. A hacker may also be able to gain access to the registry on an unpatched Windows 2000 computer if the remote registry service is running. Due to this, certain services on this computer may not be available.

Software attacks can be prevented by installing software patches that will remove the vulnerabilities. Firewall rules can also be added to filter the malformed packets before they reach the target computer.

The following section discusses a few DoS software attacks.

Ping of Death or ICMP_ECHO_REQUEST Attack

The ping of death attack is based on the ping utility of TCP/IP. In this attack, a hacker sends a chain of fragmented ping commands containing large-sized ICMP packets to the target computer. The maximum packet size that can be sent through a ping utility is 64 KB, so a hacker sends several ICMP packets (of at least 64 KB) through thousands and millions of ping commands per second (UNIX ping command with the -f option). The hacker may also modify the packet size and send packets of more than 64 KB. In order to respond to the ping requests, when the target host starts reassembling the packets, it realizes they are too big for its buffer. Consequently, a buffer overflow occurs because the target computer becomes too busy, reassembling so many packets and sending back replies at the same rate (see Figure 3.16).

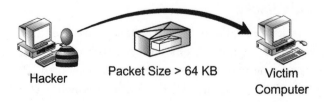

Hacker   Packet Size > 64 KB   Victim
                                        Computer

FIGURE 3.16 *Ping of death attack*

The aim of the DoS-based ping of death command is to flood the victim computer with numerous requests, thus saturating the remote site's available bandwidth. This results in denial of services by the victim computer to the other hosts on the network. To execute a successful ping of death command, the hackers need to have a considerably high-bandwidth (to support numerous ping commands) compared to the low bandwidth of the victim computer.

The following operating systems allow you to send over-sized ICMP packets through the ping command:

◆ Windows 3.11

◆ Windows 95 and NT

◆ Linux

◆ Solaris 2.4

◆ Novell Netware

Following is an example of the ping command that sends over-sized packets to the victim host:

```
ping -l 6500 -s 1 {IP address of target host}
```

In the preceding command, `-l 6500` sets the buffer size of the packet to 6500 and `-s` specifies the timestamp for hop counts.

In a UNIX platform, you can modify source codes, such as `simping.c` and `pingdd.c`, to manipulate the packet size and create a ping flood attack.

The following command will send a flooded ping to the target computer. This code would work from a Linux computer only for root users.

```
ping -fl 6777 -s 6500 {I.P address of target host}
```

The above command should be used with extreme caution, as it has the potential to bring the target computer to its knees.

You can counter a ping of death command by forbidding fragmented ping commands on your systems. This allows only regular 64-byte pings through your system and blocks fragmented pings that result in packets of larger size.

DNS Service Attacks

We previously discussed a type of DNS service attack in Chapter 1, "Security: An Overview." Let me review by quoting some lines of that chapter here again. Domain Name System (DNS) is a database that maps domain names to IP addresses. Computers that are connected to the Internet use DNS to resolve domain names to the IP addresses of the sites that need to be accessed.

To disrupt the services of a DNS server, there are several types of attacks that can be implemented. The following are a few DNS attacks:

- **DNS spoofing**. Also referred to as DNS hijacking, the hacker gains access to DNS services and makes changes to information that maps a domain name to an IP address. Due to this, users are directed to a different site than the one they want to access.

- **DNS host name overflow**. In the DNS response for a host name, there is a maximum host name length defined. DNS host name overflow occurs when there is a failure to check the permitted host name length in the DNS response. Due to this, a buffer overflow occurs when the host name is copied in the DNS server.

- **DNS length overflow**. In addition to the maximum length of the host name, the DNS response also contains a length field that has a permissible limit of 4 bytes. If a larger value is specified, a buffer overflow occurs allowing the attacker to execute arbitrary commands on the target system.

- **DNS zone transfer from privileged ports (1–1024)**. This type of overflow occurs when a hacker, through privileged ports (1–1024), uses the DNS client application to transfer *zones* from an internal DNS server. A DNS zone basically defines DNS hierarchical name space, which are used to demarcate the various DNS servers' areas of operation. In other words, they define which DNS servers have the authority to resolve name-resolution queries for a given section of DNS hierarchy.

Until now, I have only discussed various denial-of-service attacks. There is another, rather sophisticated type of DoS attack that has cropped up in the last couple years (February, 2000) and is still gaining popularity in the hacker community. This relatively new attack is referred to as the distributed denial-of-service (DDoS) attack. Although we have already briefly discussed this attack, also in Chapter 1, let us look at it again in detail.

Distributed Denial-of-Service (DDoS) Attacks

You may have noticed that both the DoS and DDoS attacks have similar names. But does this mean that both these attacks operate similarly? What is the difference between a DoS and DDoS attack? Let me explain how DDoS and DoS attacks are different as well as similar.

In an ordinary network-based DoS attack, a hacker uses application tools to flood a target computer with numerous data packets. This results in authorized users not being able to access the services on the victim computer or possibly the entire network. In such attacks, hackers make use of spoofed IP addresses or nonexistent IP addresses to hide their identity.

Like DoS attacks, DDoS attacks are also aimed at denying network services to authorized users. But the difference is in the number of computers involved in the attack. In a DoS attack, there are two computers involved, the hacker and the victim computers. However, in the case of a DDoS attack, there may only be a single hacker, but the effect of the attack is greatly multiplied by the use of several attack agents across the network (in fact, across the Internet).

You'll understand this difference better after you go through the following discussion on how DDoS attacks operate.

Modus Operandi of DDoS Attacks

In a DDoS attack, the attack process begins when the hacker breaks into several computers over a network. He does so by taking advantage of the inherent vulnerabilities in the computers or the network.

 NOTE

From now on, I'll address the computers being used in DDoS attacks as the compromised computers and the computer that will eventually be attacked as the victim computer.

After gaining access into the compromised computers, the hacker first installs software (e.g., replacement tools) that conceals traces of his existence on the computers.

Next, the hacker installs some more specialized applications that allow him to remotely control the compromised computers and give commands over the network, which, in turn, launches an attack against the victim computer or site. The complete attack process explained here is highly automated.

A vigilant hacker usually begins by breaking into a few computers. Through these computers, he breaks into few more, repeating this process several times. This repeat process prepares a base for the DDoS network that contains thousands of computers.

To launch the attack, the hacker then runs a single command from his computer, sending a command packet to all the compromised computers and instructing them to launch a particular attack against a specific victim. When the hacker decides to stop the attack, he sends another single command.

Many sources have categorized the compromised computers as handlers and agents. Handlers are those computers to which the hacker first sends the command. These computers further redirect the attack command to the agent computer that ultimately launches the attack (see Figure 3.17).

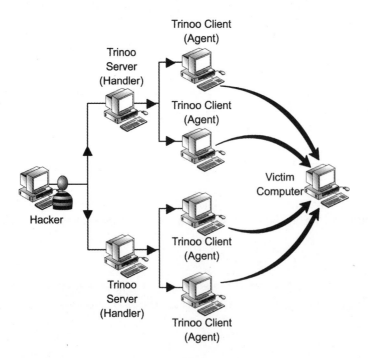

FIGURE 3.17 *The various components of a distributed denial-of-service attack*

DDoS Tools

There are several tools available to launch a DDoS attack. Most of these use distributed technology to create a large network of hosts. The following section discusses two DDoS tools, Trinoo and Tribe Flood Network (TFN).

Trinoo

Trinoo is used to launch UDP DoS flood attacks from various channels on a network. This tool basically creates a network that consists of a few servers and a large number of clients. The servers on this network are referred to as Trinoo servers and the clients as Trinoo clients.

In a DoS attack that operates on a Trinoo network, a hacker computer is connected to a Trinoo master computer (Trinoo server). By sending a single command, the hacker computer directs the Trinoo server to start DoS attacks against one or more IP addresses. The Trinoo server, in turn, passes control to the other Trinoo agents that eventually launch the attack.

 NOTE

You may map the Trinoo servers to component handlers and the Trinoo clients to a component agent.

Tribe Flood Network (TFN)

The Tribe Flood Network (TFN) tool operates along the same lines as Trinoo. Like Trinoo, TFN is also used to launch DDoS attacks against several targets across the network. The only difference is that TFN is capable of using spoofed source IP addresses. A TFN attack can be used to launch the following DoS attacks:

- ◆ UDP flood attacks
- ◆ TCP SYN flood attacks
- ◆ Ping of death attacks
- ◆ SMURF attacks

Like a Trinoo attack, in a TFN attack, a hacker computer is connected to a TFN master computer (TFN server). By sending a single command, the hacker computer directs the TFN server to start DoS attacks against one or more IP addresses. The TFN server, in turn, passes another command to other TFN clients that eventually launch the attack. In addition, the communication between TFN handlers and agents is encrypted.

Data Diddling Attacks

Data diddling attacks involve capturing, altering, and corrupting data traveling on a network or residing on the hosts. It may also involve resending data packets over the network or rerouting the data packets to invalid destinations. Hackers launch this attack by taking advantage of inherent vulnerabilities in the network protocols or the operating systems. A common data diddling attack is one in which a hacker gains access into a Web site and modifies its contents.

There are various methods, such as spoofing, sniffing, session hijacking, rerouting, and port scanning, by which a data diddling attack can be generated. In fact, you can categorize many of these methods as efficient tools for monitoring network traffic and capturing data packets on the network. Let me take each of these methods one at a time.

NOTE

Refer to Chapter 2, "Common Threats on the Web," for the discussion on session hijacking.

Spoofing

Spoofing is an attack in which a hacker computer masquerades as a computer on the target computer's network. The hacker computer's aim is to trick the target computer to believe that it is the original computer with which it is supposed to interact. The intention is to lure the target computer into sharing or sending data or gaining data modification rights.

Spoofing can either be blind or active. In blind spoofing, a hacker is not able to view the responses sent from the target computer (see Figure 3.18). This is because the hacker does not have complete information about network conditions, that is, he probably does not have the IP address for the computer that he wishes to masquerade as or the access rights that the network computers share. In such a situation, the hacker uses all possible techniques to gain access into the network. It is like throwing darts in the dark.

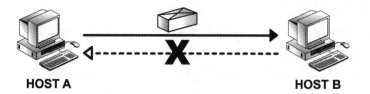

FIGURE 3.18 *A blind spoofing attack*

In active spoofing, a hacker has information about the access rights shared between the host computer (that it intends to imitate) and the target computer. This information helps the hacker view the responses from the target computer (see Figure 3.19). Because of this, the data can be easily corrupted, modified, and passed to other destinations on the network.

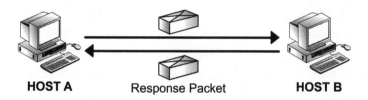

FIGURE 3.19 *An active spoofing attack*

Network spoofing attacks can be classified into the following categories:

♦ IP spoofing
♦ ARP spoofing

IP Spoofing

IP spoofing is a method in which a hacker accesses the target computer by using a spoofed IP address of a trusted host. Hackers perform IP spoofing by using either blind or active spoofing.

An IP spoofing attack (also called IP sequence guessing spoofing attack) is made during a three-way handshake connection process. To start an IP spoofing attack, a hacker first needs to forge the IP address of a trusted host on the network. He then needs to maintain a sequence number with the target computer, at which time he inserts the initial sequence number in the header information of the data packets. This task is highly complicated because when the target sends the initial sequence number as acknowledgement, the hacker must respond with a correct response, which can be accomplished only if the hacker has successfully guessed the TCP initial sequence number.

There are several services vulnerable to IP spoofing, the most being the ones that use IP address authentication—in other words, all services that run on TCP/IP networks. Apart from these, the Remote Procedure Call (RPC) services, the X Window systems, and the UNIX-based R services suite, such as `rlogin` and `rsh`, are vulnerable to IP spoofing attacks.

An IP spoofing attack can be prevented if the following security measures are adhered to:

- ◆ It is advised not to use source address authentication. It is better to use system-wide cryptographic authentication.
- ◆ Networks (or basically routers in the networks) should be configured such that they detect and reject packets on the external interface that claim to originate from an internal host.
- ◆ If external connections from trusted hosts are allowed, enable encryption sessions at the router.

ARP Spoofing

ARP spoofing is an attack in which the hacker modifies the Address Resolution Protocol (ARP) table by exploiting the communication between the IP and the Ethernet protocols. An ARP spoofing attack can be implemented on Ethernet networks operating on TCP/IP protocols.

Before I explaining how an ARP spoofing attack is conducted, I'll give you a background on the role of ARP in data transfer on a network.

Each computer connected to a network has two addresses: a MAC address (also referred to as a physical address) and an IP address (also referred to as a virtual address). A MAC address is the address of the network interface card. These addresses are globally unique; no two NICs can have same the MAC address. Ethernet protocol uses the MAC addresses to transmit data across the network independent of the application protocol residing in the higher layers. However, before transmitting data, Ethernet breaks the data into frames that contain the MAC address of the source and destination address.

IP is a protocol used by applications, independent of the network technology working below it. Each computer on a network also has a unique IP address assigned to it.

At the time of data transfer across networks, IP and Ethernet protocols work hand in hand. IP communicates on the network by breaking the data into packets. These packets are similar to frames but are different in structure. IP packets need to pass through the network layer (which, in our case, is based on the Ethernet topology). However, because Ethernet protocols only allow delivery of frames (not packets), Ethernet breaks the IP data packets into frames, which carries the Ethernet header information. These frames are passed to the router on the network, which then decides to which port the frames need to be sent. The port is chosen by comparing the destination address of the frames to an internal table, which maps port numbers to MAC addresses.

I just stated that Ethernet constructs frames from IP packets. However, at the time of construction, Ethernet only has the IP address of the destination computer and has no idea about MAC address of the destination computer. Remember, a MAC address needs to be part of the Ethernet header! Now, here comes the role of ARP.

ARP helps in locating the MAC address of the destination computer whose IP address is known. ARP does so by sending out ARP request packets, which are broadcast to all computers on the network. Each computer checks if the broadcast IP address matches their IP address. The computer whose IP address matches the broadcast address sends an ARP reply along with its MAC address.

The routers on the network maintain an ARP cache (also called an ARP table) that contains IP addresses with the corresponding MAC addresses that need to be contacted. When a router receives an ARP reply, it updates the ARP cache with the new IP/MAC association. Before the router broadcasts the IP address, it first checks its ARP cache for the corresponding IP address. If an ARP cache does not contain an IP/MAC association entry for that IP address, it broadcasts the IP address. An ARP cache thus helps minimize the number of ARP packets being broadcast on a network.

An ARP spoofing attack involves hijacking broadcast messages, changing the destination IP address with the hacker IP address, and replying with the MAC address of the hacker computer. After the router has received the MAC address, it assumes that the received MAC address is correct and transfers the data to the hacker computer. This process of spoofing is also referred to as ARP poisoning.

You can prevent ARP spoofing by ensuring that ARP cache (or table) uses proper authorization mechanisms before allowing any modifications in it. Or else, you can use static ARP caches.

Sniffing

Sniffing is an attack aimed at capturing network information. The attack involves placing *sniffer* devices at various entry points on a network. These entry points could be computers, cable wires, routers, network segments connected to the Internet, or network segments connected to servers that receive passwords.

A sniffer is a program that supervises, manages, and monitors data passing through a network. A sniffer's main purpose is to eavesdrop on network traffic. A sniffer device has the following components:

- ◆ **Capture driver**. A capture driver captures network traffic from an Ethernet wire, filters the network traffic for information that you want, and then stores the filtered information in a buffer.

- ◆ **Buffer**. A buffer is a software program that helps store data captured from a network. Data can be stored in two ways: until the time buffer is filled with information or in a round-robin method in which the data is emptied as soon as it reaches a particular level in the buffer. This implies that data in the buffer is always replaced by new captured data.

- ◆ **Decoder**. Data passing through networks does not travel in its normal readable form. It travels in a binary format that needs to be decoded. Decoders are used to decode binary data on a network so that it can be interpreted and displayed in a readable format.

These components may be different in various vendor-specific sniffer devices. Each vendor has its own set of specifications. Based on these specifications, the components might also have different names.

Having identified the basic components of a sniffer, let us now discuss how a sniffer operates on a network, which will further define the role of a sniffer.

An Ethernet network is built on shared principles: All computers on the network are connected by an Ethernet wire, which is also connected to a network card. When data is transmitted on an Ethernet network, the request is passed to all computers on the network. Though all computers receive the request, only the computer for which a data packet was sent responds. The computers that are not the actual recipients of the data packets ignore the request.

A sniffer device disables the filter and puts the Ethernet hardware (NIC) into promiscuous mode, a mode in which all computers on the network receive all the data packets, irrespective of whether or not the packets are intended for them.

Rerouting

A router is another vulnerable entry point on a network that allows unauthorized access to data packets. A router has a table containing the routing information and host configurations of other hosts on the network. Routing Information Protocol (RIP) is used to maintain the routing table. Hackers use the RIP protocol to manipulate the routing information or host configuration in a routing table.

Manipulations in the routing table may result in incorrect routing configurations of hosts on the networks, which might, in turn, lead to a loss of data packets on the network. Hackers may also impersonate router identity (a router IP address) in a manner that the hosts on a network cannot locate the external network route.

Port Scanning

Port scanning is a popular investigation technique used by hackers to penetrate a network or a host on a network. All computers, connected to a network or connected to the Internet, listen to all communications through some or the other ports. These ports act as a door where data goes out or comes in. For example, TCP and UDP ports are used by applications to establish sessions between nodes on TCP/IP networks.

In port scanning, the hacker tries to find all possible open ports on a network, then sends messages to every port on the network. Each data transmission unit contains port numbers that define the type of application ports being used. Based on the type of response received, the hacker then identifies which application port is open for exploration.

There are various port scanning utilities available. These utilities verify all possible ranges of TCP and UDP ports on a remote host. However, the technique used may differ based on the type of network topology, IDS, and the logging features enabled at the remote end.

Following are a few port scanning techniques used by hackers:

- ◆ **Vanilla.** In this technique, the hacker tries to connect to possible 65535 ports.

◆ **Strobe**. A more focused scan technique, the hacker looks for only known services to exploit.

◆ **Fragmented packets**. In this technique, the hacker operates by sending small packets

◆ **UDP**. In this technique, the hacker looks for open UDP ports.

◆ **Sweep**. In this technique, the scanner connects to same port on more than one computer.

◆ **Stealth scan**. The scanner blocks the scanned computer from recording the port scan activities.

Summary

This chapter was a general introduction to various weaknesses and vulnerabilities on a network. It was basically divided into three sections. The first section covered some history of networking, various types of networks, topologies, and discussion on protecting a private network from a public network.

The second section of the chapter gave an introduction to TCP/IP and internetworking. Very briefly, it listed the various features of TCP/IP. The section covered the TCP/IP reference model and compared this model with the OSI reference model. In the discussion on TCP/IP reference model, the functionality of the four layers—Network Interface layer, Internet layer, Transport layer, and Application layer—was clearly defined. The section also discussed the three-way handshake mechanism of the TCP protocol.

The third section of the chapter discussed in more detail the various weaknesses and vulnerabilities on a network. It covered the three main categories of network attacks: denial-of-service (DoS), distributed denial-of-service (DDoS), and data diddling. In the DoS attack, flood attacks, such as SYN flooding, ping flooding, SMURF attack, and DNS service attacks, were discussed in depth. The section also detailed the difference between DoS attacks and DDoS attacks. The brief explanation on various distributed DoS tools, such as Trinoo and Tribe Flood Networks (TFN), gave insight on how DDoS attacks operate. The section on data diddling covered the concepts of spoofing, sniffing, rerouting, and port scanning. Within spoofing, both IP spoofing and ARP spoofing were discussed in detail.

Check Your Understanding

Multiple Choice Questions

1. A bus network constitutes 20 hosts and a server. This network uses the broadcast transmission technology to transfer data. A situation arises where two hosts want to transmit data to the server simultaneously. How will the hosts behave in this situation? (Choose only one)

   a. A conflict situation arises. The network is clogged with requests from both hosts.

   b. Using the arbitrary mechanism, each device waits for a random period of time and then tries again later.

   c. The server intervenes to decide which computer transmits data first.

   d. None of the above.

2. Which topology uses the empty token mechanism to pass data packets on the network?

   a. Bus

   b. Star

   c. Mesh

   d. Ring

3. Consider the following two statements:

   Statement A: IP is responsible for retransmission of data until the data reaches its destination completely.

   Statement B: IP is responsible for transferring data to the destination by attaching destination addresses to data packets.

   Which one is true about the statements written above?

   a. Statement A is TRUE but statement B is FALSE.

   b. Statement B is TRUE but statement A is FALSE.

   c. Both the statements are TRUE.

   d. Both the statements are FALSE.

4. State whether the following statement is TRUE or FALSE:

   A three-way mechanism synchronizes both ends of connection by allotting an initial sequence number to the hosts.

5. A network is set up in such a manner that each device in the network is connected to a central device. Identify the type of network layout.

   a. Bus

   b. Tree

   c. Star

Short Questions

1. Consider a situation. Host A sends requests to Host B on a network. However, Host A does not send the requests with its own IP address. Instead, it sends the requests with a nonexistent IP address. Thinking that requests are from a known host, Host B acknowledges the requests by returning its own IP address to Host A. However, after a few seconds, Host B goes into a hanged state as its memory is clogged with half connections. Can you identify why Host B is in a hanged state?

2. A computer on a network is swamped with several spurious messages from an unknown source. On examining the network, the system administrator comes to the conclusion that not only this computer but others on the network are also behaving abnormally. The other computers do not show signs of being attacked, but their activity log shows processes that do not belong to them. The system administrator presents a report that the machine is infested with DoS attacks. Is he right in his judgment?

3. A computer on a network receives several ICMP request messages with data packets loaded in it. The computer, assuming that the requests are coming from a trusted host, starts assembling the packets. However, the computer soon realizes that the data packets are so large that it does not have the ability to handle them. As a result, its buffer capacity is flooded with data packets and it cannot send replies at the same rate. The computer soon crashes. Identify the attack that has occurred on this computer.

4. An organization has been receiving complaints from its customers that they are not able to access the organization's site. In fact, customers complain that they are redirected to a different site on the network. The organization checks with the DNS administrator to see if the contents of the site have been changed. However, the DNS administrator reports that the site content is intact. In this case, what could be the possible problem with the site?

5. Briefly explain the connection setup of the three-way handshake process of TCP.

Answers

Multiple Choice Answers

1. b. In a bus topology, an arbitration method is needed to resolve the conflict when two or more computers want to transmit data simultaneously.

2. d. A ring topology uses the empty token mechanism to transmit data across a network.

3. b. IP is not responsible for transmitting the data packets again on a network if data is lost in transit. This is the function of the TCP protocol.

4. TRUE

5. c.

Short Answers

1. Host B has undergone a SYN flood attack. In such an attack, the computer is flooded with half connections. In other words, the destination computer does not receive an acknowledgement because the requests contain a nonexistent IP address. As a result, the connection process is not completed, and the other computer remains in a hanged state.

2. The system administrator's report is not correct. The computers on the network are not infected by DoS attacks; they are infected by a single DDoS attack. A DDoS attack uses several computers to infect a single computer on the network. The other computers are used as a means of reaching the victim computer.

3. The computer is flooded with the ping of death attack.

4. Looking at the scenario, it doesn't seem that there is a problem at the organization's end. It appears that some manipulations have been made on the DNS server. The information that maps the domain names with the IP addresses has been tampered with. As a result, instead of opening the organization's site, the customers are redirected to a different site. This type of attack is called a DNS spoofing attack.

5. The steps that are used to set up a connection between two hosts (Host A and Host B) on a network are

   1. Host A sends a SYN packet to Host B.

   2. Host B acknowledges the packets by returning a SYN + ACK packet.

   3. In response to the acknowledgment, Host A sends a SYN packet to Host B.

Chapter 4

Chapter 1, "Security: an Overview" identified three areas that need to be secured on the Web: client, server, and network. The previous chapter, "Understanding Network Security" discussed one of these aspects, which is the network. The chapter identified the need for security and the components that need to be secured on the network. This chapter is a move toward the Web, which is the client, and discusses user-level security, which is based on the browser security.

This chapter has been divided into four sections. The first section, "Browser Security," briefly covers the history of browsers and why browser security is required. Next, it discusses helper applications that extend the capability of browsers. This is followed by a discussion of programming languages that are being used to write programs embedded on Web pages. This will be just an introduction because I cover the details of security-related issues of programming languages in coming sections of the chapter.

The second section, "Java and JavaScript," explores the security issues related to Java and JavaScript. The section begins with a brief on those languages. Then, relating to Java specifically, it starts by introducing how Java is a reliable language and how it provides security. Next, the section introduces JavaScript as a secure language. It compares Java and JavaScript in context of the level of security each provides. The section also talks about issues related to privacy in JavaScript.

The third section, "User Privacy," covers user privacy with respect to cookies. The section begins with an introduction to what cookies are. It then discusses security risks associated with cookies.

The fourth section, "Browser Plugins," discusses the role of plugins with respect to browsing the Internet. The section also covers ActiveX, Authenticode, and security issues related to these.

Browser Security

Browser security is becoming a cause for serious concern in recent times. Even major Web browsers have significant security flaws making users vulnerable to hackers if they visit a Web site that has malicious content. However, before discussing browser security, let's look at the history of browsers and applications that extend browser capabilities.

The History of Browsers

Scientists at CERN developed the first models of Web browsers. These browsers were developed using What You See Is What You Get (WYSIWYG) editors and were basically used for publishing white papers on high-energy particle physics.

The National Center for Supercomputing Applications created another browser that was named Mosaic 2.0. This browser had a simple user interface and the ability to display forms and simple controls, such as text fields, radio buttons, pull-down menus, and push buttons.

IBM computers in the 1970s introduced *block mode* computing, in which a host computer displayed a form on the user's computer. When the user filled the form and clicked on the Send button, the form was sent to the host computer. Editing in the form was done locally on the user's computer so that it didn't consume expensive communication and centralized CPU resources. This style of computing was mainly used in libraries, reference systems, and scholarly journals. However, it did not become very popular then because sending commands and waiting for results required a lot of other activities, such as flipping to a new page of a magazine and checking for a book in the library.

To break the block mode paradigm, Netscape developed a browser that was faster than Mosaic. This browser soon became popular because it could display GIF and JPEG images as they were downloaded. The browser did not wait for the entire image to download.

To extend the capability of its browser, Netscape introduced the `<blink>` tag that enabled the blinking of text three times within a minute. However, the `<blink>` tag was not appreciated much because the blinking text was more of an annoyance than an enhancement in the Web page. Moreover, only Netscape Navigator supports this tag.

Netscape slowly captured the market due to its Web enhancing, customization, animation, and other enhancements.

Attacks Confronted by Browsers

Malicious data can be sent through unsuspecting modes to a user through normal applications. A data-driven attack makes the user's computer vulnerable to virus attacks. These are known as data-driven attacks because malicious data is downloaded to the unsuspecting user's computer.

Social engineering attacks use interpersonal skills for extracting confidential information from users. It basically involves an attacker convincing the user to provide proprietary information or allow unauthorized access to resources. The user is unaware about the ingenuity of the malicious request.

Helper Applications

Most browsers can recognize only a fixed set of data types that include ASCII text, HTML text, GIF images, and JPEG images. However, there are many more data types other than these. It is not possible to convert other data types to the ones that display HTML text and images. For instance, a movie file cannot be converted to a data type that supports ASCII text, HTML text, GIF images, or JPEG images. In such situations, *helper applications* are used. Helper applications are programs available on the clients' side of the network that are run automatically by a browser when a data type is downloaded other than ASCII text, HTML text, GIF images, or JPEG images. Helper applications are designed to extend the capability of a browser.

Before using a helper application, you need to ensure that the following steps have been performed:

- ◆ A hyperlink that has its HREF pointing to the helper application format file has been created.
- ◆ If you are using a server, it must also be configured to pass the correct type to the browser. The browser must know how to find the software needed to interpret the file.

Consider an example where an HTML page has a link pointing to an Excel sheet. This helper application will help the browser in opening the link in Microsoft Excel. Here, it is necessary that the client's computer has Microsoft Excel installed on it or any other program that can interpret .XLS files (Microsoft Excel files). A helper application may point to the source of an application from an intranet as well as from the Internet. The user can download the application being pointed to by the helper application when the browser encounters a file requiring this application for viewing. In this example, when the user clicks on the link, the browser copies the Excel file to a temporary file, and then starts Microsoft Excel. The browser will continue to display the document from which the helper application was launched.

Helper applications enhance the presentation of information. However, their ability to interact with the Web user is very limited. They cannot be used to modify the data or take any actions based on a user's input.

Vulnerability of Helper Applications

Generally, HTML pages do not cause any security risks to the computer, especially if your computer is not on a network. However, if you use helper applications extensively, it could be a cause of security threat to your computer because, although helper applications run on the user's computer, their input comes from Web servers. A hacker can use the powerful features of a helper application to introduce a bug into the user's computer.

Also, most helper applications are downloaded while browsing sites that contain content that require information from the helper applications. A user cannot be sure about the authenticity of the source from which he is downloading the copy of the helper application. A hacker can modify the helper application and introduce malicious code within the client's computer this way.

Configuring Helper Applications

By default, most helper applications are associated with Internet Explorer at the time of its installation. Therefore, in this section, I'll concentrate on configuring helper applications in Netscape.

To configure helper applications in Netscape, follow these steps:

1. Click Edit, Preferences. The Preferences dialog box will appear (see Figure 4.1).

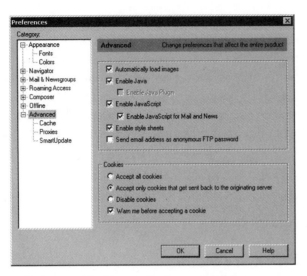

FIGURE 4.1 *The Netscape Preferences dialog box*

2. Under Navigator, select Applications from the Category tree structure. A list of applications along with their associated helper applications will appear (see Figure 4.2). You can view the details of any type of a file, add a new type of helper application, or remove a helper application in this dialog box.

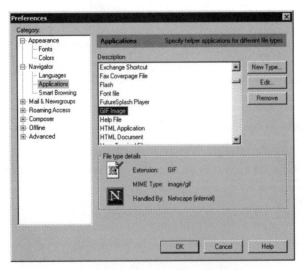

FIGURE 4.2 *The Netscape Preferences dialog box*

3. Click OK to save the change in settings.

Restrictions While Using Helper Applications

An interpreter is one of the most powerful application programs for general purpose programming languages. If appropriate inputs are provided to an interpreter, it can read, modify, open, or erase files from a user's hard disk. This can prove extremely hazardous to a user's computer. Due to these reasons, interpreters should not be used as helper applications. The following applications should not be used as helper applications for the same reason:

♦ **Microsoft Word**. Microsoft Word uses the Visual Basic extension language to execute commands on your system. Therefore, if modified, it can also be used to execute malicious commands on a user's computer. Macro viruses spread fast through this software.

♦ **Microsoft Excel**. Microsoft Excel also uses the Visual Basic extension language to execute commands on your system. As with Microsoft Word, Excel can also be used to execute malicious commands on a user's computer as can any other programs that contain Microsoft's Visual Basic scripting language.

♦ **UNIX shells** such as sh and tcsh should not be used as helper applications because they can trigger malicious commands on the computer.

♦ **Python and Tcl/Tk**. Both are scripting languages that should not be used as helper applications because these can also be used to execute malicious commands on a user's computer.

♦ **Perl**. Programs in Perl can be used to execute any commands and, therefore, may be a threat to the computer on which it is executing.

♦ **COMMAND.COM**. The DOS shell also should not be used as a helper application because it makes the system and the device driver files susceptible to threats.

Let us consider COMMAND.COM. Consider that a server is configured so that files with the extension .BAT are declared to be type application/msdos-script. If any URL includes a link to a file with the extension .BAT, the first time a user clicks the link, he will be prompted to select any appropriate application to open this file. If the user configures the browser to launch .BAT files using COMMAND.COM as the helper application, every time the browser comes across a .BAT file, it will be downloaded to the user's hard disk and executed using COMMAND.COM. Malicious commands that can be extremely hazardous to the user's computer can be included in the .BAT file.

In case the user had configured files ending with .EXE as having MIME type application/msdos-app, clicking the URL would cause the .EXE file to be downloaded and executed with COMMAND.COM. Therefore, clicking a URL that is pointing to .EXE can launch any .EXE file henceforth using COMMAND.COM. An .EXE file is a serious threat to security as the consequences can be dire if a hacker has deliberately introduced it.

Setting General Security Policies for a Browser

You can set security policies for browsers to prevent attacks, including setting various limits of security depending on the types of attacks you want to avoid.

To set security policies for Internet Explorer, follow these steps:

1. Click Tools, Internet Options. The Internet Options dialog box will appear (see Figure 4.3).

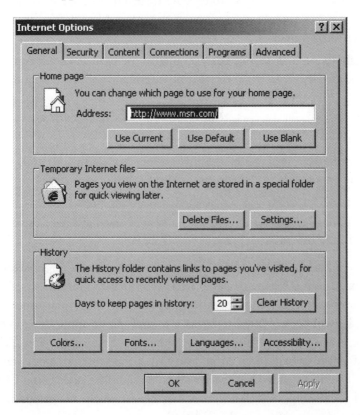

FIGURE 4.3 *The Internet Explorer Internet Options dialog box*

2. Click the Security tab. You can use the slider to set various security levels for different zones in the Security Level For This Zone box. You can configure security settings for the Internet, Local intranet, Trusted sites, and Restricted sites. The four levels of security are Low, Medium-Low, Medium, and High. The default, as shown in Figure 4.4, is Medium.

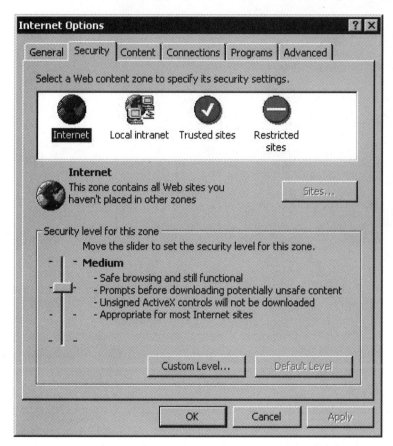

FIGURE 4.4 *The Internet Options dialog box—Medium security setting*

The various options for the security level settings are discussed as follows:

◆ **High**. Although this option makes the browser highly secured, it also makes it the least functional. For instance, cookies are disabled. This option ensures that your computer is not affected by any harmful content available on the Internet (see Figure 4.5).

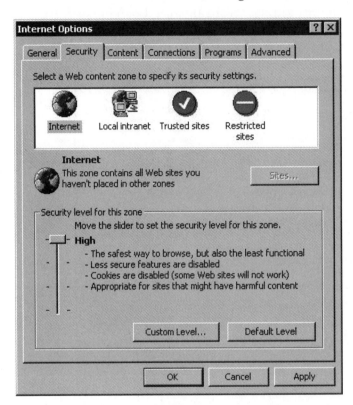

FIGURE 4.5 *The Internet Options dialog box—High security setting*

◆ **Medium**. Setting your browser to Medium security level is the ideal option. Choosing this option will ensure that you can browse safely and yet have a functional browser, unlike the High option. The browser will warn you against downloading any unsafe content. If this option is selected, ActiveX controls that are not signed will not be downloaded to your computer (see Figure 4.6).

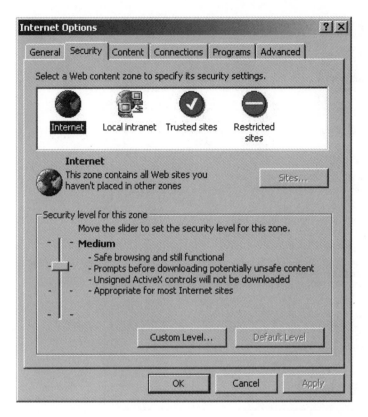

FIGURE 4.6 *The Internet Options dialog box—Medium security setting*

◆ **Medium-Low.** Selecting this option is very similar to Medium but you will not get any prompts as in selecting the Medium option. ActiveX controls that are not signed will not be downloaded. This option is most appropriate for the Intranet because you do not have to take intensive security measures. Figure 4.7 illustrates the Medium-Low security level setting in the Internet Options dialog box.

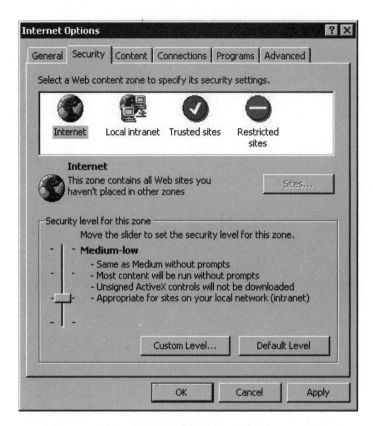

FIGURE 4.7 *The Internet Options dialog box—Medium–Low security setting*

When you move your slider from the default Medium to Medium-Low, you get a warning as shown in Figure 4.8.

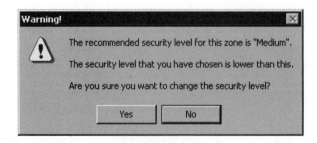

FIGURE 4.8 *The Warning dialog box*

◆ **Low**. The security level is least if you select this option. Most of the content is downloaded without any warnings. You should choose this option only if you trust the sites (see Figure 4.9). You get a warning similar to the one shown in Figure 4.8 when you choose this option.

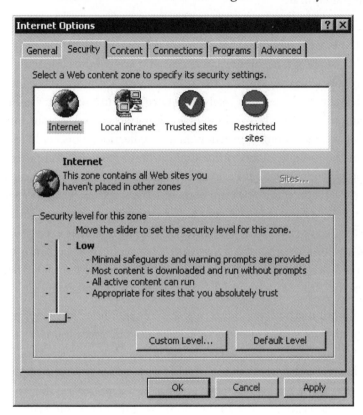

FIGURE 4.9 *The Internet Options dialog box—Low security setting*

Programming Languages

Currently there are various programming languages that are used to write programs embedded in Web pages. These programs are downloaded to Web browsers and run on the user's computer. Some of the languages used to write Web programs are Java, JavaScript, VBScript, and HTML. Microsoft has set a standard, ActiveX, for downloading applications that run on the user's computer. Details of Java, JavaScript, and ActiveX will be discussed subsequently. I'll briefly discuss VBScript and HTML as programming languages used on the Internet.

VBScript

VBScript, a scripting language, is a subset of the programming language Visual Basic. VBScript can be run on any computer that has the scripting engine provided by Microsoft installed in it.

Including VBScript within HTML tags can create dynamic HTML pages. Internet Explorer (IE) is vulnerable to threats from VBScript. A VBScript is very similar to a Visual Basic program. Hence, attackers who are comfortable with Visual Basic can easily introduce bugs into VBScript. Because VBScript is a client-side scripting language, it can be used to easily introduce bugs in the client's computer. The most common is the buffer overflow bug. The attacker uses various methods and commands that lead to buffer overflow in an application. This could lead to a system failure or the running of a harmful application in the user's computer. Even malicious VBScript codes can be used to infest a user's computer. The most widely spread occurrence of a harmful VBScript code was the *loveletter* worm. When this worm attacks a computer, an e-mail is sent to the user with the worm as an attachment. When the user opens the attachment, the VBScript code is executed, causing damage to the user's computer. This worm also replicates itself into various folders of the hard drive to ensure that it is reloaded when the computer reboots. This worm uses the Address book in Microsoft Outlook to replicate itself.

There is no foolproof method for countering the vulnerabilities in VBScript. Programmers, administrators, and users should take certain precautions to prevent unauthorized persons from gaining access to resources. Programmers should set a check for the length and type of input provided by a user for their application code. This ensures that a hacker does not attempt to introduce a buffer overflow bug on the server that is hosting the application. Programmers should run a check for all Web pages that were created in the past. They must also adhere to standard security checks. Administrators should ensure that all the users in the network have installed the latest version of the antivirus kit. Users should ensure that the security level of their browser is set appropriately to prevent any attacker from introducing malicious code into their computer. They should be cautious about any attachments received and should check the source before opening them.

HTML

Hyper Text Markup Language (HTML) is the basic language used to develop Web pages. It is not a dynamic language and is generally opened in a Web browser. It uses a set of tags such as <HEAD> and </HEAD> to give structure to a Web page. A simple Web page that says *Hello World* will look like this:

```
<html>

  <head>
  </head>
  <body>
         <p> Hello World </p>
  </body>
</html>
```

Initially, when HTML was used only to display text, there were no security threats. However, due to additional functionality and features to meet increasing requirements, complexities in the language have increased opportunities for hackers to attack vulnerabilities in HTML. HTML is very vulnerable to attacks such as buffer overflows, HTML e-mail attachments, remote access, and IE scripts. In the buffer overflow attack, there is an overflow of the buffer of a variable in the HTML library that is used by IE, Outlook Express, and Windows Explorer. In Outlook Express 5.0 for Macintosh, attachments are downloaded from an HTML message without warning the user. This is referred to as the HTML e-mail attachment vulnerability. In a remote access attack, an attacker can execute malicious commands through Microsoft Networking. This happens because the window.showHelp() method in IE 5.x does not restrict HTML help files (.CHM) to be executed only from the local host. The help file can be executed from remote hosts and hence makes it prone to hacking. In IE script vulnerability, the Microsoft database file in the ActiveX object tags of HTML documents is opened by IE 5.x without warning the user. This gives a hacker the opportunity to execute malicious commands on the user's computer. Constant attempts are being made to increase the security level of HTML-based programs.

Several extensions were also added to the HTML specifications, including a password field. Unfortunately, this field does very little to enhance real security. After the location of all subsequent pages on a site are opened, hackers can bypass the password protection of the page. They can directly load all the pages that are loaded after a user provides the correct password.

Although user's passwords are ultimately stored in encrypted form, they are not passed in encrypted form in basic HTTP authentication. In basic HTTP authentication, the password is passed over the network not encrypted but also not as plain text—it is "encoded." Anyone watching packet traffic on the network will not see the password in the clear, but the password will be easily decoded by anyone who happens to catch the right network packet.

Java and JavaScript

Sun Microsystems developed the Java programming language. Java is based on the principles of C++ and reflects object-oriented programming (OOP). Java was designed for the stand-alone environment and hence has more functionality compared to its Web based counterpart JavaScript. JavaScript was developed by Netscape Communications Corporation. It is a scripting language that is embedded within HTML tags. Although Java and JavaScript's mode of execution pattern is completely different, JavaScript derives most of its syntax from its parent, Java.

Java

Java is based on the OOP concept. Programmers in Java can define objects and use them for programming purposes. Java needs a Java Runtime Environment (JRE) on the client computer to run and execute a program. Java was not initially developed for writing programs on the Internet. Due to its increasing popularity, Sun and other vendors supplied tools that could be used to create Java applets, which could be used to create applications on the Internet. Java-enabled browsers can run Java using a plugin. Some of the browsers have built-in support as well.

The syntax for Java is similar to C++. Concepts such as dynamic binding, garbage collection, and a simple inheritance model prove Java's lineage with the OOP concept. Java is platform-independent. Java programs are not compiled for any particular microprocessor. They are compiled into a processor-independent byte code. Java Class Loader is used to load the byte code into the computer's memory. Finally, the byte code is run on a Java Virtual Machine (JVM). The JVM can run Java programs directly on the OS or can be embedded inside a browser, allowing programs to be executed as they are downloaded from the Internet.

Java can also be compiled into a computer code and run on a target computer. However, in this case it loses its advantage of being computer-independent but retains its ability to manage memory automatically.

Security in Java

Initially Java was not developed as a secure language. When Java was used for writing programs for the Internet, security became a concern. On the Internet, any user can download any bit of code and execute it. There are chances that the code may contain malicious programs. Java uses many techniques to limit the activities of downloaded programs. Some of the techniques are

◆ Sandbox

◆ Byte-code verifier

◆ SecurityManager class

◆ Java Class Loader

Sandbox

Java programs are not permitted to directly tamper with the hardware of a computer or to make any direct call to the OS. Java runs on a virtual machine within a restricted virtual space. This concept is called *Sandbox* because it is similar to a child's game in which the child can play without getting hurt or hurting others.

Byte-Code Verifier

The byte-code verifier in Java checks whether any downloaded byte code is necessarily a compiled Java program or not. It ensures that the downloaded byte code does not violate any access restrictions and does not manipulate any pointers.

SecurityManager Class

If the Sandbox concept was completely implemented, the functional aspect of Java programs would decrease tremendously because it would be extremely difficult for Java programs to communicate with the external world and derive relevant data. To overcome this hurdle, Java uses a series of special classes that permit programs running inside the Sandbox to communicate with the external world. For example, Java programs use the Java class FileOutputStream to open a file from the user's hard disk to write into it.

Java uses a mechanism wherein programs downloaded from an external and unreliable source run with fewer privileges than a program executed from the user's hard disk. The creators of Java created a special class, SecurityManager to implement this. SecurityManager is invoked before any unsafe task is performed. SecurityManager decides whether the task should be performed or not.

Java Class Loader

Most of the security checks in Java are programmed within Java. The next task before the creators of Java was to ensure that no malicious piece of code could disable any of these checks. Any malicious piece of code can disable the `Security-Manager` class or tamper with it in a manner that would permit the code to run. This can happen when a malicious piece of code exploits a bug in the JRE. To avoid these kinds of attacks, the creators of Java introduced Class Loaders. The Class Loader analyzes the class to ensure that they do not violate the JRE.

Loopholes in Java Security

Most security issues in Java are implementation errors and design flaws. Implementation errors are bugs in the JRE. Security flaws in the implementation errors can be broadly classified as

◆ **Class Library bugs**. These bugs give malicious programs access to a user's personal information.

◆ **Bugs in JVM**. These bugs tamper with Java's type system. If the type system has been tampered with, the JVM can be tuned to execute arbitrary code.

Initially, numerous design flaws were detected in Java. Design flaws are more serious compared to implementation errors because fixing design flaws might affect genuine programs that depend on these flaws to work properly. One major flaw was that the complete dependency of the security system in Java was based on maintaining the integrity of the Java type system. The integrity of the Java type system, in turn, depends on the proper functioning of the byte-code verifier and the `SecurityManager` class. Both, the byte-code verifier and the `SecurityManager` class run into numerous lines of code, making it susceptible to errors. Following are some of the known security flaws in Java.

Buffer Overflow Bug

One of the earliest of the identified bugs is a buffer overflow in some Windows 95/NT versions of the Java Virtual Machine. Some variables in the Java library do not check for buffer overflow, making the user's computer vulnerable. The buffer overflow bug can cause your system to crash.

Execution of Arbitrary Computer Instructions

In this bug, using the Netscape caching mechanism, a binary library file is first downloaded to the user's hard disk. Then, the Java interpreter is used for loading the file into memory and executing it. This bug is present in Netscape 2.0 and 2.01 versions. It has been fixed in the 2.02 and higher versions.

Utilizing Local Resources by Storm Attacks

In these kinds of attacks, the disk space of a computer is utilized excessively. The computer is prevented from performing any genuine tasks. For example, triggering the opening of many windows in a short span of time will divert the computer's resources. These kinds of attacks can be harmful and can cause annoyance to the user.

Bypassing Java SecurityManager with Malicious Byte Code

This bug can be used to bypass Java SecurityManager and execute malicious programs. The bug is present in IE 3.01 and earlier versions and in Netscape Navigator 3.01 in JDK 1.1. A patch for this bug is available for Java library licensees.

Utilizing Network Resources by Denial of Service

These kinds of attacks are similar to storm attacks but aim at the network instead. In this, network traffic is diverted to a particular server. This results in excessive utilization of server resources and forces the server to deny services to genuine requests.

Professor Edward W. Felten and his team identified the following about Java and Java-enabled browsers:

◆ Denial-of-service attacks could be effected in two ways. First, by locking certain internal elements of the Netscape and HotJava browsers, thereby preventing further host lookups via DNS. Second, by forcing CPU and RAM over-utilization, thus grinding the browser to a halt. Further, the origin of such an attack could be obscured because the detrimental effects could be delayed by issuing the instructions as a timed job. Therefore, a cruiser could theoretically land on the offending page at noon, but the effect would not surface until hours later.

◆ DNS attacks could be initiated where the browser's proxies would be knocked out, and the system's DNS server could be arbitrarily assigned by a malicious Java applet. This means that the victim's DNS queries could be rerouted to a cracked DNS server, which would provide misinformation on host names. This could be a very serious problem that could ultimately result in a root compromise (if the operator of the victim machine were foolish enough to browse the Web as root).

◆ At least one version (and perhaps more) of Java-enabled browsers could write to a Windows 95 file system. In most all versions, environment variables are easily culled from a Java applet. Java applets could snoop data that many feel is private, and information could be gathered about where the target had been.

Making Network Connections with Arbitrary Hosts

Netscape Navigator 2.0 contained another Java bug, which restricted applets from contacting arbitrary hosts. This bug has been fixed in the 2.01 version.

Applets should communicate only with the server from where they originated. In this bug, when an applet is downloaded to a user's computer, it can connect to any computer on the user's local area network. It can connect to another computer even if the LAN was protected by a firewall. Most LAN setups trust local computers, giving access to services that are not given to distant computers. For example, an applet can open up a connection to the organization's discussion forum and transmit the information back to a foreign host. Taking advantage of this bug, applets can be even used to collect information on the network topology and name services from behind a firewall.

An attacker, to tamper with Java's Domain Name System (DNS), can tap this security hole. The DNS can be manipulated to allow contacting a particular host. The attacker using his own DNS server can create a false DNS entry to trick the Java system into thinking that a script is allowed to talk to a host that it is not authorized otherwise.

Session Hijacking

In this attack, the DNS server can be modified to divert all requests to another server. The other server to which the requests are sent might contain malicious programs that could crash systems.

Transferring Information by Disclosure Attacks

In these attacks, information from a client computer is disclosed to a remote computer.

Setting Java Security Policies

You can set three kinds of security policies for Java:

◆ Not run Java completely.

◆ Run Java with various kinds of privileges depending on the source of the programs. Programs running from the user's hard disk would not have any restrictions. However, programs running from the Internet would have many restrictions.

◆ No restrictions for any Java program.

Setting Security Policy for Java in IE

To set the security policy for Java in IE, perform the following steps:

1. Click Tools, Internet Options. The Internet Options dialog box appears.

2. Click the Security tab.

3. In the Security Level For This Zone box, click the Custom Level button. The Security Settings dialog box appears as shown in Figure 4.10.

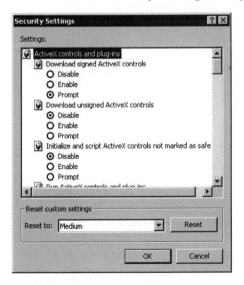

FIGURE 4.10 *The IE Security Settings dialog box*

4. Scroll down to the part that contains Microsoft VM, Java Permissions. You can opt between Custom, Disable Java, High Safety, Low Safety, and Medium Safety (see Figure 4.11).

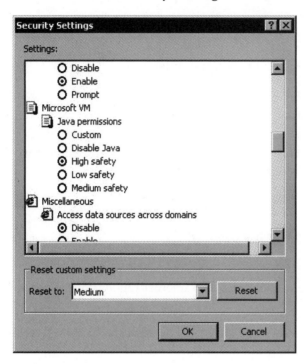

FIGURE 4.11 *Java Permissions options in the IE Security Settings dialog box*

The various options under Java Permissions are

◆ **Custom**. You can specify individual settings for each type of access that a Java applet can request by selecting this option.

◆ **Disable Java**. You can prohibit Java applets from running on your computer by selecting this option.

◆ **High Safety**. Select this option if you want to permit the least amount of access to the Java applets.

◆ **Low Safety**. Select this option if you want to provide the greatest amount of access to the Java applets.

◆ **Medium Safety**. Choose this option if you want to provide a moderate amount of access to the Java applets.

To completely disable Java applets from running on your computer, select Disable Java, as shown in Figure 4.12.

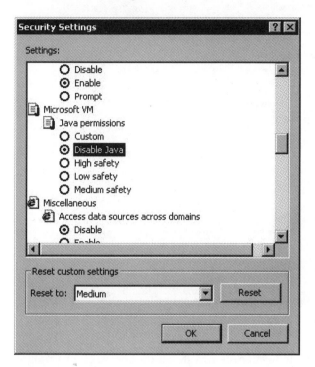

FIGURE 4.12 *Java permissions disabled in the IE Security Settings dialog box*

5. Click OK to save your settings. The Security Settings dialog box will close.

6. Click OK to close the Internet Options dialog box.

Setting Security Policy for Java in Netscape

To set the security policy for Java in Netscape, perform the following steps:

1. Click Edit, Preferences. The Preferences dialog box will appear.

2. In the Categories tree structure, click Advanced. The default selections in the Advanced area will appear as shown in Figure 4.13.

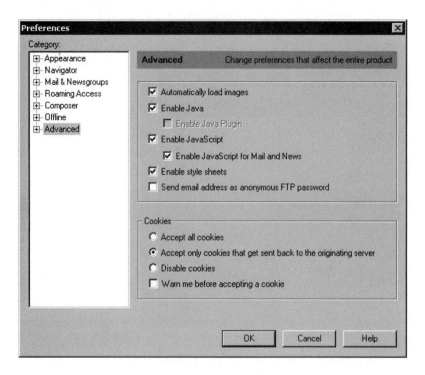

FIGURE 4.13 *The Netscape Preferences dialog box*

3. Deselect the Enable Java check box if you do not want Java programs to run on Netscape.

4. Click OK to save your settings.

JavaScript

JavaScript is a scripting language that was originally known as LiveScript. It is a precompiled language that can be used on both the client side as well as the server side on the Internet. JavaScript is directly inserted into HTML pages by using the following code within the <HTML> tags:

```
<Script Language="JavaScript">

code.....
</Script>
```

Unlike Java, JavaScript cannot be used to create stand-alone applications, as it does not have a run-time environment. It is always executed in browsers. JavaScript was designed by Netscape Corporation for Netscape Navigator 2.0 and higher versions. It is also compatible with Microsoft's IE 3.0 and higher versions. JavaScript for IE 3.0 and higher versions is known as JScript.

JavaScript is a language developed for controlling the browser. Using JavaScript, you can open and close windows, adjust browser settings, manipulate form elements, and download and execute Java applets.

JavaScript executes on the client's computer, which makes it prone to malicious attacks. The developers of JavaScript have adopted many mechanisms to ensure that it is not vulnerable to security breaches.

Programs written in JavaScript are safer compared to programs written in Java and other programming languages because

- There are no methods in JavaScript that can open connections with other computers on the network.

- There are no methods in JavaScript that can directly access the user's file system.

- The `SecurityManager` object defines the various activities that a remote computer is allowed in a host computer. It does not permit the functioning of any suspicious operation.

- `SecurityManager` does not allow JavaScript to execute any arbitrary system commands, to load or open driver files, to load system libraries, or even modify .DLL files.

Security Flaws in JavaScript

Due to enhancements and increased functionality, security flaws are slowly creeping into JavaScript, too. In Java, attackers can modify data on the user's hard disk. In JavaScript, most attacks are related to infringements on the privacy of the user. A large number of security loopholes have been identified in JavaScript. Some of the known flaws in JavaScript implemented with Netscape and Internet Explorer are discussed below.

Vulnerability to Denial-of-Service Attacks

JavaScript can be used to take up system memory and processor time excessively, thereby causing denial to genuine requests. Incorrectly written programs or even purposeful inconsistencies in coding can cause the program to go into an infinite loop, for example, calling the `alert()` method in a tight loop. Every time the loop is executed, an alert window appears on the user's screen. There is no maximum limit for the number of times this method can be called. The only option might be to shut down the browser.

Reading Arbitrary Files from a User's Computer

A bug in the implementation of JavaScript allows a Web page to read arbitrary files from a user's computer and transmits the arbitrary files across the Internet. This bug is found in Netscape Communicator 4.5 and 4.04–4.05 versions. However, Internet Explorer is not affected by this bug. This bug affects both the Windows and UNIX versions of Communicator. Any HTML page can be the source of this bug, or it can be transmitted through e-mail attachments.

Vulnerability in Using Frames

This bug allows data availability across browser frames. For example, if you are using two frames in your browser and accessing a different site in each, this bug has the ability to read information from one frame to another. This is potentially risky, as a downloaded JavaScript program from one unsafe frame can access and obtain information from another window. Although JavaScript cannot recover the URLs of Web pages, it can access a list of URLs of all the inline images, URLs of all applets, inline information about images such as width and height, and URLs of ActiveX controls. Therefore, JavaScript can be used to silently monitor visited sites and obtain details of those sites.

Accessing a User's Browser Settings

JavaScript code implemented on Netscape Navigator 4.0–4.04 can be made to access the preference details of a user's browser. The details stored in a file called preferences.js also contain other information, such as the user's e-mail ID, identity of the mail servers, FTP passwords, and so on.

A hacker can use this bug to obtain personal information about a user without his explicit permission and can be used for malicious activities. For example, a hacker could obtain your e-mail ID and spam your Inbox. However, a hacker can obtain FTP and POP e-mail passwords only if the user saves his settings. Therefore, it is always better to enter information every time one logs in. Although this precaution cannot prevent the availability of the user's e-mail ID, it can avoid the transit of other information, such as FTP passwords.

Breaking into a User's Hard Disk

This is called a Freiburg attack. JavaScript coding deployed on IE 4.0 working on Windows 95/NT allows a hacker in a remote location to access the content of various files located in a user's local computer. Firewalls cannot prevent this attack even if they are set at a high security mode. However, Macintosh versions of IE 4.0 are not affected by this attack.

This bug uses JavaScript to create a 1 x 1–pixel wide invisible frame. The JavaScript program running in the invisible frame scans the user's local computer while the user is browsing the Internet.

The Netscape Cache Browsing Bug

A bug in the Windows Home edition version of Netscape Navigator 3.04, 4.07, and 4.5 allows a remote user to access data in the History folder of a user. The hacker can derive a list of sites visited by the user based on this folder. This bug does not affect Mac- and UNIX-based systems.

The Cuartango Security Flaw

IE 4.0–4.01 and prerelease versions of IE 5.0 allow JavaScript programs to cut and paste text into file upload fields. This enables hackers to steal files over the Internet through the implementation of JavaScript. Any Web page or e-mail message can steal any file from the user's disk. This is known as the Cuartango bug.

Monitoring the User's Session

Earlier versions of IE 4.0 and Netscape Navigator 4.02 allow JavaScript code to capture the URLs of various documents the user visited as well as the contents of fill-out forms, cookies, and other information about the user's session, even if he is connected with a 128-bit SSL connection. This bug intrudes into the user's privacy but cannot modify the data or software on the user's computer without explicit permission.

This bug uses JavaScript to open an invisible window. The user cannot see the window and, so he is not aware that a JavaScript program continues to run even after the user has exited the page that launched the script. This bug could also open a new browser window and attract the user into using the window for subsequent browsing.

Uploading File Hole

JavaScript implemented on Netscape Navigator enables browsers to upload any local file on the user's hard disk. The hacker must know the name of the file in advance to take advantage of this bug. Most browsers have the same file name, therefore, it is not a very difficult task to find it. Sensitive information such as login names and system passwords are stored in files with known names. If hackers in remote locations can access these files, the computers can become vulnerable to any kind of attack. Netscape Navigator 2.0, 3.0, and 3.01 and Netscape Communicator 4.0 are all affected by this bug. The user can close this hole by selecting Warn Before Submitting A Form Insecurely in the Security Options dialog box.

Earlier Known Bugs

There have been many bugs in earlier versions of Netscape. Some of them are as follows:

- Earlier versions of Netscape Navigator allowed JavaScript codes to send e-mails without the user's explicit permission. The user can avoid this bug by choosing Warn Before Sending Mail in the Security Options dialog box. This option is available only in later versions of Netscape browsers.

- A hacker can use JavaScripts to trick a user into uploading a file from his local hard disk to an arbitrary computer on the Internet. Although the initiation of the transfer happens from the user's end, the hacker can cleverly mask it into something very unsuspecting.

- A hacker can use JavaScript to monitor all the sites visited by a user during a session.

Setting Security Policy for JavaScript in Internet Explorer

To set the security policy for JavaScript in Internet Explorer, perform the following steps:

1. Click Tools, Internet Options. The Internet Options dialog box will appear.

2. Click the Security tab.

3. In the Security Level For This Zone box, click the Custom Level button. The Security Settings dialog box appears.

4. Scroll down to the portion on Scripting, as shown in Figure 4.14.

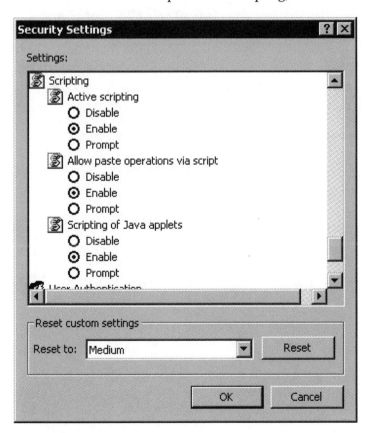

FIGURE 4.14 *The Internet Explorer Security Settings dialog box*

5. Select the appropriate option—Disable, Enable, or Prompt—from Scripting of Java Applets. It would be advisable not to choose the Prompt radio button because every time you visit a site with JavaScript you will be prompted by a dialog box that might soon become very annoying. Select Disable if you do not want JavaScript to run on your computer. You can choose Enable if you want JavaScript to run on your computer.

6. Click OK to save your settings. The Security Settings dialog box will close.

7. Click OK to close the Internet Options dialog box.

Setting Security Policy for JavaScript in Netscape

To set the security policy for Java in Netscape, perform the following steps:

1. Click on Edit, Preferences. The Preferences dialog box will appear.

2. Click Advanced from the Categories tree structure. The default selections in the Advanced area will appear as shown Figure 4.15.

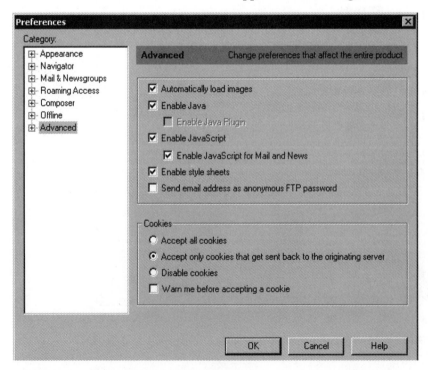

FIGURE 4.15 *The Netscape Preferences dialog box*

3. Deselect the Enable JavaScript check box if you do not want JavaScripts to run on Netscape. You can deselect the Enable JavaScript for Mail and News option and select the Enable JavaScript option alone.

4. Click OK to save your settings.

User Privacy

Most sites use a technology called *cookies* to retain a visitor's information for future use. Cookies are small text files that reside on the hard disk of a user's computer. These files contain information and details of Web site visits. For example, when a user wants to send an e-card, he provides the Web site with his name, e-mail address, and optionally his address, too. This information gets stored in a cookie on the hard disk. Next time when the user visits the same site for sending an e-card, it will recognize him and display the information provided by him earlier, which saves time.

Cookies are used to keep track of a user's browsing habits. They provide information about the sites he has visited. This information is at times used for market research. Web sites use this information to determine their target audience for advertising.

Types of Cookies

Session and Persistent Cookies

There are two types of cookies, session and persistent cookies. Cookies stored in memory are known as session cookies. Cookies stored on your hard disk are known as persistent cookies. Session cookies are used to store information only within a session and are deleted from the cache when the user ends the session. To enable session cookies in IE, perform the following steps:

1. Click Tools, Internet Options. The Internet Options dialog box will appear.

2. Click the Security tab.

3. Click the Custom Level button from the Security Level For This Zone box. The Security Settings dialog box appears.

4. Scroll down to the portion on Cookies. Under Allow Per-Session Cookies (Not Stored), if you select Enable , your computer will accept session cookies (see Figure 4.16). You can choose to disable this option too. Selecting the Prompt radio button is not advisable, as it might cause unnecessary annoyance.

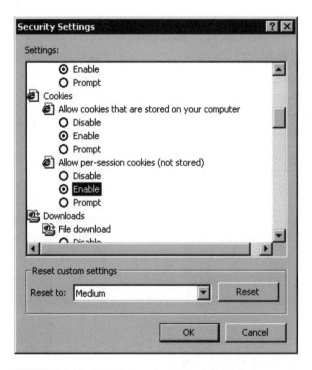

FIGURE 4.16 *The IE Security Settings dialog box*

First-Party and Third-Party Cookies

First-party cookies are generated by the host domain. Third-party cookies are generated by any other domain. Let me take an example to differentiate between the two. Let's assume that www.yahoo.com has banner ads advertising www.designyourwear.com and www.credit4all.com. When you visit Yahoo!, all three sites place their cookies on your computer. The cookies set by www.yahoo.com are first-party cookies, and the cookies set by www.designyourwear.com and www.credit4all.com are third-party cookies. Cookies are uniquely set for a user profile and can be retrieved only by the host domain that set the cookie. There is a known security leak in IE 4.0 and IE 5.0 where a Web site could retrieve cookies set by another domain. This has been corrected in IE 5.5 and higher versions. However, the user can proactively close this bug in Netscape by performing the following steps:

1. Click on Edit, Preferences. The Preferences dialog box will appear.

2. Click Advanced from the Categories tree structure. The default selections in the Advanced area will appear.

3. Select Accept Only Cookies That Get Sent Back To The Originating Server to ensure that your computer accepts only first-party cookies (see Figure 4.17).

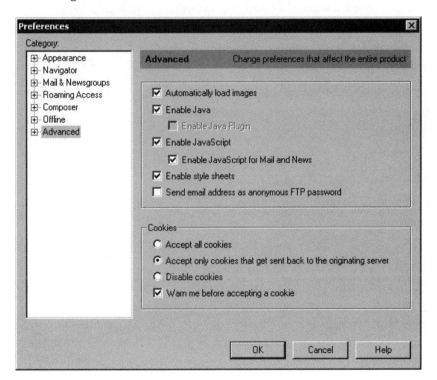

FIGURE 4.17 *The Netscape Preferences dialog box*

4. Click OK to save your settings.

Advantages of Using Cookies

Cookies can be used for personalization. For example, consider the site www.yahoo.com. This site allows a user to personalize his home page to display only required information. The user can choose to have only news, weather forecasts, and mail links in his home page. This personalization is stored in a cookie on the user's hard disk. Every time the user visits www.yahoo.com, only the personalized page will appear. Therefore, cookies are useful in customizing a browser and providing personalized content.

Cookies can save time by preventing repetitive entries. For example, if a user shops online at www.amazon.com, the information provided by him while making the purchase will be stored in a cookie. When the user visits the site again, the cookie helps the Web page server to recall the information provided by him in his first visit. This simplifies the process and saves time.

Cookies cannot be used to obtain information about a user or his computer system. It can only be used to retrieve information provided by the user. Cookies cannot contain viruses, and Web sites cannot use cookies to induce viruses.

Cookies—A Security Privacy Risk

Though cookies can be used to personalize a browser, they can prove a serious threat to security, too.

A cookie can be viewed by the user and the Web site that issued the cookie. Most companies do not share cookie information with third parties. However, it is possible there are companies that give third parties access to cookie information without the permission or knowledge of the user. This can lead to unnecessary harassment. For example, if the mail ID given by the user in some Web site is shared by that Web site with a third party XYZ, XYZ can use that mail ID and target the user with advertisements that he may not be interested in.

Two different sites can share cookies between them. One site can provide to another the cookie information provided by a user during a Web visit and vice versa. Netscape has a solution to prevent this. However, Internet Explorer does not. (Refer to the section on first-party cookies for the solution provided by Netscape.)

The cookie information stored in your computer is not encrypted. Therefore, anybody who can access a computer's hard disk can access its cookie information, too.

Certain Web sites use a secure ID/password to access sensitive data stored in cookies. However, not all Web sites follow this. Some sites store sensitive data without any security, and this data can be accessed by anybody who has access to the computer.

Managing Cookies

You can change the privacy settings for cookies based on the amount of security required.

Configuring Privacy Settings for Cookies

The latest browsers support various levels of settings. The Privacy Settings slider of Internet Explorer consists of six levels: Block All Cookies, High, Medium, Low, and Accept All Cookies. Medium is the default level.

◆ **Block all.** This option blocks cookies from all Web sites. The existing cookies on the hard disk cannot be read by the Web site that created it.

◆ **High**. This option blocks cookies that have a compact privacy policy specifying the usage of personal information without the user's explicit consent. It also blocks cookies that do not have a compact privacy policy.

◆ **Medium high**. This option blocks first-party cookies that have a compact privacy policy specifying the usage of personal information without the user's implicit consent. It also blocks third-party cookies that do not have a compact privacy policy or use personal information without the user's explicit consent.

◆ **Medium** (Default). This option blocks third-party cookies that do not have a compact privacy policy or that have a compact privacy policy specifying the usage of personal information without the user's implicit consent. It downgrades first-party cookies that have a compact privacy policy that specifies the usage of personal information without the user's implicit consent.

 NOTE

Downgrading deletes cookies when the browser is closed. It leashes the first-party cookies that do not have a compact privacy policy. *Leashing* is restricting access to the cookies to only the first-party domain.

◆ **Low**. This option leashes first-party cookies without a compact privacy policy. It also downgrades third-party cookies without a compact privacy policy or that have a compact privacy policy that specifies the usage of personal information without the user's implicit consent.

◆ **Accept all**. All the cookies will be saved in your computer.

 CAUTION

Changing privacy preferences will not affect the cookies already present in a computer unless Accept All Cookies or Block All Cookies is selected.

Configuring Privacy Settings for Cookies in Internet Explorer

To set the privacy policy for cookies in Internet Explorer, perform the following steps:

1. Click Tools, Internet Options. The Internet Options dialog box will appear.
2. Click the Security tab.
3. Click the Custom Level button from the Security Level For This Zone box. The Security Settings dialog box appears.
4. Scroll down to the portion on Cookies, as shown in Figure 4.18.

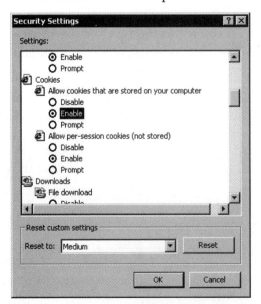

FIGURE 4.18 *The IE Security Settings dialog box*

You can select Enable under Allow Cookies That Are Stored On Your Computer if you want to store cookies in your computer. You can select Disable if you do not want to store cookies in your computer. If you select Prompt, every time you visit a site, the browser will prompt you whether or not to accept the cookie from the site. This can become very annoying.

5. Click OK to save your settings.

Cookies in IE can be disabled by setting the security level for the Internet to High. To do this, perform the following steps:

1. Click Tools, Internet Options. The Internet Options dialog box will appear.

2. Click on the Security tab.

3. Move the slider to High in the Security Level For This Zone box. This will also ensure all cookies are disabled.

Configuring Privacy Settings for Cookies in Netscape

To configure privacy settings for Cookies in Netscape, perform the following steps:

1. Click on Edit, Preferences. The Preferences dialog box will appear.

2. Click Advanced from the Category tree structure. The default selections in the Advanced area will appear (see Figure 4.19).

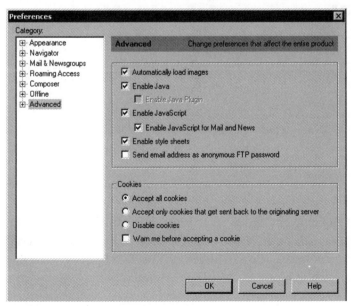

FIGURE 4.19 *The Netscape Preferences dialog box*

There are three options in the Cookies box: Accept All Cookies, Accept Only Cookies That Get Sent Back To The Originating Server, and Disable Cookies. If you want your computer to accept all cookies, select Accept All Cookies. All cookies from visited Web sites will be saved on your computer.

3. If you want the browser to warn you before accepting any cookie, select Warn Me Before Accepting A Cookie Option. It is suggested you not select this option, as frequent warning messages can become annoying.

5. Click OK to save your settings.

Configuring Privacy Settings on a Per-Site Basis for Cookies

In Internet Explorer, you can set preferences for cookies on a per-site basis. Setting per-site preferences will override the default settings of a user for the selected sites in the Per Site Privacy Actions dialog box. However, this does not work if you have selected the Accept All Cookies or Block All Cookies option. Per-site privacy options take precedence over all privacy options other than Accept All Cookies and Block All Cookies. This option is available only in higher versions of browsers.

Browser Plugins and ActiveX

Unsuspecting users can easily become targets of virus attacks when they download malicious programs from the Internet. When a program is downloaded, the user has limited control over the execution of the program. Hackers can write programs to crash the computer or erase the files on the system.

A browser plugin is a software application used to manage a particular kind of document. For example, when a user opens a link containing an MS Word document, most browsers pass the file to the MS Word plugin. In most of the cases, content is passed to the plugin without the user's knowledge or consent. This makes plugins vulnerable to virus attacks. For example, in IE 3.0 and 4.0, using the Microsoft Office plugin, an attacker could run arbitrary code on the client computer. Plugins are manually downloaded and stored by users in a special directory located in the browser's program directory. The Web browser scans this directory when it starts up to assess what plugins are available.

Two popular plugins are Macromedia Shockwave and Adobe Acrobat. Macromedia Shockwave is used to play animated sequences and Adobe Acrobat is used to display .PDF files.

To prevent an attack through a plugin, you should disallow plugins that you do not use because they have full access to your computer and are written and supplied by third parties. Whenever you have to download a new plugin, ensure that you download it from a reliable source.

A plugin does not come with the program's source code, and therefore, it is difficult to determine whether the plugin is reliable or not. Instead, you should assess the plugin's source and determine its reliability.

Plugins can damage the hard disk as soon as you start downloading them. The original plugin would have been an authentic plugin, but a copy of it might have been tampered with. The plugin can introduce a general-purpose program (that might not be malicious) that can be misused by an attacker.

ActiveX is an alternative developed by Microsoft for Netscape's plugins. ActiveX controls are .COM objects that download executable files from the Internet. ActiveX includes protocols and APIs. The entire collection is known as an ActiveX control with a file extension .OCX. There are many similarities between Netscape's plugins and Microsoft's ActiveX controls. However, there are a few differences, too, as follows:

◆ Plugins are manually installed and ActiveX controls are automatically installed.

◆ ActiveX controls can be digitally signed using Authenticode to ensure the source of the .OCX file. The plugins in Netscape do not have any such utility.

ActiveX controls can perform simple activities as well as complex activities. It can be used to view a .GIF file as well as implement databases. There are two types of ActiveX controls:

◆ **.OCX files containing native computer code that is written in C, C++, or Visual Basic.** The source code of the control is compiled into an executable file and is downloaded and executed on the user's computer.

◆ **.OCX files containing Java byte code.** The source code is written in Java or any other language and compiled into a Java byte code. These controls are downloaded to browsers and executed on a virtual machine.

There are two kinds of ActiveX controls, as discussed. Different ActiveX controls have different security implications. The first control is used predominantly for downloading and running a native computer code. It is at the programmer's discretion to use the ActiveX API or use the native OS API. There is no known methodology to audit the ActiveX control's functions on most computers' OS.

In the latter one, the ActiveX control downloaded as Java byte-code restrictions can be applied. These controls can be set to run within Java Sandbox. In this case the functions of the ActiveX control can be clearly audited.

Ensuring Security in ActiveX Controls

ActiveX components have complete access to a user's computer. To ensure that ActiveX components are safe, Microsoft has introduced digital signatures for them, and each ActiveX control has one associated with it. A digital signature verifies the contents and source of a file. It is a declaration from the author that the software is free from any kind of virus or malicious component. Digital signatures cannot be altered and can only be obtained by purchasing a certificate from a Certifying Authority (CA). The CA is a trusted third party that certifies the identity of the source and issues a certificate, which serves as verification to the author's credential.

Signing a Code

Files with extensions .OCX, .EXE, .DLL, .VBD, or .CAB can contain a digital signature. To obtain a digital signature for your piece of code, there are two main steps involved. First, you should apply for a certificate. Second, you should sign your code. The steps are as follows:

1. Apply for a certificate from a CA. CAs, as discussed, verify the identity of an author and provide a certificate that proves the authenticity of the author.

2. Obtain the latest tools for signing files and checking signatures.

3. Organize the files that need to be signed. Signing any .OCX, .EXE, .DLL, or .VBD does not require any special preparation. While signing a .CAB file, the following entry should be added to the .DDF file:

```
.Set ReservePerCabinetSize=6144
```

4. Use signcode.EXE for signing your files. Following is an example:

```
Signcode -prog filename -name displayname -info http://www.myaddress-inc-10.com -
spc mycredentials.spc -pvk myprivatekey.pvk
```

5. Test the signatures. For testing a signed .OCX, .EXE, .DLL, or .VBD
   file, run `chktrust filename` where `filename` is the name of the file that
   you signed. For testing a signed .CAB, run `chktrust -c`
   `cabfilename.cab` where `cabfilename` is the name of the file that you
   signed.

If the signing was a successful process, either of the above tests will display the
certificate.

Using Authenticode

Authenticode is a technology used to prevent the distribution of harmful pieces
of code. Authenticode is used to verify the author of the code for Internet users
who are downloading it. Authenticode also ensures that the code has not been
tampered with or altered after the application of the digital signature.

Authenticode has evolved from public key signature technology. In public key signature, key pairs are used to encrypt data. Key pairs are used for encrypting and
decrypting files. The public key and the private key are used to ensure the privacy
of files. The public key is used for encrypting data and the private key is used for
decrypting data. Authenticode is a revised version of public key signature technology. Public key signature technology can be used for small files, such as an
e-mail message, and Authenticode is used for larger files.

The Authenticode process includes the following steps:

1. When a file is signed by the author, a number known as a *hash* is calculated. The hash is the total number of bytes of the file. Using a private
   key, a hash is encrypted and inserted into the file. The author deploys
   the file to a Web server.

2. When a user downloads the file, the hash is recalculated. If the number
   matches with the number encrypted in the file, the content of the file is
   verified.

3. The public key is used by the browser to identify the author and the CA
   who provided the certificate.

4. The author's identity is verified by the CA, and a certificate is issued that contains the author's name encrypted with the private key.

5. The private key is used by the browser to decrypt the file. Installation of the file follows this.

This security model places the responsibility for the computer system's security squarely on the user. If the browser downloads an ActiveX control, the .OCX file that does not have a digital signature or that has been signed but certified by an unknown CA, a dialog box appears warning the user that the action may be unsafe. The user can choose to abort the download or to continue. Though ActiveX supports digital signatures as a security measure, it takes a moderately experienced user to check the source of the component. Therefore, some organizations prefer to completely disable ActiveX controls rather than permit their users to decide whether an ActiveX control is safe to download or not.

Authenticode can be used for different purposes based on the type of ActiveX control.

Using Authenticode for Controls Distributed in Native Computer Code

Authenticode can be used to decide whether a control should be downloaded or not. Authenticode signatures are verified only when the control is downloaded from the Internet. A control from the local hard disk is assumed safe to run.

Using Authenticode for Controls Distributed in Java Byte code

Authenticode can be used to decide whether a control should be downloaded or not. In IE 4.0, Authenticode can be used to determine the access permission to be given to the Java byte code when it is running.

Security Threats in ActiveX Controls

Security threats from ActiveX controls arise when a user accesses a site that has an ActiveX control registered on the user's computer. The ActiveX control automatically downloads to the user's computer. Earlier versions of IE were vulnerable to security threats due to ActiveX controls. The latest version of IE has a more foolproof security check to counter threats from ActiveX controls.

A hacker can use different methods to trap the loopholes in ActiveX controls. Some of them have been discussed.

Using Direct Commands

A hacker can write malicious code within the ActiveX control. When the control is downloaded, the code is executed. The code could perform any operation that could result in dangerous consequences to the user's computer. This code will run only if the browser does not check whether or not the code is safe to download and the security settings of the browser have been kept as Low.

Using Indirect Commands

A hacker can write code within an ActiveX control that could, if downloaded affect another application in the user's computer. The control can corrupt the user's hard disk. For example, supplying an unchecked buffer to provide a large amount of data to a variable in the ActiveX control. This results in a buffer overflow when the control is initialized.

Posing As a Secure ActiveX Control

A browser generally checks for the digital signature of a control. If the security setting is set to Medium, a user can opt to download the control or not. A hacker can trick the browser to believe that the ActiveX is safe and can be downloaded. The unsuspecting user would then download the malicious code that could prove a serious threat to his computer.

Setting Security Policies for ActiveX Controls

ActiveX has increasingly become popular as it has a vast number of functionalities. The popularity of ActiveX controls has also made it prone to security threats. To prevent hackers from misusing ActiveX controls, many security checks have been put in place. To ensure that there is no security threat, users have to take some proactive steps by changing settings in theirs browsers.

To set the security policy for ActiveX controls in Internet Explorer, perform the following steps:

1. Click Tools, Internet Options. The Internet Options dialog box will appear.
2. Click the Security tab.

3. Click the Custom Level button from the Security Level For This Zone box. The Security Settings dialog box appears.

4. Scroll down to the portion on ActiveX Controls and Plug-Ins, as shown in Figure 4.20.

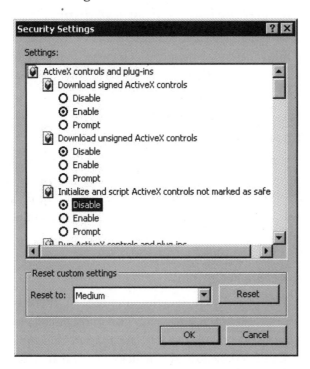

FIGURE 4.20 *The Internet Explorer Security Settings dialog box*

Under Download Signed ActiveX Controls, there are three options: Disable, Enable, and Prompt. If you select Enable, only signed ActiveX controls will be downloaded to your computer. If you select Disable, even signed ActiveX controls will not be downloaded to your computer. Selecting the Prompt option is not advisable because the warning boxes can be a nuisance.

Under Download Unsigned ActiveX Controls, there are three options: Disable, Enable, and Prompt. If you select Enable, all unsigned ActiveX controls will also be downloaded to your computer. If you select Disable, unsigned ActiveX controls will not be downloaded to your computer.

Selecting the Prompt option is not advisable because the warning boxes can be a nuisance. It is advisable to select Disable because this would prevent the downloading of unsigned ActiveX controls.

Under Initialize And Script ActiveX Controls Not Marked As Safe, there are three options: Disable, Enable, and Prompt. If you select Enable, ActiveX controls not marked as safe will also be initialized and downloaded to your computer. If you select Disable, ActiveX controls not marked as safe will not be downloaded to your computer. Selecting Prompt is not advisable because the warning boxes can be a nuisance. Selecting Disable is most advisable because it will ensure that ActiveX controls not marked as safe will not be downloaded to your computer.

Under Run ActiveX Controls And Plug-Ins, there are four options: Administrator Approved, Disable, Enable, and Prompt. If you select Administrator Approved, only ActiveX controls and plugins approved by the Administrator will run on your computer. If you select Enable, you can run ActiveX controls and plug-ins in your computer. If you select Disable, you cannot run ActiveX controls and plug-ins in your computer. Selecting the Prompt option is not advisable because the warning boxes can be a nuisance (see Figure 4.21).

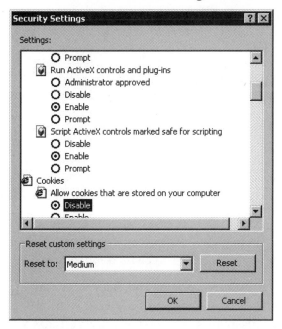

FIGURE 4.21 *The IE Security Settings dialog box*

Under Script ActiveX Controls Marked Safe For Scripting, there are three options: Disable, Enable, and Prompt. If you select Enable, only ActiveX controls marked as safe will be initialized and downloaded to your computer. If you select Disable, ActiveX controls marked as safe also will not be downloaded to your computer. Selecting Prompt is not advisable because the warning boxes can be a nuisance. Selecting Enable is most advisable because it will ensure that only ActiveX controls marked as safe will be downloaded on your computer.

You can also set the security policy for ActiveX controls by changing the security level settings for the Internet zone:

1. Click Tools, Internet Options. The Internet Options dialog box will appear.

2. Click the Security tab.

3. If the slider is set to Medium in the Security Level For This Zone box, unsigned ActiveX controls will not be downloaded. Even if the slider is set to Medium-Low, unsigned ActiveX controls will not be downloaded. If the slider is set to Low, all ActiveX controls will be downloaded.

4. Click OK to save your settings.

Summary

This chapter was a general introduction to user-level security on the Internet. It was divided into four sections. The first section covered the history of browsers, security settings in various browsers, and security issues in using VBScript and HTML as a programming language for Web programs.

The second section gave an introduction to Java and JavaScript as programming languages. The section also discussed the security flaws in Java and JavaScript. The section also covered the security policies to be set for using Java and JavaScript as a programming language for the browsers.

The third section covered the usefulness of cookies and the security threat caused by them. It also discussed the security settings to be used for cookies.

The last section of the chapter discussed plugins and ActiveX controls, covering their uses. It also discussed the security threats that a user is vulnerable to while using them. The section also entailed a discussion on the security settings to be used.

Check Your Understanding

Multiple Choice Questions

1. You want to point a helper application to an application that will open only text-based data. Which application will you choose? (Choose only one.)

   a. Microsoft Word

   b. Notepad

   c. Perl

   d. None of the above.

2. How would you set up Netscape to permit only first-party cookies?

   a. Choose the Enable Cookies option.

   b. Choose the Disable Cookies option.

   c. Choose the Accept Only Cookies That Get Sent Back To The Originating Server option.

   d. None of the above.

3. Consider the following two statements:

   Statement A: The default security setting for any zone in IE is Medium.

   Statement B: Choosing the Medium security option enables the downloading of unsigned ActiveX control.

   Which one is TRUE about the preceding statements?

   a. Statement A is TRUE but statement B is FALSE.

   b. Statement B is TRUE but statement A is FALSE.

   c. Both the statements are TRUE.

   d. Both the statements are FALSE.

4. State whether the following statement is TRUE or FALSE:

   Setting the security level to Low will ensure that a user can browse the Internet safely.

Which of these programming languages can be used to create stand-alone applications?

a. Java

b. JavaScript

c. VBScript

Short Questions

1. What is the concept of Sandbox in Java?

2. You are not connected to the Internet, but you are connected to an extensive intranet and do not want to be bothered by warning messages. What should be your security settings in IE?

3. You are connected to the Internet, and you use Netscape for browsing. You want to accept only cookies that will be sent to the host domain and not to any third-party domain. What should your setting be?

4. You wish to download a piece of code from the Internet. What should you use to verify the source of the code?

5. How will you enforce security settings for the behavior of ActiveX controls in IE?

Answers

Multiple Choice Answers

1. b. The other two options should be used as a helper application.

2. c. Only this option ensures that the browser accepts only first-party cookies

3. a. The default security setting for any zone in IE is Medium. Choosing Medium will ensure that unsigned ActiveX controls will not be downloaded.

4. FALSE

5. a. Only Java can be used to create stand-alone applications.

Short Answers

1. Java programs are not permitted to directly tamper with a computer's hardware or to make any direct call to the OS. Java runs on a virtual machine within a restricted virtual space. This concept is called *Sandbox* because it is similar to a child's game in which the child can play without getting hurt or hurting others.

2. The setting should be Medium-Low. In this setting the functionalities remain the same, but the user does not receive the warning messages about the third-party cookies that are being accepted by the system.

3. You should choose Accept Only Cookies That Get Sent Back To The Originating Server from the Preferences dialog box.

4. A technology known as Authenticode.

5. Using the various options available in the Security Settings dialog box. You can open the Security Settings dialog box from the Internet Options dialog box.

Chapter 5

A crucial part of the Web that needs to be secured is the host. Many people confuse host security with client security. *Host security* refers to the security of computers on which severs are running. It is important to secure Internet servers because they host all essential services being accessed from different parts of the world. Servers are the single connecting point for millions of people across the world. If an attacker manages to get control over any server on the Internet, it may result in the leakage of crucial information, disruption of services, and malicious content sent to users.

This chapter discusses strategies for securing servers on the Web, and covers three aspects: operating system security, Web server security, and the security of extensive CGI programs. The first section of the chapter emphasizes how important it is to secure the operating system of a host. It also explores various features provided by the two most widely used operating systems on the Web: Windows 2000 and Linux. It also covers operating system vulnerabilities.

The next section discusses the security aspect of the most commonly deployed servers, IIS 5.0 and Apache, and briefly lists their features.

The last section of the chapter discusses CGI programming, an extension to the servers on the Web. The section also discusses programming techniques that you can use to make CGI programs secure.

Securing Operating Systems

Why do you need to secure operating systems on hosts? An operating system is the heart of a computer. If an attacker manages to get control of the host operating system, the host cannot provide secure services. I'll begin this section by discussing the essential security features of an operating system, then introduce the various security features of two widely used operating systems, Windows 2000 and Linux.

Essential Security Features of an Ideal Operating System

The essential features of an ideal operating system are authentication, access control, accountability, auditing, security partitioning, integrity, confidentiality, and reliability. Let us explore each of these features separately.

Authentication

Authentication is a mechanism that enables an operating system to identify a user and provide the assurance that the person is who he or she claims to be. Authentication involves ensuring that only a valid user with preassigned credentials can access the resources on a computer.

An authentication mechanism may be based on the following categories:

◆ **Password**. Combined with a user name, this is the most widely used but relatively insecure method of authentication. Another example of such authentication is the PIN number validation performed at ATM machines.

◆ **Biometric mechanisms**. Fingerprints, retinal scans, and voice prints are examples of biometric mechanisms that provide high-level authentication.

◆ **Location**. Network adapter addresses and global positioning satellite–based systems provide authentication information based on a user's location.

An efficient authentication system is generally a mix of at least two of the preceding mechanisms. For instance, to access your bank account, you require both the physical possession of an ATM card and the knowledge of a PIN number. Maintaining the confidentiality of authentication information is extremely important. If the PIN number of an ATM card is written on the card itself, the purpose of the number is lost. Similarly, if user names and passwords float as plain text on a network, the authentication process is defeated.

 NOTE

Refer to Chapter 6, "Secure Authentication and Messaging" for detail about various authentication mechanisms available. The chapter discusses cryptography, which is the foundation of authentication. It also discusses authentication as a solution to security threats on the Web.

Access Control

After an operating system determines a user's validity, it must determine what information the user is allowed to access. An *access control* mechanism restricts the use of resources by authorized users. Typical enterprise operating systems support access control mechanisms that specify the names of users who can read, write, modify, or copy particular system objects.

Access controls can be deployed at several levels and can be based on various system-level models. In other words, an access control can be deployed at the byte level or the system level. Following are a few access control mechanisms:

◆ **Mandatory access control.** In this model, a centralized decision-making authority determines what should be accessible to whom. The owners of the object do not have the right to control access to the object.

◆ **Discretionary access control.** In this model, owners of objects have the right to define and modify the access controls specified for the objects.

◆ **Role-based access control.** In this model, access control rights are assigned based on the roles of the users.

The access controls supported by an operating system can be assessed on the following factors:

◆ The level on which they are applied in the system

◆ The strength of mechanisms used to enforce the controls

◆ The level of integration into system management mechanisms.

Accountability

Accountability ensures that the actions of an entity are identified uniquely with the entity that performed them. The entity can be a user, an operating system resource, or an external system, such as a computer or a network resource.

To measure the accountability of an operating system, you can consider the following factors:

◆ The strength of the mechanism used to ensure accountability

◆ The ability of the operating system to make decisions based on this information

Auditing

Auditing is the ability to monitor activities on a system in order to determine if a policy violation has taken place or a suspicious activity is a cause for alarm. It operates by recording the sequence of steps of an event (when it occurred) with the help of support documents generated by the operating system and an application (such as event logs) to facilitate the examinations made on the event.

Audit systems, such as intrusion detection systems, use operating system audits for making an analysis. Audit details provided by operating systems also help trace the source of a security problem and plan remedial action.

The auditing ability of an operating system can be evaluated on the following basis:

◆ The strength of the mechanism used to perform audits. The first step a hacker takes to jeopardize the auditing capabilities of an operating system is to either turn off audit functions or delete audit logs.

◆ The volume of audit data that the operating system can produce and handle.

Security Partitioning

Every system entity (whether a user or a computer resource) is allocated to a security partition or domain. A security domain is a logical partition that consists of all objects an entity is authorized to access. A user domain may include file storage space, I/O devices, and application programs. A process domain may include system resources that it is authorized to use. The purpose of creating a security domain is to ensure that an entity operates within its defined domain.

The efficiency with which operating systems can enforce security domain separations is based on the following:

◆ The strength of security partitioning mechanisms that limit the access of users outside their domains.

◆ The manner in which domains are managed is also a crucial indicator of the effectiveness of a domain partition. If the domains are difficult to administer, administrators will frequently default to very broad definitions that minimize the impact of changes but greatly reduce the level of security provided.

Integrity

Ensuring integrity means ensuring that unauthorized users do not modify the contents of an object on a system. Access control is an integrity mechanism that prevents the unauthorized modification of resources on a system. There are other integrity mechanisms that detect unauthorized change instead of preventing the change, such as checksums, cyclic redundancy checks, hashes, and digital signatures.

In computer systems, integrity is applicable to both stored data, such as system and executable files, and data in transaction, such as messages. Ensuring the integrity of data is an important function of operating systems.

The efficiency with which operating systems can enforce integrity is based on the following factors:

- ◆ The strength of the integrity mechanisms used
- ◆ The level to which integrity is applied in the system

Confidentiality

Maintaining confidentiality of information implies ensuring that it is only disclosed to authorized users, regardless of who owns the information. Mostly, confidentiality in computer systems is maintained through the use of encryption to encode and decode data.

The confidentiality mechanisms provided by operating systems can be assessed based on the following factors:

- ◆ The strength of the protection mechanisms used
- ◆ The flexibility of the protection mechanisms
- ◆ The integration of the mechanisms with other system security controls
- ◆ The effect of the mechanisms on system operations

Reliability

Reliability of an operating system refers to security of data accessed by users on a computer or a network. In other words, reliability refers to an operating system's ability to protect its data from external and internal threats and attacks.

Reliability essentially means that an operating system should be designed in a manner that users are able retrieve data and resources even after a disaster. The data should remain intact even after a breakdown. A few features of a reliable operating system are the ability to make regular backups, retrieve data after a breakdown, and ensure less down time in case of a breakdown.

INFORMATION TECHNOLOGY SECURITY EVALUATION CRITERIA (ITSEC)

ITSEC is a global endeavor by several governments, such as France, Germany, the Netherlands, and the United Kingdom, focused toward security evaluation. These criteria help assess the security of operating systems by issuing various specification levels. These specifications are referred to as the *target of evaluation* (TOE). A TOE may or may not include all standards specified by ITSEC, which follow:

- **Identification and authentication.** An operating system should have a set of rules and procedures to identify a user.

- **Access control.** An operating system must have a set of procedures to control users' access to that which they are authorized.

- **Accountability.** An operating system should have well-defined mechanisms to track and monitor the activities performed by users or processes.

- **Audit.** An operating system should provide procedures and mechanisms to track the logs of both anticipated and unanticipated events.

- **Object reuse.** An operating system should allow the reuse or multi-use of operating system resources, such as disk space and memory. The reuse should not compromise the security of resources. The reuse mechanism essentially involves managing resources without the overuse or failure of resources.

- **Accuracy.** An operating system should ensure the accuracy and legitimacy of data being transferred between processes, users, and objects.

- **Reliability of service.** Reliability of service implies providing appropriate services at the appropriate time. This essentially requires the operating system to provide available resources when an authorized user or process requires it.

- **Secure data exchange.** An operating system should provide the security of data not only on the system but also while it is being exchanged over a network.

Having discussed the essential security features of an ideal operating system, I would like to discuss the security features provided by Windows 2000 and Linux.

Security Features of the Windows 2000 Operating System

Windows 2000 is an operating system developed by Microsoft Corporation. There are several editions available, and it can be deployed on both stand-alone and network computers. The most commonly used editions are Windows 2000 Server for servers and Windows 2000 Professional for desktops. Both editions provide several features to secure data and resources on a computer. The following section discusses the security features of Windows 2000 Server.

Authentication

The Windows 2000 authentication mechanism has several subcomponents that work together to authenticate users who want to access the system. These components include an authentication interface and the Kerberos protocol. The authentication interface accepts user credentials, and Kerberos validates these credentials.

Authentication Interface

To enable users to submit their credentials for logging on to a computer or a network, Windows 2000 provides two types of authentication interfaces, a logon screen and smart card authentication.

Logon Screen

The first interface that a user encounters in a Windows 2000 system is the logon screen. The logon screen appears when the user presses the Ctrl+Alt+Del key combination. This screen prompts for a user name and the password. If the user is a member of a domain, the user is also suppose specify the domain name. The logon information is verified against the user information stored in the Active Directory. If the information exists in the Active Directory, the user is allowed to connect to a computer, a domain, or a network.

Smart Card Authentication

The other interface used to provide security in computer systems is the smart card. A smart card is an electronic card that stores a user's logon information, such as a private key and an authentication certificate. If a user wants to log on to a computer by using a smart card, the user inserts the card in a card reader device. The computer then asks the user to enter a digital personal identification number (PIN). After the PIN is verified, the user is allowed to logon to the computer.

The main advantage of a smart card is that a user does not need to remember a user name and password information because this information is stored in the card. The user just needs to type the PIN on the smart card authentication screen. This process, therefore, involves the least risk because an intruder does not get a chance to guess the user name or the password, which are safely stored in the smart card.

Before discussing Kerberos, this section will discuss the concept of the domain controller and the Active Directory services deployed on a Windows 2000 Server. This is because the domain controller and the Active Directory play an important role in Kerberos authentication process.

Domain Controllers and Active Directory Service

A *domain* is a collection of computers used to centralize the activities on a network. A domain may have several controllers and client computers. A domain controller is basically a computer running Windows 2000 Server that has the Active Directory services running. The Active Directory Installation Wizard installs and configures components that provide Active Directory services to network computers and services. A domain controller stores information about directory data and user domain interaction, including the user logon process, authentication, and directory searches.

Active Directory is a service on a Windows 2000 Server that stores security information about the various objects on a domain. It is a centralized storehouse that allows a domain controller to access, retrieve, and modify an object and its attribute.

Active Directory provides the option of installing several domain controllers on a domain. Active Directory frequently replicates the information contained in a domain in another domain. In this way, multiple domain controllers ensure that in case the Active Directory service fails, there is a continuous availability of domain resources to various domain users.

Kerberos Protocol

Kerberos is the default authentication protocol in Windows 2000. It is a set of predefined steps that helps users successfully log on to a Windows 2000 domain (see Figure 5.1). The steps are as follows:

1. A user either enters the logon name, the password, and the domain name through the logon screen or inserts a smart card into the client computer. The computer sends these credentials to a domain controller.

2. The Kerberos protocol on the domain controller validates the user's credentials against those stored in the Active Directory. If the credentials match, it creates a ticket-granting ticket (TGT) for the user. TGT is a ticket granted to a user after successful verification of the user's credentials.

3. Next, Kerberos encrypts the TGT by using a secret key, which is an encrypted form of a user password. In addition to the TGT, a session key is also created and encrypted for the user's session. The session key is valid until the user is logged on to the domain. The domain controller then sends the encrypted TGT and the session key to the client computer from where the user is attempting to log on.

4. After receiving the encrypted TGT and the session key, the client compares the TGT with the user's credentials at its end. If the credentials match, it sends back the logon credentials with the TGT to the domain controller.

5. On receiving the client credentials along with the TGT, Kerberos issues an encrypted service ticket to the client. This ticket enables a client to connect to a server on the domain and access its resources.

6. On receiving the service ticket, the client sends data or a resource access request to the resource server along with the encrypted service ticket.

7. The encrypted service ticket is decrypted at the server end using the secret key of the user. This enables the server to verify the user's credentials and provide the user with access to resources controlled by the server.

In addition to authenticating the client, the server might also need to authenticate itself to the client. This is referred to mutual authentication, in which the server sends back its server certificate that is encrypted using a secret key. After both the client and the server authenticate each other, they exchange data.

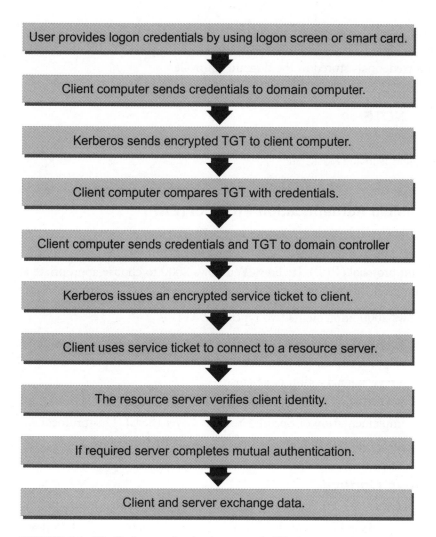

FIGURE 5.1 *The Kerberos authentication process in Windows 2000 Server*

In addition to the default Kerberos protocol, Windows 2000 supports the NT LAN Manager (NTLM) protocol and Extensible Authentication Protocol (EAP). The following section discusses these in detail.

NT LAN Manager (NTLM) Protocol

NT LAN Manager (NTLM) was implemented in Windows NT, an earlier version of Windows. Windows 2000 also supports this protocol to allow Windows NT users to connect to a Windows 2000 network and its resources. NTLM works on the challenge-response protocol. It accepts the user name, password, and domain name. The credentials accepted are encrypted and verified against the logon credentials stored in the domain controller.

 NOTE

For more details on the challenge-response protocol, refer to Chapter 6 "Secure Authentication and Messaging."

Extensible Authentication Protocol (EAP)

Extensible Authentication Protocol (EAP) is another authentication protocol supported by Windows 2000. EAP is basically a protocol derived from the Point-to-Point protocol (PPP). It allows Windows 2000 to choose appropriate authentication mechanisms based on the type of client that is requesting a connection.

Windows 2000 implements two types of EAP:

◆ **EAP-MD5**. The EAP-MD5 protocol implements the technique of response-challenge handshake authentication. This protocol is based on a reverse-encryption mechanism.

◆ **EAP-Transport Layer Security (TLS)**. The EAP-TLS protocol is an implementation of Secured Sockets Layer (SSL). This protocol is used on computers that are part of network authentication.

Access Control

Access control is a mechanism that determines the limit of authority of a user or a group on various local and domain resources on a network. In Windows 2000, access control is a two-fold mechanism that determines the authority of a user based on

◆ User rights
◆ Object permissions

A user right may permit or deny a user's access to an object. By contrast, an object permission is assigned to an object that defines the level of modifications a user can make to an object. The difference between the two seems small, so let me provide an example. Suppose a user has a right to modify the content of a file. This is a user right. However, the file has a read-only attribute assigned. This is an object permission. In such a situation, the object permission will supersede the user right. The user will not be allowed to modify the file. User rights in conjunction with object permissions indicate the effective rights a user has to access an object.

Only the owner of an object may grant or deny permissions to a user for accessing it. The owner of an object is the one who created the object. The ability of an owner to specify permissions for an object ensures that only authorized users access the object.

Windows 2000 maintains a security descriptor to manage access to an object and to identify the rights that a user has to that object. The security descriptor monitors access to an object by maintaining its audit information. Security descriptors are part of the Active Directory. This means that object access information is available to all the computers on network, including domain controllers, servers, and clients in a domain.

Access control in Windows 2000 is hierarchical, which implies that all rights assigned to a group are automatically assigned to the member users of that group.

The following are mechanisms through which Windows 2000 keeps track of user rights and object permissions.

User and Group Identification

Each user account and group in Windows 2000 has a corresponding object in the Active Directory. These objects are identified by unique IDs, referred to as Security Identifiers (SIDs).

Access Control List (ACL)

Windows 2000 maintains an access control list (ACL) for every Active Directory object. An ACL is fundamentally a part of the security descriptor of an object. It contains SIDs of users and groups that have rights to access the object. An ACL has several components that store information about the rights of users or groups in a structured manner. These components are as follows:

◆ **Access control entry (ACE)**. An ACE is a row in an ACL that uniquely identifies a user or a group SID. It contains information about the rights and permissions that an SID has on an object or objects.

◆ **Access mask**. Access mask is the value of the rights of a user or a group in terms of 32 bits. An access mask is part of an ACE. Active Directory uses the access mask to identify user rights when a user requests access to a resource. The access mask determines the level of access that a user has for an object.

Access Token

After the authentication process, an access token is created for a user. This token stores the unique user SID, group membership details, and details about the rights and permissions applicable to the user. Now, to verify if a user has permission to access an object, Windows 2000 checks the details stored in the access token assigned to the user and the ACL of the object. This determines the effective permission that a user has on an object.

Auditing

Windows 2000 allows you to audit system, user, and file access activities on a computer or a network, and it provides several tools and techniques for doing so. The following is a description of a few of the auditing tools provided by Windows 2000.

System Access Control List (SACL)

Like objects, Windows 2000 also creates an ACL for all events that need to be audited for an object. This ACL is referred to as SACL, which is part of the security descriptor of an object.

Event Viewer

The Event Viewer in Windows 2000 allows you to view events logged by the system or applications. It also allows you to filter events to enable you to specifically view the most critical events. Before I explain these, let me explain the three types of logs that are generated by systems and applications: security log, application log, and system log.

Security Log

A security log records the events related to user activity, which include information about successful as well as unsuccessful events. The following are examples:

- User logon and logoff and success or failure
- User accessing resources, such as printers or hard disks
- User creating files and folders
- User modifying files and folders
- User deleting files and folders
- User modifying permissions for files and folders

All the events recorded in a security log are referred to as audit messages. All audit messages may not be stored in a single security log on a computer. This implies that if an object on one computer is being accessed from another computer on the network, the security log of the object will be recorded on the computer from which it is being accessed. This enables Windows 2000 to create a security log for each computer on a network separately.

Application Log

An application log records events related to programs and applications running on a computer. This log enables you to figure out the cause of an application functioning improperly on a system. For instance, because the log monitors applications every minute, any error generated or any abrupt halt in an application is recorded instantly. This gives log analysts sufficient information, such as the type of error and the time of occurrence, to monitor the functioning of an application.

System Log

A system log records events generated by an operating system and its services. Examples include successful or failed network connections, errors generated while starting a system service, or problems with device drivers. A system log can also track events that might be affecting system performance. In addition, log entries might be used to track the effect of service failure on various users logged on to a computer.

Events

Now that you understand the types of logs that are generated by systems and applications, I'll explain the types of events you can examine in the Event Viewer:

♦ **Error**. This event indicates that an error has occurred in an application or system service. Such errors need immediate attention to continue the proper functioning of an operating system.

♦ **Warning**. This event indicates that a minor problem has occurred in an application or system service. Events generating warnings do not need immediate action but are an indication of an approaching problem. Therefore, when an event log shows a warning, it is recommended that you verify the application or service generating it to ensure that no critical problem arises later.

♦ **Information**. This event provides information about an activity occurring on a system. The basic purpose of recording such an event is to monitor the successful completion of tasks, for example, the successful initiation of a service.

♦ **Success audit**. This event provides information about an event success that was indicated to be an auditable event. For example, if a record of all print jobs sent to a printer is required, the audit log would record information about all the successful print jobs sent to a printer as a successful audit.

♦ **Failure audit**. This event provides information about an event failure that was indicated as a auditable event. For example, the audit log would record information about all the failed print jobs sent to a printer as a failure audit.

Filtering Events

All the event logs generated might not be of use at a particular time. For instance, you might just want to view error and success audit events because they are critical to your current security strategy. The Event Viewer allows you to filter events based on specific criteria. It provides several options that enable you to filter specific events:

♦ **View events from**. This selection allows you to view events logged after a specified date.

◆ **View events to**. This selection allows you to view events logged prior to and including a specified date.

◆ **Information**. This selection allows you to view information type events.

◆ **Warning**. This selection allows you to view warning type events.

◆ **Error**. This selection allows you to view error type events.

◆ **Success audit**. This selection allows you to view success audit type events.

◆ **Failure audit**. This selection allows you to view failure audit type events.

◆ **Source**. This selection allows you to view events based on the application, resource, or action that generated the events. For example, all events related to print jobs sent to the printer can be viewed using this criterion.

◆ **Category**. This selection allows you to view events based on category. For example, the modification of properties and permissions for an object is an event category.

◆ **User**. This selection allows you to view events generated by a specific user logged on to a computer or a network.

◆ **Computer**. This selection allows you to view events generated by a specific computer on a domain or a network.

◆ **Event ID**. This selection allows you to view events based on the unique number assigned in the audit log. Filtering events based on event ID is not an efficient method of viewing events.

In addition to filtering events based on a criterion, Event Viewer also allows you to sort events in ascending or descending order based on the various columns in the event log. The default sort order is descending based on the event date and time. However, you can change the sort order. Event Viewer also allows you to view specific detail recorded in an audit log by simply double-clicking the event entry.

File System Audit

File system audit is another important audit mechanism used in Windows 2000. It allows you to monitor access and modifications made to the files and folders on a computer. A file system audit is enabled in a group audit policy, which specifies various events that need to be audited for various files and folders.

The following are various events you can track for a file:

◆ Reading, modifying, or deleting files

◆ Viewing or modifying file attributes

◆ Viewing or modifying file permissions

◆ Executing a file

◆ Modifying or taking file ownership

The following are various events you can track for a folder:

◆ Traversing or deleting files

◆ Viewing or modifying folder attributes

◆ Viewing or modifying folder permissions

◆ Creating files and subfolders

◆ Modifying or taking folder ownership

Audit Policy

To run and handle audit events, you need to create and apply an audit policy. An audit policy needs to be applied to the Organizational Unit (OU) of the user, group, or other objects whose events need to be audited. Windows 2000 does not allow auditing events if an audit policy is not created and applied first.

A Windows 2000 audit policy needs you to specify the category of events that need to be audited. The following are the categories that you can specify in an audit policy:

◆ **User account**. This category allows you to specify events related to user logon and logoff.

◆ **User account management**. This category allows you to specify events related to creating and deleting accounts. It can also include events that relate to modifying user account properties and permissions.

◆ **System events**. This category allows you to specify events related to system services.

◆ **Object access**. This category allows you to specify events related to the objects accessed by a user.

◆ **Policy modification**. This category allows you to specify events related to any modifications made to the policies on a system.

Reliability

Reliability is comparatively new and one of most talked about features of Windows 2000. It includes the disaster recovery tools that avoid a system breakdown and other tools that ensure minimum system down time in the case of system failure.

Robust Architecture

Windows 2000 is said to have a robust architecture because of its following unique features:

- ◆ It ensures the effective and efficient management of system resources, such as memory, hard disk, and processor time.

- ◆ It implements techniques such as processor time slicing, multiprocessing, and thread management to ensure equal distribution of time and control among the applications running on it.

- ◆ It ensures that no application has a monopolist control over the system or resources and no application exerts excess load on a specific resource to cause a system breakdown.

- ◆ All its system files are digitally signed, which enables Windows 2000 to inform its users about unauthorized file modification.

- ◆ It allows you to use device drivers (selective) from vendors other than Microsoft, which are exhaustively tested and validated by Microsoft to prevent the system from crashing if there is a device driver failure.

Diagnostic Tools

Windows 2000 provides several diagnostic tools that enable you to monitor a system's state and prevent problems from occurring. A few of the Windows 2000 diagnostic tools are Task Manager, Performance Monitor, and System Log.

Task Manager

The Task Manager is a Windows 2000 diagnostic tool that tracks system processes and application performance. It helps you terminate applications that have stopped responding to system commands by allowing you to view nonresponding applications and giving you termination rights. In this way, it saves the computer from logging off abruptly or shutting down completely.

In addition, the Task Manager allows you to prioritize one application process over another that might cause a system to slow down. It also allows you to assess the activity of running processes by using several parameters, graphs and data on CPU, and memory usage (see Figure 5.2).

The Task Manger contains the following three tabs:

- **Applications tab**. Displays the status of programs running on the computer. On this tab, you can end, start, or raise the priority of a program.

- **Processes tab**. Displays information about processes running on the computer. It displays information such as CPU and memory usage, page faults, the handle count, and a number of other parameters.

- **Performance tab**. Displays a summary of a computer's performance, such as graphs depicting CPU and memory usage and details about the number of handles, threads, and processes running on the computer. In addition, it provides details about physical, kernel, and commit memory.

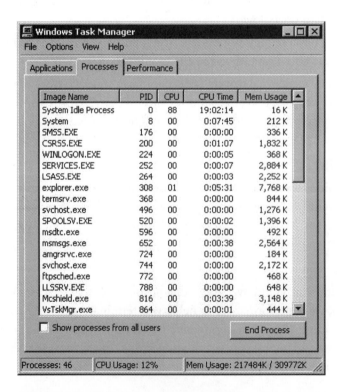

FIGURE 5.2 *The Task Manager with the Processes tab activated*

Performance Monitor

The Performance monitor is a diagnostic tool that enables you to evaluate the performance of your computer or other computers on a network (see Figure 5.3). It allows you to perform the following functions:

◆ Collect and view real-time performance data on a local computer or on several remote computers

◆ Analyze current or formerly collected data through a counter log

◆ Represent performance data in the form of graphs, histograms, or reports

You can access the Performance monitor from the Performance utility of Windows 2000.

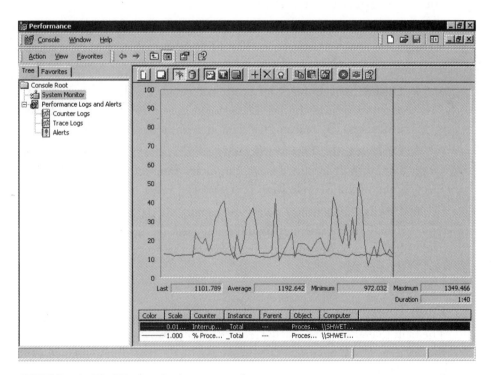

FIGURE 5.3 *The Windows Performance monitor*

System Log

As already discussed, a system log is an auditing tool that allows you to view information about system events. This tool can also be used for diagnostic purposes and recovery in the case of a breakdown.

Backup

Windows 2000 has a powerful backup mechanism that enables you to maintain system and data files, registries, and Active Directory data. Backups may be made using several devices, such as CDs, Zip drives, and tapes.

One of these services in Windows 2000 is the backup agent. This service can be configured to take a combined backup of all the servers on a network. It is configured to automatically back up data on a tape device at regular intervals. The advantage of using this service is that you need not manually make data backups. You configure the backup agent and monitor it at regular intervals to ensure that continuous data backups are made.

Disk Management Utilities

A disk management utility is another diagnostic tool that allows efficient disk management and fast data access. This utility also enables you to detect and eliminate data access errors on a disk:

◆ **Disk defragmenter**. This utility rearranges the data stored on the hard disk into logical chunks. Data stored in a scattered form results in slow disk access. By rearranging data, it enables faster data access.

◆ **Disk cleanup**. This utility removes unnecessary files from a computer's hard disk. It usually deletes temporary Internet files and deleted files lying in the Recycle Bin.

◆ **Chkdsk**. This utility tracks and repairs the data stored in bad sectors of a disk. Chkdsk operates by traversing each sector on the disk, checking for bad sectors, moving data from bad sectors to good sectors, and repairing data links.

Fault Tolerance

The fault tolerance feature helps recover an operating system and system and data files in case of a breakdown. The following are a few fault tolerance techniques used by Windows 2000:

◆ **Redundant Array of Independent (or Inexpensive) Disks (RAID)**. RAID is a mechanism that combines several disks to store data. This ensures that data is recovered in case one of the disks in RAID is corrupted. Windows 2000 implements RAID-5, which stores data and parity information.

◆ **Uninterrupted Power Supply (UPS).** UPS is a technology that provides continuous electricity in case of power failure, which provides users adequate time to shut down their systems. It prevents an abrupt shutdown that may lead to system crashes or loss of data.

Windows 2000 also enables you to integrate the UPS service with the operating system to secure files from being lost in case of a sudden shutdown. A UPS service detects the power supply call from the hardware component attached to the computer in the case of a power failure, which, in turn, informs the operating system. The operating system then informs the users of the limited time they have to save data and shut down the computer successfully.

System Recovery

The reliability features of Windows 2000 help avoid system failure and data loss. However, a system can break down. In such an event, the failed system and the data it stored need to be recovered.

The following are mechanisms that Windows 2000 provides for system recovery:

◆ Safe mode

◆ Last known good configuration

◆ Recovery console

◆ Boot disks

◆ Emergency repair disk

Safe Mode

Safe mode is a boot up technique that starts the computer with minimum configurations. A system should be started in safe mode when the system hangs up in normal mode. A blank screen after logon, the logon screen not appearing, or applications not responding are indicators of a system being in a hanged state.

Last Known Good Configuration

Last known good configuration is a system recovery option that starts the computer with the last saved configuration settings in the registry. This option is useful in situations when a faulty configuration has caused harm to the registry settings. An example of faulty configuration would be the presence of an incorrect SCSI disk driver.

Recovery Console

A recovery tool is a CUI-based operating system administration tool that enables you to recover a system that cannot be recovered by using safe mode or the last known good configuration option. This tool allows you to detect and analyze system problems and various operating system resources.

The recovery tool is available in the Windows 2000 CD. It can be installed using the /cmdcons option.

Boot Disks

Boot disks are operating system startup disks present in a Windows 2000 computer to enable the booting process when all possible recovery options fail. After the system boots by using these disks, you can access the hard disk and repair the system or run the recovery console.

Emergency Repair Disk (ERD)

An ERD is a special boot disk that stores the system files necessary for a Windows 2000 computer to boot. ERD is typically used to restore critical system information, such as a SAM (Sequential data access via meta-data) database, registry keys, and Windows 2000 initialization files.

Security Configuration

When installing an operating system, certain settings are configured automatically. These settings enable a user to perform common tasks, navigate through the system, and use its resources easily. The include security settings, but they are not very stringent. A user can easily manipulate and reconfigure a system setting. You need to reset these in order to have a secure and controlled operating system.

Windows 2000 allows you to perform the security configuration of the system by using templates. A security template is comprised of predefined settings that verifies and configures a computer's security settings. Usually, the predefined settings are in the form of policies that correspond to different system configurations.

The settings can be configured using the Security Configuration and Analysis tool. This tool allows you to create new security templates and apply existing templates.

A security template can be used to configure the following policies:

◆ **Password Policy**. This allows you to specify different types of restrictions for a password. These settings include minimum password length, minimum and maximum password age, password history, password complexity, and reversible encryption requirements for passwords (see Figure 5.4).

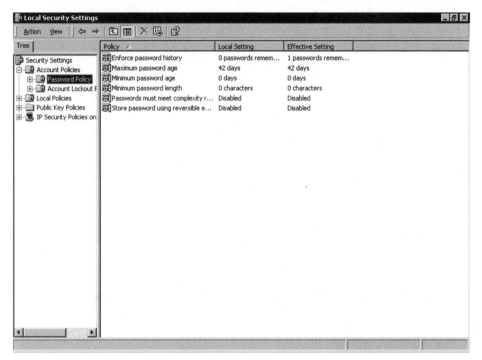

FIGURE 5.4 *The Password Policy*

◆ **Account Lockout Policy**. This allows you to specify settings for account lockout duration, the number of logon attempts before account lockout, and resetting account lockout. An account lockout is a security mechanism that restricts unauthorized users by locking the system after a certain number of unsuccessful logon attempts (see Figure 5.5).

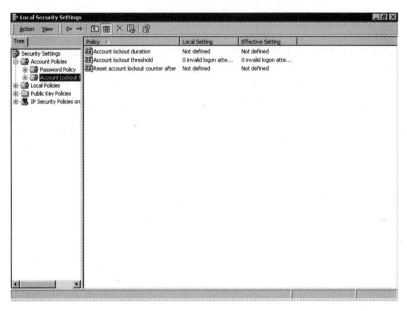

FIGURE 5.5 *The Account Lockout Policy*

◆ **Audit Policy.** This allows you to specify the user and system activities that need to be audited. You can also specify success and failure audits for an activity (see Figure 5.6).

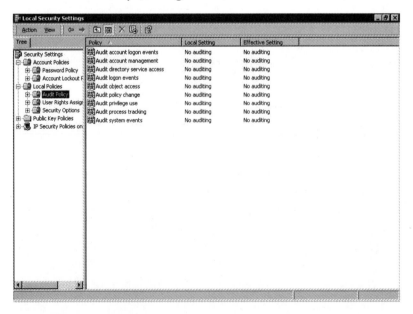

FIGURE 5.6 *The Audit Policy*

◆ **User Rights Assignment Policy**. This allows you to set the rights and permissions of users (see Figure 5.7).

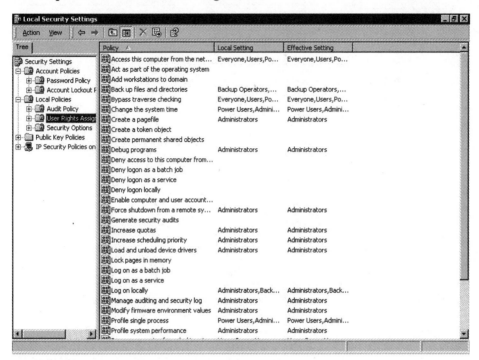

FIGURE 5.7 *The User Rights Assignment Policy*

◆ **Security Options Policy**. This allows you to specify security settings, such as restricting anonymous connections, allowing or denying access to install printers, enabling the digital signing of data exchange, disabling Ctrl+Alt+Del, logging off a user after the requisite session time, and disabling floppy and CD devices. These settings enable you to control the extent of access that a user has on system resources (see Figure 5.8).

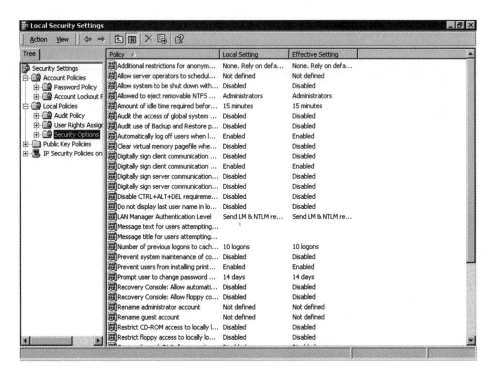

FIGURE 5.8 *The Security Options Policy*

In this section, we discussed security features of the Windows 2000 operating system. However, Windows 2000 is not secure with its default installation settings. Even a little negligence by a system administrator can make these operating systems highly vulnerable. In addition to existing vulnerabilities, new vulnerabilities appear regularly. Therefore, it is necessary for system administrators of Windows-based networks to take certain steps to protect networks from hacking activities.

Vulnerabilities of Windows 2000

You are already aware of the security features that Microsoft has added to Windows 2000 operating system. However, a Windows 2000 system is not secure with its default installation settings. A system administrator needs to be extremely cautious when configuring these security settings.

The following section lists a few of the known vulnerabilities in Windows 2000. The section also provides solutions or best practices that a system administrator should follow to prevent these vulnerabilities.

Password Hacking

You are already aware of the importance of maintaining the privacy of passwords to maintain the security of a system. Windows 2000 stores passwords, in the form of hash values, in a database called the Security Accounts Manager (SAM). The SAM database can only be accessed through the HKEY_LOCAL_MACHINE registry hive under the SAM key by writing a program or using a Registry editor. Ordinarily, the operating system does not allow a user to access the database because it limits the permissions on the key to the built-in SYSTEM account. Therefore, by default, it locks the database to protect it from unauthorized access. Only administrative users can trick the operating system to provide SAM-key access under the user context of the SYSTEM account. However, there are certain hacking utilities, such as L0phtCrack, that allow password cracking using the SAM database. To crack passwords using these utilities, the hacker manages to access the SAM database by the following methods:

◆ If a remote registry access is enabled on a target computer, hackers import passwords from the Windows registry.

◆ If the hacker has physical access to the target Windows 2000 computer with NTFS file system, a hacker copies the SAM database.

Microsoft also provides a utility named SYSKEY that protects passwords from cracking activities. In Windows 2000, the SYSKEY utility is installed and activated by default. However, the updated versions of L0phtCrack, LC3, have the ability to crack passwords protected by the SYSKEY utility also.

The hacker may remotely gain access to a SAM database in which the SYSKEY utility is installed by using another program called pwdump3. However, hackers must have administrator privileges on the target computer.

Most Windows 2000 computers are vulnerable to password cracking attacks. However, hackers require administrator privileges or physical access to exploit these vulnerabilities. Therefore, a system administrator must be extremely cautious while granting access rights to the users of a Windows 2000 computer. In addition, administrator accounts should also be protected by keeping difficult to guess passwords.

Default Accounts

Windows 2000, by default, creates an account under the name of "Administrator" at the time of installation. By default, the password of this account is blank. A

Windows 2000 system does not allow you to delete this account. However, it does allow you to change the password.

The most common method of gaining access to a Windows 2000 computer is through the Administrator account. Therefore, to avoid unauthorized access, it is essential to change the name and password of the Administrator account.

File Sharing

When you share a folder in Windows 2000, the default sharing permissions are Everyone Full control. Granting Full Control access to all users on the network implies that any user can modify content of the files shared in this folder. Negligence on the part of users creates a major security hole for hackers.

You need to ensure that restrictions to access a folder are properly maintained. To ensure that Full Control permissions are not assigned to users, it is important to clear the Full Control option and change the it to Read Only.

Trust Relationship

Windows 2000 operating systems have a feature called *trust relationship*. This feature allows the authenticated users of Windows 2000 domain to access the resources on another domain without being authenticated by the other domain. The domain that trusts the users of another domain is referred to as a *trusting* domain and the domain with trusted users is referred to as a *trusted* domain.

How does a trust relationship between domains operate? If the SIDs of the users are authenticated by the trusted domain, the trusting domain allows the users to access resources without any reauthentication.

However, there is a risk involved in such authentication. It is possible that the SIDs of users in the trusted domain can be manipulated or replaced. Therefore, if the trusting domain allows trusted domain users to access resources without reauthentication, the security of the trusting domain network is compromised.

The manipulation of SIDs on the trusted domain is only possible if a hacker has administrator privileges. In addition, hackers need to have in-depth knowledge of low-level operating system functions and data structures. The Windows 2000 operating system uses a mechanism called SIDHistory to allow users with administrator privileges to insert or modify SIDs into the authentication details. However, this interface does not have a programming interface. For a hacker to exploit the vulnerability of SIDHistory, he needs to make binary modifications to its data structure.

Windows 2000 provides patch programs called SID filters to counter the vulnerability of SIDHistory. You can install the SID filters from Windows 2000 Security Roll-Up Package 1. SID filters must be installed on domain controllers of trusting domains. In addition, you need to activate them for trusted domains as well.

Event Viewer Buffer Overflow

The Event Viewer tool of Windows 2000 may result in buffer overflow if the following are generated by a system at a given point:

◆ Several services or applications are running

◆ A service or an application generates multiple errors

◆ A service or an application goes into a hanged state

An Event Viewer buffer overflow may result in the Event Viewer not functioning properly. As a result, it may provide a hacker the opportunity to modify the Event Viewer and use the target computer to perform hacking activities.

The use of this vulnerability by a hacker depends upon his privileges on the target system. A hacker with administrator privileges can make maximum use of this vulnerability.

Microsoft provides a solution to this vulnerability in the form a patch, which can be installed from http://www.microsoft.com/Downloads/Release.asp?ReleaseID=27842. However, before installing the patch program, you need to install Service Pack 1 and Service Pack 2 of Windows 2000.

NBNS Protocol Sniffing

Windows 2000 uses the NetBIOS Name Server (NBNS) protocol to manage name conflicts between computers on the network. The NBNS protocol does not support the authentication process. Instead, it uses the Name Conflict and Name Release mechanisms to solve the name conflict. In the Name Conflict mechanism, the computers, when registering or refreshing names in the network, check if another computer with same name exists. In the Name Release mechanism, the computers release the names of the computers when they are not in use.

Hackers exploit the NBNS protocol to initiate a denial-of-service attack on the network computer. They operate by spoofing the NBNS traffic and misleading the computers to believe that its name has conflicted with some other computer on the network. As a result, the target computer is not able to register its name.

If the target computer's name is already registered, its name is cancelled. When other computers try to access resources and services of the target computer, they receive a name conflict error.

Microsoft provides a solution to this vulnerability in the form a patch, which can be installed from http://www.microsoft.com/Downloads/Release.asp?ReleaseID=23370.

RPC Service Failure

The Remote Procedure Call (RPC) service running on a Windows 2000 computer allows an application to call a subroutine executing on a remote computer on the network. However, the RPC service poses a serious vulnerability because it does not authenticate the inputs submitted to it for processing. Hackers take advantage of this, denying legitimate use to the authorized users.

Hackers operate by sending RPC requests with invalid inputs to computers running Windows 2000. Because the computer cannot check the validity of the input, it processes it. The invalid input may cause harm to the computer by halting it for a short or a long duration. The duration of the halt depends on the number of invalid inputs sent to the computer.

Microsoft also provides a patch for this vulnerability on the site http://www.microsoft.com/Downloads/Release.asl?ReleaseID=31434.

SMTP Authentication Vulnerability

The authentication process of the SMTP service of Windows 2000 Server has an inherent vulnerability: It does not authenticate even unauthorized users. Hackers can take advantage of this by sending malicious e-mail messages. However, this vulnerability does not enable the hacker to obtain administrator privileges on the target system.

If SMTP services are not required on a Windows 2000 computer, it is recommended that you disable this service to prevent hackers from exploiting it. However, if you use the SMTP service, you need to install the following patch:

http://www.microsoft.com/Downloads/Release.asl?ReleaseID=31181.

Telnet Vulnerabilities

A flaw in the telnet service of Windows 2000 enables users to start idle sessions. By exploiting this flaw, hackers configure the telnet service to start multiple idle sessions in order to initiate a denial-of-service attack on the target computer. The target computer is flooded with so many idle sessions that it is unable to allow a legitimate user to initiate a valid telnet session.

Another vulnerability is that telnet allows normal users to execute system commands that can terminate services. Hackers also use this vulnerability to initiate denial-of-service attacks against the telnet service.

Taking advantage of the vulnerabilities discussed above, hackers can only deny services to legitimate users. They cannot manipulate privileges or data on the target system. Usually restarting the telnet service or the telnet server solves the problem.

Another vulnerability exists in the procedure that telnet follows at a session initialization. When a telnet session is initiated, the telnet service creates a named pipe and uses it for the initialization process. However, if telnet finds an existing named pipe, it uses that instead of recreating a new one. Hackers take advantage of this by guessing the names of the pipes and replacing the existing named pipes on the server with pipes that contain malicious content. They also associate this pipe with a program that allows them to access the target system remotely. When a user starts a session requesting the creation of the named pipe that has been replaced by the hacker, telnet initializes the session with the named pipe containing malicious content. As a result, the associated program with the pipe is executed and the hacker gains access to the target system.

The preceding vulnerability is not easy to exploit if hackers don't have the ability to code and load programs on the telnet server. In addition, they can exploit this vulnerability only if telnet is started and running on the target system.

Microsoft has developed the following patch to prevent hackers from exploiting this vulnerability:

http://www.microsoft.com/Downloads/Release.asl?ReleaseID=30508.

IP Fragments Reassembly

The component that handles the reassembly of IP fragments also contains a flaw. It results in the target system consuming all the CPU time in processing the IP packets that have been modified by hackers. The processing of such packets results in denial of services to authorized users. It may also result in the system crashing. Mostly, this vulnerability is exploited on computers that have a Web server installed.

Microsoft has developed the following patch to prevent hackers from exploiting this vulnerability:

http://www.microsoft.com/Downloads/Release.asl?ReleaseID=20827.

This section discussed the security features and vulnerabilities in the Windows 2000 operating system. The next section discusses the security features of Linux.

Security Features of the Linux Operating System

The Linux operating system was developed by Linus Torvalds and is fundamentally based on the UNIX operating system. Linux can be deployed on a stand-alone or a network computer. A Linux host on a network can act as a file server, a print server, a Web server, a DNS server, or an e-mail server. In addition, it can also be configured to act as a router or firewall for a network.

Authentication

Like other operating systems, Linux has predefined procedures and mechanisms to authenticate users so that they can log on to a computer and access its resources. The Linux system allows users to specify their credentials by using one of three authentication interfaces: the X-windows-based console, the character user interface (CUI) console, or the Linux client terminal. Through these interfaces, the user provides a user name and a password. A common authentication mechanism used by Linux is PAM.

PAM (Pluggable Authentication Modules)

When Linux was developed, it followed a simple authentication mechanism. If a program, such as su, passwd, login, or xlock, wanted to authenticate a user, it would map user information from /etc/password. If it wanted to change a user's password, it would edit the /etc/passwd directory. This method later presented several problems for system administrators because authentication mechanisms were no longer limited to password verification. Each program requiring user authentication needed to know how to get proper information when dealing with different authentication schemes. If a user authentication scheme had to be changed, all these programs had to be recompiled.

Pluggable Authentication Modules (PAM) is a solution to this problem as it provides the Linux system with different forms of authentication modules. It also enables a system administrator to set an authentication policy without having to recompile authentication programs. In addition, it gives application developers the flexibility to concentrate on developing their own programs without being concerned about matching an authentication scheme.

The configuration settings for PAM are stored in various files under the /etc/pam.d/ directory or in /etc/pam.conf file. The pam.conf file is still read if no /etc/pam.d/ entry is found, but its use has decreased. Each application has its own file under the /etc/pam.d/ directory. Each file of an application has five elements: service name, module type, control flag, module path, and arguments. I'll explain these elements quickly.

Service Name

The service name of every PAM-enabled application is the name of the application that is requesting an authentication module. The information about the service name is stored in the application's configuration file in the /etc/pam.d directory.

Examples of service names would be a program named login defining the service name login and ftpd defining the service name ftpd.

Module Type

PAM includes four different types of modules for accessing a particular application or service in Linux:

- **auth module**. This (commonly known as authentication module) provides actual authentication by verifying user names and passwords. It also sets information such as group membership or Kerberos tickets.
- **account module**. This checks whether the authentication account of a user has expired, whether the user is allowed to log on at this hour of the day, and so on.
- **password module**. This is used to modify and maintain user passwords. This module works in association with the auth module to authenticate users.
- **session module**. This is used to implement settings before user authentication takes place. The settings include user environment settings that may put restrictions on users accessing a service during a session.

Control Flag

When authenticating a user, an application, or a service, PAM might implement multiple authentication module types, such as `auth`, `account`, and `password`. A control flag is used to establish the authentication status after each module executes. It indicates whether to halt or continue the authentication process. There are four types of control flags:

- ◆ **required**. All modules must be successfully verified for the authentication process to complete. This implies that if a module flagged as required fails the authentication process, the user is not notified until all the other required modules are checked.

- ◆ **requisite**. All modules must be successfully verified for the authentication process to be successful. However, if a module flagged as requisite fails the authentication process, the user is immediately notified with a message indicating the first failed required or requisite module.

- ◆ **sufficient**. If modules flagged as sufficient fail the authentication process, they are ignored. However, if a sufficient flagged module is successfully verified and no required flagged module above it has failed, then no other module of this type is checked and it is considered to have successfully been checked.

- ◆ **optional**. Modules flagged as optional are not important for the overall success or failure of authentication. The only time they play a role is when no other optional modules have succeeded or failed.

Module Path

A module path indicates the location where an authentication module is stored on a disk. All PAM modules are stored in the /lib/security directory. Usually, a module path specifies the full path to a module, such as /lib/security/pam_stack.so. However, if the full path is not indicated, then the module is assumed to be in the /lib/security directory, the default location for PAM modules.

Arguments

Arguments are additional information passed to pluggable modules during authentication for a particular module type. There are four types of arguments:

◆ **debug**. A module with a `debug` argument needs to write debug entries to the system log.

◆ **no_warn**. A module with `no_warn` argument does not pass any warnings to an application that is requesting authentication.

◆ **user_first_pass**. A module with the `user_first_pass` argument authenticates a user based on the password specified in the previous module in the authentication process. A user may be denied authentication if the password is not properly communicated between the two modules. In addition, if the previous module does not validate the password, the module with the `user_first_pass` argument will deny authentication to the user.

◆ **try_first_pass**. A module with the `try_first_pass` argument functions like the module with the `user_first_pass` argument. The difference is that this argument requires a module to reprompt a user for a password if there is improper password communication.

Access Control

Linux controls access to resources by categorizing users as owners, groups, and other system users. Following are a few mechanisms that allow Linux to control access to its resources.

Security Descriptor and an ACL

Linux uses security descriptors for managing each file and folder stored in it. The security descriptor monitors information about file flags (file rights) and file owners. It contains ACLs of various types for every file and folder. An ACL type may be for auditing a file or a folder or for defining the rights of users to a file or a folder. Each ACL contains ACEs for each user or group that is allowed access to a file or a folder.

File Access Rights

A Linux file system grants three types of access rights on files and folders to a user. These rights are read, write, and execute. Each user has a separate set of rights. Usually, the owner of a file has full access rights, which implies that only the file owner or the root user can grant any rights on the file to other users. The following are the attributes of a file:

- **SUID**. A user accessing an executable file has limited permissions that are assigned by the owner of the file. However, in case of a file set with the SUID attribute, the user of the file has the same permissions as the owner of the file.

- **Sticky bit**. A directory that has the sticky bit attribute gives users the right to modify and delete only those files from the directory that they have created. A sticky bit attribute is set on a directory and applies to all the files stored within a directory.

- **SGID bit**. The SGID bit attribute provides the inheritance of group ownership rights to a directory. This implies that a user who creates a directory automatically owns all the files in a directory that has the SGID attribute.

Auditing

To track and monitor the number of users logged on to a host and the resources they are accessing, Linux provides a logging mechanism. In addition, Linux provides commands and logs that enable you to view user and network activities. A few of these commands and logs are as follows.

lastlog/last/lascomm

Auditing tools in Linux record data in files such as `/var/log/wtmp` and `/var/log/lastlog`. These files contain information about the name of a terminal from where a user logged on, the IP address of that terminal, and the date, time, and duration of the logon.

A number of commands can help you sort the data stored in the audit log files:

- `lastlog`. The `lastlog` command is used to track user logons. This command provides the option of using two parameters, −tn and -u. The -tn parameter prints only logins more recent than n days ago. The -u parameter prints only logon information for user name.

- `last`. The `last` command prints the last time a user logged on to a system.

- `lascomm`. The `lascomm` command prints the user name, terminal, number of CPU seconds consumed, and both date and time of execution.

xferlog/syslog/klogd

`xferlog` is an audit log file in Linux that stores information about the FTP file transfers taking place on the host. `xferlog` is located in the `/var/log` directory. The following command enables you to view the details of this log file:

```
less /var/log/xferlog
```

The details displayed by this command include the FTP user name, file name, transfer time, type of file transferred, and the host from which the file was retrieved. In addition, it also provides information about how the user was authenticated and whether the user uploaded or downloaded a file.

In addition to the `xferlog` audit log file, Linux provides `syslogd` and `klogd` log files to log events. The logs created by these files are stored in the `/var/log/` directory. The `syslogd` log stores information about various programs and applications running on the Linux system. The `klogd` log file stores information about the kernel's activities.

Reliability

Like Windows 2000, Linux also offers several tools and techniques to quickly recover the system and data in case of a breakdown. This section discusses the reliability feature.

Data Backup and Archiving

Linux provides both backup media and backup techniques to enable you to make a safe backup of data when a system breaks down. The backup media supported by Linux include CDs, tape drives, Zip drives, and optical disks. The following are the backup techniques deployed by Linux:

◆ **Incremental backup**. This technique backs up only those files and directories that have been modified after the last backup. This technique is most useful when you have less disk space available to spare for backup. In addition, because the technique only backs up last modified files, its use involves a smaller amount of time.

◆ **Complete backup**. This technique backs up entire data without considering when the last backup was made. This technique is more secure than an incremental backup because it enables you backup entire data instead of smaller chunks.

Linux also provides several tools that automatically make backups. One of these is the Advanced Maryland Automatic Network Disk Archiver (AMANDA). AMANDA is a disk backup and archiving utility that makes backups at scheduled times. This utility can be used to make backups on a tape driver from multiple hosts on a network.

In addition to backup tools, Linux provides data archiving tools that enable you to compress data. One such tool is Tar, which creates data archive packages for directories. It ensures that the original directory structure is retained even after packaging so that data can be restored in the same directory structure as before.

Boot Disks and CDs

Linux provides system boot disks to start the system in the minimum possible time after boot failure. Boot disks help you start your system and restore system files. It contains information such as boot drivers, boot images, and minimal system configuration.

Using the `mkbootdisk` command in Red Hat Linux and its derivatives, you can create system boot disks. In addition, you can use the Linux installation CD and repair your boot-failed system by using the `rescue` command.

Data Restore

After recovering a failed Linux system, you would probably like to restore the data that you have backed up. To do this, you would use the restore utility corresponding to the tool you used to back up the data.

Security Configuration

Like Windows 2000, Linux also allows you to configure security settings. However, Linux does not have a specific security tool that is part of the operating system. Linux allows you to make security settings by executing shell scripts.

Having discussed the security features of Windows 2000, let me also introduce you to various vulnerabilities that exist in the Linux operating system.

Vulnerabilities of Linux

Most hacking attempts to a Linux system are initiated by physical methods. Therefore, it is essential to ensure that hackers don't gain physical access to your Linux servers. You can restrict access by keeping the servers under lock and key.

Vigilant selection of starting options and BIOS setup may avoid physical access to a Linux server. However, it does not ensure security. For example, a difficult-to-guess password may protect a system but does not ensure complete security. In addition, changing the BIOS setting to boot a computer from only the boot floppy disk does not mean that hackers cannot exploit the system. Hackers can use bootable floppy disks of Linux to start your computer and use it for their purpose.

An option that can prevent physical intrusion is setting a BIOS password. In fact, a BIOS password ensures that the hacker cannot enable the option of starting the computer by using a floppy disk.

A common Linux vulnerability is the permissions that users have on the /etc/passwd file, which stores encrypted login passwords and cleartext logon names of users. By default, all users in Linux have the read permission to the /etc/passwd file. This implies that a hacker who manages to gain access to a Linux system can easily read the /etc/passwd file and obtain logon names and passwords. Even though the passwords are encrypted, they can be easily cracked using password cracking tools.

While configuring an operating system, even a slight negligence on the part of system administrators may also lead to security holes. This is especially true for a Linux system installed with default configurations, accounts, and user privileges and services. The next section discusses the vulnerabilities in the root and default accounts.

Root Account

The root account is the most important user account in Linux. It is most preferred by hackers because it provides all access privileges on the system. Therefore, it is especially necessary to choose a difficult-to-guess password for the root account.

System administrators need to ensure that the root account is not used for critical activities that can be also performed using another account. Most user accounts (other than the root account) do not have permissions to perform activities that are important to the system. Even if accounts have permissions, most of them display warning messages about the criticality of the activity. The root account allows you to perform activities without showing warning messages. Storing and performing activities might result in an accidental data loss from the root account, as it does not even display a warning before performing an activity.

Another potential risk is a system left unattended after logging into the root account. A hacker within the organization can exploit this situation to perform any number of activities. Therefore, it is always necessary to log out of the root account immediately after your work is complete or when you are away from your computer. A good practice to counter this problem is to specify root account timeout options so that, even if the system is left unattended for some time, the user is logged out automatically.

It is always recommended that you not give any user root account privileges. If it becomes necessary to provide such privileges, system administrators should grant only a limited number.

Also, you should not configure Linux systems to allow remote logins through the root account because it is easy for hackers to guess the remote password and access the system. If the need arises to access the Linux system from remote locations with root privileges, the user should log in as a normal user, and then use the /bin/su command.

Default Accounts

When Linux is installed, certain accounts and groups are created by default, which include adm, lp, halt, sync, news, uucp, operator, games, ftp, and gopher. A few of the default groups are adm, lp, and popusers.

After the root account, the other method by which users can log on to the system is through default accounts. Therefore, security risks increase as the more default accounts are activated.

To prevent hackers from accessing the default account, it is recommended to delete all default accounts and groups.

Having discussed the risks that a Linux system has from open and unattended root and default accounts, let me brief you on the vulnerabilities associated with various utilities of Linux.

Utility Vulnerabilities

Utilities that accompany various flavors of Linux (such as Red Hat Linux and other UNIX-based operating systems) are vulnerable and a source of security breaches. The following section briefly discusses these utilities and the security threats that they pose to systems.

r Utilities

The r utility allows users to remotely access Linux and other UNIX-based operating system. The most common r utilities are rlogin and rsh. The rlogin utility allows users to connect to remote hosts from a terminal of local hosts. The rsh utility allows trusted users to execute commands on local hosts from remote hosts.

The r utilities are insecure due to several reasons. First and foremost, they use a mechanism called rhosts that allow users to connect from remote locations. The second reason is that r utilities transfer data in plain text. Insecure medium (rhosts) along with unencrypted data make r utilities highly vulnerable.

It is recommended that you disable r utilities to prevent an attack occurring due to these vulnerabilities.

Groff Vulnerability

Groff is a utility used in Red Hat Linux for document formatting. If a buffer overflow occurs in the preprocessor of this utility, it gives hackers the opportunity to gain access rights to the lp account in the target system. However, to exploit this vulnerability, the hacker needs to execute the groff in the LPRng printer spooler.

Mutt Buffer Overflow

Mutt is text-based e-mail client software used by UNIX-based operating systems. Versions earlier than 1.2.5.1 of mutt software have vulnerabilities that allow hackers to overwrite the data stored in memory due to a buffer overflow problem. Red Hat Linux (from version 6.2 to 7.2) is also affected. Hackers can send malicious content in e-mail messages to client computers, allowing hackers to modify bytes in the memory.

To prevent hackers from exploiting the vulnerabilities of mutt software, you need to update the version from the following link:

http://www.redhat.com/support/errata/RHSA-2002-003.html

OpenSSH Vulnerability

The SSH utility provides a secure connection to a remote computer and is used to execute commands and transfer files to and from remote computers.

OpenSSH is an implementation of SSH1 and SSH2. OpenSSH secures network traffic from unauthorized access attempts by implementing authentication and monitoring network sessions.

The UseLogin directive in OpenSSH allows a remote user to gain root access to the Linux operating system. Users who have an SSH connection on a Linux computer, which has OpenSSH installed, can execute commands from remote locations. When a user executes a command from a remote host, OpenSSH opens root privileges and executes a command. However, OpenSSH fails to close root privileges, which is a major loophole that allows hackers to gain root access to Linux systems.

GID Man Exploit

The ultimate_source() function of the earlier versions of the GID man package undergoes buffer overflow quite often. Hackers use this vulnerability to gain root access to the target Linux systems. They exploit the vulnerability by creating a man page that contains file names with escape characters.

This vulnerability affects Red Hat Linux versions ranging from 5.2 to 7.1. To protect Red Hat Linux systems from this vulnerability, you need to update the GID man package from http://www.redhat.com/support/errat/RHSA-2001-072.html.

PAM Buffer Overflow

A buffer overflow may occur during a PAM implementation of the /bin/login service, which stores the buffer value in the PAM call. When the PAM implementation process of /bin/login communicates with some PAM modules set with nondefault options, the process overwrites this buffer value. This may occur in a buffer overflow that might, in turn, allow a hacker to obtain account details of another user.

The buffer overflow vulnerability affects Red Hat Linux versions 7.1 and 7.2 and Mandrake Linux versions 8.0 and 8.1.

The discussion on the security features and vulnerabilities of Windows 2000 and Linux is complete. I will now discuss the features of the most commonly deployed Web servers: IIS and Apache.

Securing Web Servers

Deploying a secure Web server implies securing your host Web sites and applications from the outside world. This section is a discussion on the various security features provided by IIS and Apache.

Internet Information Server (IIS)

IIS is the default Windows 2000–based Web server. It not only provides Web services but also acts as an FTP server. As a Web server, IIS allows you to create and manage Web sites and publish content on the Internet. As an FTP server, IIS allows you to upload and download files from FTP servers.

This section provides you with a thorough understanding of IIS. You'll learn how it provides security against innumerable security attacks that have time and again plagued networks.

NOTE

In this chapter, IIS 5.0 (the current version) will be referred to as IIS, unless mentioned otherwise.

Security Features of IIS

IIS provides the following security features that help safeguard sites and content on the hosts:

◆ **Encryption**. IIS contains strong encryption techniques that provide integrity, authentication, and confidentiality to your data. The high encryption pack now comes installed with IIS and has further leveraged its encryption capabilities. You can now use 128-bit encryption to export your data internationally.

◆ **Authentication**. This is one of the core security features of IIS. This mechanism authenticates users by mapping them to Windows 2000 user accounts. Some of the authentication mechanisms supported by IIS are anonymous authentication, digest authentication, Integrated Windows authentication, and certificate authentication.

◆ **Access control**. After a user has been authenticated, access control mechanisms are deployed to determine the level of access that can be granted. IIS does this by using several access control filters, such as file system permissions, network address permissions, and Web server access permissions.

◆ **Auditing**. As you already know, auditing allows you to monitor your system as well as user accounts. Auditing in IIS allows you to keep a track of authorized or unauthorized access to your resources.

◆ **Certificate services**. IIS uses certificates mainly for authentication purposes. IIS supports SSL and TLS security protocols. IIS uses the SSL protocol's client authentication feature to authenticate users

Due to the constraint of the scope of this book, the following sections discusses only the authentication and access control features provided by IIS.

Authentication

IIS authentication mechanisms provide a comprehensive security solution. Authenticating users in IIS invariably involves mapping users to Windows user accounts. Authenticated users are then allowed to access the various services, such as FTP, HTTP, SMTP, and NNTP. In this way, users accessing resources are authenticated before they are granted any kind of access.

Some authentication mechanisms supported by IIS are

◆ Anonymous authentication

◆ Basic authentication

◆ Digest authentication

◆ Integrated Windows authentication

◆ Certificate authentication

Anonymous Authentication

Anonymous authentication is, in effect, not an authentication mechanism because the user who is accessing the resources need not provide his identification details, such as user name and password. In this process, when a user tries to access any resource, IIS maps the user to a local account, referred to as `IUSR_computername`, where `computername` is the name of the computer on which IIS is running.

IIS manages and controls the password for this account because, by default, IIS is configured for password synchronization. As a result, in anonymous authentication, IIS impersonates the user and logon by using the `ISUR_computername` account. However, the account needs to have the right called Access This Computer From The Network.

This account is defined with a password at the time of setup. However, you can change the account in the IIS administrative tool. It is recommended to change the Anonymous User account in case you are hosting multiple Web sites. In this way, you can define one Anonymous User account per Web site.

Basic Authentication

Basic authentication, as is suggested by the name, is the most basic or simplest form of authentication in which the user is prompted for a user name and password. After the user enters his user name and password, the information is sent over the network, which where this form of authentication suffers from some inherent vulnerability. The password is sent as base64-encoded, which is so weak that it is even referred to as plain text or clear text. As a result, basic authentication is also known as a clear text logon.

To implement IIS basic authentication, you need to have Windows 2000 accounts in the Active Directory. When a user connects to a Web site, user name and password information is obtained by IIS from the HTTP authorization header, and calls the LogonUser API. IIS then impersonates the user to logon. The LogonUser API determines the manner in which the account has been logged on. For example, it can be logged on locally or through an external or remote network.

 NOTE

When the account is logged on locally, information about the user is maintained so that if the domain controller cannot be accessed, then the account can perform an offline logon.

Although basic authentication is a very unsecured protocol, its weaknesses can be overcome by combining it with SSL/TLS protocols. When basic authentication and SSL/TLS are working in conjunction, then all the data is first encrypted by

SSL/TLS. This adds a very strong security feature to the otherwise security deficient basic authentication mechanism. Moreover, being a part of the HTTP suite, basic authentication is supported by a large number of browsers.

Digest Authentication

Digest authentication is a part of HTTP1.1 protocol. Digest authentication does not send a user's credentials in clear text format. The following steps describe the working of the digest algorithm:

1. Some information is sent from the server to the browser. This information, also referred to as the challenge, contains the identity of the client's computer, the domain, and the time.
2. The browser prompts for a user name and password.
3. The password and information are hashed to produce a digest. This digest is sent back to the server along with the information.
4. The server also hashes the password with the same information, and a similar copy of the digest is created.
5. After the server receives the digest, it compares both the digests.
6. If both the digests match, only then is the authentication deemed successful.

For a proper digest authentication to take place, the following points should be kept in mind:

◆ The computer running Windows 2000 Server should be an Active Directory domain.

◆ Users should have their accounts in the Windows 2000 domain.

◆ All passwords should be reversibly encrypted before the domain controller stores them. This can be done by configuring all those accounts that use digest authentication with the Store Password Using Reversible Encryption option enabled. After setting this option, the user needs to then change his/her password. If the password is not changed, the complete process will not work.

◆ IIS should be configured to use digest authentication.

◆ The `iissuba.dll` file should be present in the domain controller.

Integrated Windows Authentication

Integrated Windows authentication is based on two protocols, namely KerberosV5 and challenge-response. The following steps describe how the integrated Windows authentication is accomplished:

1. If a user has logged on to a domain, the browser tries to gather the user's credentials from the logged on information itself.

2. If it is unsuccessful, that is, the user has not logged on, then the browser keeps on prompting the user for his credentials or returns an error.

Certificate Authentication

To authenticate users, IIS can use certificates and then map the user accounts with the users. For this, users need to first obtain a certificate from a CA, then the browser can use this certificate to prove that it possesses the private key. IIS supports the SSL/TLS protocols for certificate authentication tasks. An SSL enabled IIS provides the following options:

◆ **Require Secure Channel (SSL).** Allows you to communicate only over the HTTPS interface.

◆ **Enable client certificate mapping.** Allows you to map certificates to user accounts. You can edit these mappings in the following two ways:

  • **One-to-one mapping.** Allows you to specify a certificate and the user account to which it will be mapped.

  • **Many-to-one mapping.** Allows you to map several certificates to a single user account.

◆ **Configure Client Authentication.** Allows you to manage and configure client authentication with the following options:

  • **Accept Client Certificates.** Allows IIS to map the client's certificate with Windows user accounts when the client accesses the network over an HTTPS interface and presents a certificate.

  • **Require Client Certificates.** IIS requires that the clients present a valid certificate before accessing the network.

  • **Ignore Client Certificates.** Allows the client to access the network without any certificate.

You can use the Web Server Certificate Wizard in the Internet Services Manager to create and manage server certificates.

Access Control

After authenticating users, IIS uses some access control filters, such as Web server access permissions, file system permissions, and IP address permissions. Before discussing each of these, let me first describe the access control process of IIS.

Access Control Process

Following are the steps in the access control mechanism of IIS:

1. A client sends a request to access resources from IIS.
2. The client may or may not be asked to authenticate itself.
3. IIS then verifies the client's IP address. In case of Web access, a client's DNS will also be verified. IIS may be configured to deny access to some particular IP addresses. As a result, all IP address denied access are filtered and an HTTP 403 error is returned to the client.
4. After this, IIS checks the user account that has been mapped to the user during the authentication process. If the user name and the password is valid, the process carries on. Otherwise, an HTTP 403 error results.
5. Then, IIS checks the compatibility between the Web or FTP access permissions and the type of access (read, write) requested by the client.
6. If any third-party security modules have been specified by the administrators, then IIS contacts them.
7. The last check performed by IIS is to see the compatibility between NTFS permissions and the type of access requested. If any incompatibility is reported in the case of a Web request, IIS reports an HTTP 401 request.
8. Finally, if all conditions are satisfied, IIS agrees to the client's request.

Access Control Filters

IIS supports the following three types of access control filters:

◆ **Network address access control**. You can configure IIS to deny or permit access on the basis of IP addresses, range of IP addresses, and

FQDNs (Fully Qualified Domain Names). You can select either a single computer (identified by an IP address), a group of computers (identified by the IP address and the subnet mask), or a domain name (identified by the computers FQDN or a subdomain of the form *.subdomain.com).

♦ **Web server permissions**. Web server permissions and FTP permissions allow you to specify the operations that can be carried on the resources. These permissions are applicable to all clients. In case there are a set of conflicting permissions, then the permissions that are more restrictive take precedence.

♦ **NTFS (NT File System) permissions**. This is applied after all other permissions have been applied. These permissions are responsible for finally controlling access to resources. When you configure NTFS permissions, you need to first convert your disk partition from FAT to NTFS because access control permissions that restrict access to resources are only available in the NTFS.

Apache

Apache is a powerful Web server being used extensively in the Internet scenario, and its security features are commendable. It is one of the most preferred Web servers because it can be used with a wide range of operating systems, such as UNIX, Linux, and Solaris. A binary version of Apache is also available for Windows operating systems. Apache also allows you to work with several scripting languages. Apache and PHP are considered to be one of the best combinations. Apache is built on a modular design.

In this section, I will discuss Apache's security features, such as various authentication and access control mechanisms used to protect information. First, I will discuss basic and digest authentication mechanisms, then move on to the host-based access control, which ensures that only authorized people are allowed to access resources. Then, I'll discuss the authentication-based access control. Finally, I'll discuss .htaccess files and their role in ensuring security.

Securing through Authentication

Apache provides two types of authentication mechanisms:

♦ Basic authentication

♦ Digest authentication

Basic authentication is the simplest form of authentication available. In this mechanism, the password is exchanged between the client and the host in a plain text format.

Digest authentication is an alternate method of protecting content on a Web server. Digest authentication is considered to be more secure than basic authentication.

The main feature of digest authentication is that passwords specified by users are not sent across the network. Instead a *digest* is sent to the server, which is a value derived by combining the following:

◆ **User name**. The identity of the user sending the request.

◆ **Password**. The secret pass phrase specified by the user.

◆ **Requested resource**. The resource on the server requested by the user.

◆ **Server**. The identity of the server that contains the requested resource.

◆ **Nonce**. A special key that is generated by the server and sent to the client.

Validating credentials in the case of digest authentication is very different from basic authentication. In digest authentication, the Apache Web server maintains a copy of user names and passwords. Whenever a client specifies a user name and password, the server performs a few calculations using an MD5 hash algorithm and used to generate a *one-way hash* with the user name, password, and other information.

NOTE

Terms, such as MD5, used in the preceding explanation are well covered in Chapter 6, "Secure Authentication and Messaging."

Securing through Access Control

Apache provides several control mechanisms to restrict access to both files and directories on the host computer. Following are Apache's most commonly used access control mechanisms:

◆ Host-based access control

◆ .htaccess files

Host-Based Access Control

In host-based access control, the request from a user is accepted only if the computer sending the request is allowed to access the resource on the server computer. Host-based access control can be implemented by specifying IP addresses or domain names in the configuration file. If any specified IP address or domain name is restricted, the server will deny access to the requested resource. Host-based access control can be implemented using

◆ Domain names

◆ IP addresses

.htaccess Files

One of the most common requirements of any Web server administrator is to enable the Web server to behave in the same way that all documents in a particular directory or a directory tree are treated. One such configuration would be to prompt a user for a password before accessing the contents of a particular directory. Another possible configuration would be to allow or disallow directory listing for a particular directory. However, the requirement doesn't end with that of the Web server administrator. Even Apache users require that they are able to customize their space on the Web server.

This is made possible by using .htaccess files, which are configuration files that allow you to specify exclusive configuration options for a particular directory. This helps the server administrator to customize the behavior of the Apache Web server or allow users to customize the space allocated to them. It is fairly simple to use .htaccess files: All the administrator has to do is include the required configuration directives. Of course, the file should be located in the directory for which the configuration is meant.

Relevance of .htaccess Files

Configurations you specify in .htaccess files can also be used under the <Directory> section in the main configuration file, which also ensures that necessary settings are available to the directory. Besides, the <Directory> section is a preferred choice of administrators because the configurations specified there get loaded directly into the system's memory when it is started.

If directives can be specified in the main section of the configuration file, then what use is the .htaccess file? The following situations highlight the relevance of .htaccess files for access control:

◆ There are situations wherein several developers need to work together to create a site's content. In such a scenario, the developers might want to make configuration changes to the server as the need arises. However, these developers do not have access to the main configuration file. Also, contacting the administrator for every small configuration could waste a lot of time. Therefore, it is best to allow these developers to make required configuration changes to the server without involving the site administrator. This is made possible by using .htaccess files.

◆ Another advantage of using .htaccess files is their ability to make local configuration modifications to affect the behavior of directories without having to involve the entire server. Moreover, if you use .htaccess files, you need not restart the system with every configuration change.

When to Avoid Using .htaccess Files

There may be situations in which .htaccess files are not the best option, such as the following:

◆ When only a single administrator is looking after a complete Web server, it is recommended to maintain only the configuration files. This is because .htaccess files are scattered all over the system and it is, therefore, very difficult to maintain them. On the other hand, since there is only one main configuration file, an administrator can easily maintain it.

◆ Whenever a user wants to access a file or a directory on the server, the authenticity of the user is checked. In such situations, whenever .htaccess files are used, each directory that is a part of the path to the file are checked for the presence of .htaccess files. If the server encounters any .htaccess files, these files are parsed to check whether the user has adequate permissions on the directory. In situations where the requested file is located farther down in the directory structure, it might take a long time to process the .htaccess files for each directory before sending a response to the client. Therefore, it is recommended to not use .htaccess files in such situations.

Securing CGI Programs

Common Gateway Interface (CGI), is one of the first and still the most popular server-side scripting language. It is used to extend the capabilities of a host server, and also executes as subtasks of Web servers. A CGI program written in languages, such as C, C++, Perl, and UNIX shell scripts, accepts user input in environment variables and creates a response by creating an HTML document. CGI programs have the capability of interacting with databases and displaying results to users. They allow complex financial calculations and also allow you to create programs that enable users to chat with each other on the Internet. In fact, almost all innovative and dynamic uses of the Internet, ranging from search engines to Web pages, that interact dynamically were originally developed using CGI.

Problems with CGI Scripts

CGI scripts create problems because their extensibility is powerful. The scripts are so authoritative that if not written properly, they can completely compromise the security of the server on which they run.

CGI scripts can introduce security holes in the following two ways:

◆ Scripts not written well may deliberately or accidentally provide loopholes that may leak information that helps hackers break into the host system.

◆ Scripts that accept user input, such as the contents of a form or a "searchable index" command, may be susceptible to attacks by remote users.

CGI scripts may be a potential security risk even if a server is run as *nobody*, or an *httpd user* account. This is because a weak CGI script has sufficient privileges to leak the system password file, scrutinize network information maps, or initiate a logon session on a port. To administer such activities, all that needs to be done is execute a few commands in Perl. In fact, even a server running in a chroot directory can allow a faulty CGI script to provide enough information sufficient to compromise a system.

NOTE

Web servers with Windows 2000 and Linux operating systems that allow multiple users access at multiple authorization levels run under a restricted account. These accounts are usually referred to as *nobody* or *httpd user* accounts. CGI programs residing on Web servers running under these accounts are also run under the same restricted user account.

Unfortunately, not all operating systems provide restricted user accounts. This implies that a meager level security for CGI is also not available that was once provided by these restrictions. For instance, on Windows 3.1, Windows 95, and Macintosh operating systems, it is not easy to restrict the reach of a CGI program.

Restrictions on Using the cgi-bin Directory

The cgi-bin directory is the place where all CGI scripts are ideally saved. However, his directory may also become a source of intrusion into a system if care is not taken while using it. The following should be kept in mind while saving programs in the cgi-bin directory of a server.

Extensive programs, such as interpreters, shell scripts, and script engines, should not be installed in the cgi-bin directory or any other place on the server that is easily accessible through a simple request to any Web server process. Programs installed in such places give attackers the opportunity to explore other content on the host very easily. For example, on Windows-based systems, the Perl executable perl.exe should never be placed in the cgi-bin directory. If a hacker manages to get access to this directory, the complete system is open to attack. Unfortunately, several Windows-based Web servers are configured to place this file in the cgi-bin directory because it is easier to set up Perl script on these. Another example of inappropriate use of the cgi-bin directory is placing of the Web search engines in this directory. If a system is not configured properly, it is easy to know the details stored in the cgi-bin directory. To make matters worse, if search engines are placed in such vulnerable places, they can be used to find other vulnerable machines on the network.

CGI scripts distributed with Web servers are another security hole for hosts because most of these scripts have security flaws. These scripts are a security threat because users tend not to delete files from a cgi-bin directory. Even if new versions of the Web server are installed, these scripts continue to exist in this directory for months or even years. The following are a few examples of CGI scripts distributed with Web servers and pose a threat to security of systems:

◆ `webdist.cgi`, **part of IRIX Mindshare Out Box versions 1.0–1.2**. This script helps users install and distribute software across the network. Due to the inadequate CGI parameters defined in the script, the script allows remote users to execute commands on the server system with the permissions of the server daemon. The bug in this script was not fixed till June 12, 1997. You can contact Mindshare for details on patches and workarounds. Until then, it is recommended that you disable the execute permissions of this script.

◆ `files.pl`, **part of Novell WebServer Examples Toolkit v.2**. This script fails to check user input properly. Due to this bug, it allows users to view any file or directory on the host on which it runs. This leads to a compromise of confidential documents and gives hackers sufficient information to break into a system. It is recommended that you delete this script.

◆ `nph-test-cgi`, **all versions**. This script is included in several versions of NCSA httpd and Apache demons. Through this script, remote users can obtain the file listing of any directory on the Web server. This script should be either disabled by removing execute permissions or completely removed from the system.

◆ `nph-publish`, **versions 1.0–1.1**. This script allows remote users to place writable files on the server.

◆ `phf phone book` **script, all versions**. This script is distributed with NCSA httpd and Apache. The script allows remote users to execute commands on the server and retrieve files.

Apart from applications mentioned in the preceding discussion, it is recommended that you store other CGI scripts in the `cgi-bin` directory. Although there's essentially nothing wrong in storing CGI scripts in other places around the document tree, it's better to store them in the `cgi-bin` directory. This is because CGI scripts are potentially large security holes and it is easy to keep track of what scripts are installed on your system if they're kept in a central location. This is particularly true in an environment where there are multiple Web authors. It's too easy for an author to inadvertently create a buggy CGI script and install it somewhere in the document tree. By restricting CGI scripts to the `cgi-bin` directory and by setting up permissions so that only the Web administrator can install these scripts, you avoid this chaotic situation.

There's also a risk of a hacker managing to create a .CGI file somewhere in your document tree and then executing it remotely by requesting its URL. A `cgi-bin` directory with tightly controlled access reduces this possibility.

Comparison of C, Perl, and Shell Scripts as Scripting Languages for CGI

Compiled languages, such as C and C++, are safer than interpreted languages, such as Perl and shell scripts. The main reason is the issue of a remote user gaining access to the source code of the script. The more the hacker knows about how a script works, the easier it is for him to find flaws in it and exploit it for his needs. A script written in compiled language is compiled on the server and, therefore, only the byte code of the script is placed in the `cgi-bin` directory. Even if the hacker gains access to the `cgi-bin` directory, the source code is not accessible and, therefore, any manipulation of the script is not possible. However, an interpreted script is easily exploited if the hacker accesses its source code.

A properly configured server generally does not return the source code to an executable script. However, this can happen in several situations. Consider the following example where a Web administrator's normal course of action leaves a big security hole on the server. To modify an interpreted CGI script, a Web administrator opens the file in a text editor. After making modifications, the file is saved and closed. Unfortunately, the text editor has the option of making an activated backup copy. As a result, the backup copy of the executable script is created some place in the directory tree. Though a remote user cannot obtain the source code by fetching the script, he can now obtain the backup copy by blindly requesting the following URL:

```
http://your-site/a/path/your_script.cgi~
```

This is the reason for limiting CGI scripts to the `cgi-bin` directory and ensuring that it is separate from the document root directory.

The second reason why C is preferred as a CGI scripting language is speed. Whenever a CGI program is executed, it is loaded into memory and executed. If the CGI program is written in Perl, the entire Perl interpreter needs to be loaded and compiled before every execution. These two processes take a large amount of time.

The third reason that compiled code is safer than interpreted code is the size and complexity of the interpreted scripts. Extensive software programs, such as shell and Perl interpreters, are known to have flaws that may turn out to be security holes.

The fourth reason is ease of use. It is easy to send data to system commands and capture their output from scripts. In contrast to this, invoking a system command in C is not easy. In fact, it is said that writing complex CGI programs in a shell script is inviting trouble. A shell scripting language is an appropriate choice for only small and trivial CGI programs.

After everything previously said about compiled and interpreted languages, there is still no guarantee that a compiled program is completely safe. A script written in a compiled language, such as C, can also have flaws. This has also been clearly indicated by the experiences of NCSA httpd version 1.3. Although interpreted scripted languages have a number of problems, they are shorter and more modular when compared with compiled programs. In addition, Perl contains a number of built-in features that were basically introduced to catch potential security holes in scripts. For example, Perl's *taint check* mechanism captures several flaws in CGI scripts and makes Perl scripts safer in some respects.

PERL TAINT CHECKS

One of the most common security holes in CGI scripts is the unintentional passing of unchecked user variables to the shell of the system. Perl provides a solution to this in the form of a taint-checking mechanism, which treats any variable that is set by values from outside the program as infected or tainted. It also restricts the interaction of such variables with the shell.

Using a special version of an interpreter called `taintperl`, you can enable the taint checking mechanism in Perl version 4. The following command enables the taint checking mechanism:

```
# ! / usr /local /bin /taintperl
```

In Perl version 5, you need to pass the `-T` flag to the interpreter as shown in the code below:

```
# ! / usr /local /bin /perl -T
```

If a tainted variable is used to set the values of another variable, the other variable also becomes tainted. The use of tainted variables is restricted by various functions of Perl that interact outside the program, such as `eval()`, `system()`, `exec()`, or `piped open()`. If you try to use these variables in such functions, Perl automatically exits the program by giving a warning.

Tainted variables cannot be used with such functions even if shell metacharacters are scanned using `tr///` or `s///` commands. The only method to untaint a tainted variable is by pattern matching and extracting the required matched substrings.

Safe Practices While Coding CGI Scripts

Over the years, several general rules have been listed for coding in any language. The following are a few safe practices for code using CGI scripts:

- ◆ **Understand the relevance of a program.**
- ◆ **Carefully design the program before scripting.** After identifying a program's relevance, you need to carefully plan certain aspects of programming. For instance, you need to consider the environment in which the program will be executed, the input that will be accepted from the user, output expected from the program, the files used, and the arguments passed. Before scripting the program, ideally, you should write a pseudocode of the program in English or any native language.
- ◆ **Avoid disclosing too much information about your site and server host.** Scripts that easily reveal system information are not considered good scripts. For example, the `finger` command prints out the physical path to the user's home directory. In fact, the `finger` demon should be completely disabled or removed from the system if you want to avoid information leaks.
- ◆ **Evaluate all possible values provided by the user.** Many times, a programmer comes to know that his script contains security loopholes only when a user passes unexpected values or unforeseen formats to the program or a function within the program. A programmer can avoid such problems by using a CGI program to check all the arguments used in the program. The verification of arguments slows down the CGI script but protects it from hostile users. When the arguments in a program are being checked, special attention should be given to the following points:
  - Check the length of the arguments being passed by the user. Ensure that values passed to the arguments do not result in buffer overflow and crash the system.
  - If you plan to use a selection list, ensure that the value provided by the user is a legal value.
  - Clean the values entered by the user by filtering unwanted characters for each application.

◆ **Verify arguments passed to system functions**. Even if your program is making a call to system functions, you need to ensure the sanctity of the arguments being passed to ensure that functions return the expected results. Consider the following example. To check if your program is opening a file in a current directory, you may want to use the index() function in C or Perl to verify if the file name contains a forward slash character (/). If the file contains a slash that it shouldn't, the program should not open the file.

◆ **Log error messages to track programming bugs and security problems**. C and Perl follow the POSIX programming specification, which necessitates every system call to provide return code. This specification is a blessing in disguise because it allows programmers to log error messages returned from system functions. Many programmers are of the view that system functions, such as write(), chdir(), or chown() cannot fail in any circumstance. However, they are wrong. A system function can fail. When a call to a function fails, the errno variable provides the return code and the reason for the failure. Programmers can use this variable to identify system call failure and track programming bugs.

◆ **Ensure that crucial portions of your program are small, modular, and easy to understand**.

◆ **Read through your code**. Attack your code as if you were an outsider. Think of all possible ways that your program may react if it encounters unexpected input, if there is a delay between two system calls, and so on.

◆ **Use full path names for any file name argument**. This practice should apply to both commands and files.

◆ **Dump core files only while testing**. Core files fill up a file system, and they may contain confidential information. If an attacker knows this, he can use such information to break into a system. Instead of making your program dump core files, you should have your program log the appropriate problem and exit. For instance, you may use setrlimit() to limit the size of a core file to 0.

◆ **Do not create files in world-writable directories**. If your CGI script needs to run under the nobody user, then files created in the program should be saved under a directory with the same rights.

◆ **Place timeouts on the real-time used by the CGI script**. A CGI script may be blocked because of several reasons; for example, a read request from the user's end may hang or the user's Web browser may not accept information that you send to it. A solution to such problems is to place timeouts in the script wherever the script makes real-time processing. If the script is taking more time than allotted, then it should exit by giving an appropriate message.

◆ **Place timeouts on the CPU time used by the CGI script**. A faulty CGI script may result in an infinite loop. You should, therefore, place a limit on the total CPU time that a CGI script can use.

◆ **Do not make the user send the password in plain text over the network connection**. If your CGI script needs to accept a user name and a password, you should use cryptography enabled Web servers so that only encrypted passwords are exchanged over the network. Otherwise, you may use client-side certificates to provide authentication.

◆ **Let your script go through a bug bash session**. It is best to get your scripts reviewed by other competent programmers. After a script is reviewed, a walk-through session with other programmers can help find logical errors in the script. In trying to explain every part of the code with a logical reason of why an action is performed in a certain manner, you'll be able to find loopholes in your script.

Specific Practices for Specific Programming Languages

This section lists rules that are applicable to specific programming languages, in particular Perl and C.

Practices for Perl

◆ **Use Perl's taint feature for all CGI scripts**. As stated earlier, this feature will prevent unchecked values entered by remote users to interact with the shell of the system.

◆ **Use Perl's emulation mode for SUID users**. For scripts using the SUID users account, it is preferable to use the Perl's emulation mode running on older versions of Linux.

◆ **Always set the PATH environment variable**. Even when you are not using the SUID account, it is always recommended to set your program's PATH environment variable.

◆ **Untaint all file names**. Remember that Perl ignores tainting for file names that are opened as read-only. However, ensure that all file names are untainted and not the ones that you need to modify.

◆ **Ensure that the Perl interpreter and all its libraries are installed**. If these are installed, they cannot be modified by anyone other than the administrator. A person who can modify the Perl libraries can modify any other Perl program.

Practices for C

◆ **Avoid making assumptions about the size of user input**. A security loophole in C has been the ability to overflow character buffers when reading in user input. Consider the following example:

```
#include <stdlib.h>
#include <stdio.h>
static char user_input[1000];
char* read_input(){
        int input_size;
        input_size=atoi(getenv("CONTENT_LENGTH"));
        fread(user_input, input_size, 1, stdin);
        return user_input;
}
```

The preceding code assumes that user input will never exceed the size of the static buffer, which is 1,000 bytes. This is a security flaw in the code, which a smart hacker can easily bypass. The hacker can break this type of program by providing input, which is several times more than the size specified. As a result, the buffer overflows and crashes the program. Many times, hackers use the buffer overflow mechanism to execute commands remotely. The following code avoids buffer overflow by returning NULL if there is not enough memory place:

```
#include <stdlib.h>
#include <stdio.h>
static char user_input[1000];
char* read_input(){
```

```
      int input_size;
      input_size=atoi(getenv("CONTENT_LENGTH"));
      char* user_input=(char*) malloc(user_input);
      if(user_input != NULL)
            fread(user_input, input_size, 1, stdin);
      return user_input;
}
```

After input from the user has been read safely, the risk of overflow is reduced but not eliminated completely. There are a number of C library functions, such as `sprintf()`, `fscanf()`, `sscanf()`, `vsprintf()`, `realpath()`, `getopt()`, `getpass()`, `streadd()`, `strecpy()`, and `strtrns()`, that may cause buffer overflow even after user input is read. These functions may result in overflow at either a destination buffer or an internal static buffer on some system.

Table 5.1 lists the functions that you should avoid and also provides an alternative function for each of these functions.

Table 5.1 Functions That May Generate Buffer Overflow

Avoid	Use Instead
gets()	fget()
strcpy()	strncpy()
strcat()	strncat()

◆ **Make maximum use of available tools**. For instance, if you are using the ANSI C compiler, you should use prototypes for calls.

◆ **Generate maximum warnings**. As stated in the section "Safe Practices While Coding CGI Scripts," a program should generate the maximum error and warning messages to capture bugs and flaws in the program. For instance, you can generate warnings in the GNU C compiler by specifying the -Wall option. If the compiler you are using does not generate warnings, you can use the lint program to check mistakes in the program.

◆ **Check if a file already exists before creating a new one**. If you want to create a new file with the open call, then you should use O_EXCL ¦ O_CREATE flags to cause the routine to fail.

Guidelines for Writing CGI Scripts That Execute with Additional Privileges

Several times, you need to assign permissions to CGI scripts that are different from those assigned to the Web server. On UNIX computers, you can do this by assigning SUID and SGID permissions to CGI scripts. These permissions allow the scripts to execute with the permissions of the files' owner instead of the Web server. On Mac, DOS, and Windows 95 computers, no such option is available. Scripts generally execute with the same privileges and can access everything on a system.

Because scripts execute with additional privileges, they are vulnerable to hacker attacks. The following suggestions are based on the vulnerabilities of these scripts:

◆ Superuser permissions (SUID root and SGID wheel) should be assigned only if your program needs to perform some functions that can only be performed by the superuser. Consider the following example. You may need the SUID root permission if you want your CGI script to interact with system databases, such as /etc/passwd. However, if your CGI script simply wants to access a custom database, you may create a special UNIX user for that application and give that script SUID permissions for that the particular user.

◆ If your script needs SUID or SGID permissions, you should use permissions for the intended purposes as early as possible. Whenever the purpose, you may revoke those permissions and grant the UIDs and GIDs that initially invoked the process.

◆ Avoid writing SUID scripts in shell languages, especially in csh or its derivatives.

◆ Consider creating a different user name or group for each application to prevent unanticipated interactions and misuse.

◆ Consider assigning full path names to all files you need to open.

Summary

This chapter discussed the strategies for securing servers on the Web. It covered three aspects of server security: operating system security, Web server security, and the security of extensive CGI programs. The first section of the chapter discussed the importance of securing the operating system of a host, as well as the various security features provided by the two most widely used operating systems on the Web: Windows 2000 and Linux. The section also covered the vulnerabilities of both operating systems.

The next section of the chapter discussed the security aspect of the most commonly deployed servers: IIS 5.0 and Apache, and also briefly introduced their security features.

The last section of the chapter discussed CGI programming, an extension to the servers on the Web. It also discussed programming techniques that you can use to make CGI programs secure on a host.

Check Your Understanding

Multiple Choice Questions

1. In a system audit, which one of the following events is not tracked for a folder?

   a. Traversing or deleting files

   b. Modifying or taking file ownership

   c. Viewing or modifying folder attributes

   d. Viewing or modifying folder permissions

2. In anonymous authentication, IIS maps the user to a local account known as _____.

   a. `IGST_computername`

   b. `IADM_computername`

   c. `IUSR_computername`

   d. `IUSR_domainname`

3. Consider the following two statements:

   Statement A: Safe mode is a bootup technique that starts the computer with minimum configuration.

   Statement B: Last known good configuration is a system recovery option that starts the computer with last saved data.

   Which one is TRUE about the statements written above?

   a. Statement A is TRUE but statement B is FALSE.

   b. Statement B is TRUE but statement A is FALSE.

   c. Both the statements are TRUE.

   d. Both the statements are FALSE.

4. State whether the following statement is TRUE or FALSE:

   A domain controller is a directory service on a Windows 2000 server that stores security information about the various objects on a domain.

5. Which one of the following are not attributes of a file in Linux?

   a. SUID

   b. GUID

   c. Sticky bit

   d. SGID bit

Short Questions

1. Why is Windows 2000 termed as a robust operating system? Highlight the features of Windows 2000 that make it robust.

2. What is the role of the `auth` module in Linux's PAM authentication process?

3. Differentiate between the `required` and `requisite` flags used in Linux's PAM authentication mechanism.

4. What is the effect of a buffer overflow in the `Groff` utility?

5. Briefly list safe practices that you should follow while coding CGI scripts.

Answers

Multiple Choice Answers

1. b. Modifying or taking file ownership is a function of file.

2. c. The local account in anonymous authentication is `IUSR_computername`.

3. c.

4. FALSE. A domain controller is not a directory service on a Windows 2000 server that stores security information about the various objects on a domain. That's the definition of the Active Directory. Rather, a domain controller is a computer running Windows 2000 Server running Active Directory services.

5. b.

Short Answers

1. The following features make the Windows 2000 operating system robust:

   • It ensures the effective and efficient management of system resources, such as memory, hard disk, and processor time.

   • It implements techniques such as processor time slicing, multiprocessing, and thread management to ensure that there is equal distribution of time and control among the applications running on it.

   • It ensures that no application has a monopolist control over the system or resources and that no application exerts excess load on a specific resource to cause a system breakdown.

   • All its system files are digitally signed. This enables Windows 2000 to inform its users about unauthorized file modification.

   • It allows you to use device drivers (selective) from vendors other than Microsoft.

2. The auth module provides authentication in PAM by user names and passwords. It sets information such as group membership and Kerberos tickets.

3. All modules flagged as required must be successfully verified for the authentication process to complete. This implies that if a module flagged as required fails the authentication process, the user is not notified until all the other required modules are checked.

   All modules flagged as requisite must be successfully verified for the authentication process to be successful. However, if a module flagged as requisite fails the authentication process, the user is immediately notified with a message indicating the first failed required or requisite module.

4. If a buffer overflow occurs in the Groff utility, it gives hackers the opportunity to gain access rights of the lp account in the target system.

5. The following are the safe practices that one should follow while coding CGI scripts:

   - The programmer should have a clear understanding of the relevance of the program.

   - The design of the program should be created before scripting starts.

   - All possible values provided by the users should be evaluated.

   - Arguments passed to system functions should be verified.

   - Error messages should be logged to track programming bugs and security problems.

   - Crucial portions of the program should be small, modular, and easy to understand.

   - One read-through of code is necessary.

   - Full path names for file name arguments should be used.

   - Timeouts should be placed on the CPU time used.

   - The script should go through a bug bash session.

PART III

Security Countermeasures

Chapter 6

*Secure
Authentication
and Messaging*

While logging onto systems locally or through networks, we authenticate ourselves several times a day. For example, while interacting through e-mails, shopping online, or visiting a private Web site, we provide some sort of evidence of who we claim to be. This is nothing but confirming our identity to the system. *Authentication* is a technique that verifies whether a network user has an identity that he or she claims to possess. In other words, it is a mechanism that validates a user's identity of or a process attempting to connect or log on to a system. Differentiating the identity of a process or a user from a malicious process or an active intruder is a difficult task. It involves complex mechanisms that are based on cryptography.

In this chapter, we will study a few commonly used authentication mechanisms that validate users on insecure computer networks. Cryptography lays the foundation for authentication mechanisms. Therefore, I'll begin the chapter with an overview of cryptography. Then, I'll discuss various authentication methods deployed to implement authentication features in systems and networks. As a part of this discussion, I'll cover the challenge-response protocols, the KDC authentication mechanism, the complete architecture and working of Kerberos V5, message digest functions, and digital signatures.

Before beginning with cryptography, there is an important issue that needs to be addressed. Some people confuse authentication with authorization. *Authentication* addresses the important question of whether or not a user is the person who he or she claims to be and that he or she is not an imposter. Authenticating a user ensures that only a valid user with preassigned access credentials can connect to a computer. Authentication is the first step toward enabling a user to access resources.

Authorization verifies whether the user's attempt to access a particular application or file is permitted or not. Authorization is the next step after authentication. Once the user is authenticated and tries to access an application or file, permission is granted based on the rights attached to that application or file for that particular user. Consider this example. A client process connects to a file server. It sends a request, "I am Maria's process and I want to modify the file status.doc." At the server end, there are two questions that need to be answered:

◆ Is this actually Maria's process?

◆ Is Maria allowed to modify `status.doc`?

The first question is a part of the authentication process. The second question is part of the authorization process. Only if the answer to both questions are answered in the affirmative is the request of the client executed. Only after the first question is verified does the server attempt to verify the second question. Verifying the answer to the second question involves checking the list of authorized users who can access the file.

Authorization or access control is also very important. But because it is specific to operating systems, it cannot be covered in as much detail as authentication mechanisms. Authorization mainly covers concepts related to auditing, file and folder permissions, user rights, and disk quotas. The scope of this chapter is limited to concepts related to authentication.

What Is Cryptography?

Cryptography is a mechanism that protects information by enciphering and deciphering messages in secret code or cipher. Historically, cryptography was used to provide secure private communication between individuals, military forces, government agencies, and diplomatic groups. However, today cryptography is the foundation of modern security technologies that protect network information and resources.

History of Cryptography

As stated earlier, traditionally, the main aim of cryptography was to protect sensitive information from falling into the wrong hands. It involved exchanging coded messages between parties to ensure that the communication was concealed from opposing sides or enemy eyes.

In its traditional form, cryptography mainly involved transforming the original message, called plain text, into an encrypted message, called cipher text, by using another message, called a cipher. The cipher either substituted or rearranged the letters in the original message. The letters in cipher were generally tousled to such an extent that it became unreadable and meaningless.

> **NOTE**
>
> The process of transforming a message into unreadable form is called *encryption*. *Decryption* is its reverse, the transformation of the encrypted message back into its original form. Encryption and decryption require the sharing of secret information, usually referred to as the *decoding key*.

Only the person who had the decoding key could decrypt the ciphered text back to its original plain text. The originator of the message needed to share the decoding key (encryption mechanism) with its intended recipients who were authorized to know the contents of the coded message. The decoding key needed to be shared in a secure manner, otherwise unauthorized groups might have captured it, which would have defeated the very purpose of encryption. Security would have been compromised because, with the decoding key, the cipher text could be converted to plain text and the content of the message easily read.

I'll give you a sample notation for linking plain text, cipher text, and the encryption key. Consider the following notation that depicts the encryption of a message:

C=E$_k$ (P)

The preceding notation suggests that the encryption of plain text P using key K gives the cipher text C. Similarly, consider the following notation that depicts the decryption of a message:

Dk (E$_k$(P)) = P

The preceding notation suggests that E and D are mathematical functions where $D_k(E_k(P))$ decrypts the ciphertext $E_k(P)$ into plaintext P (see Figure 6.1).

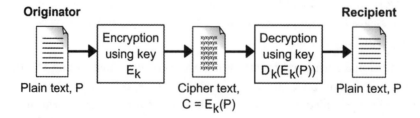

FIGURE 6.1 *Cryptography model*

NOTE

The algorithms used in this chapter are proprietary and publicly shared.

Modern Cryptography

As against historic cryptography, today's cryptography is more than just secret writing. It goes beyond simple cryptographic functions, such as encryption and decryption. Beyond simple encryption functions, it provides mechanisms to bind documents to its creation at a particular time, to access shared disk drives, and to create high security mechanisms. As stated earlier, cryptography has become an integral part of authentication process also.

In addition, cryptography also has other uses also. Cryptographic tools can be used to create protocols and mechanisms that provide users services, such as paying through electronic money and not exposing it at the same time.

Modern cryptography is fundamentally aimed at providing solutions for problems difficult to solve. A problem may be difficult because its solution requires secret information, such as encrypting and decrypting message or signing some digital document. The problem may also be difficult because it requires finding complex values, such as hash values for a message.

The Goal of Cryptography

Cryptography is generally associated with security and confidentially of information. However, the goal of cryptography is beyond confidentiality. The following are the four basic functions that cryptography aims to provide:

◆ **Confidentiality**. Implies that only authorized users can view or use classified information. It is necessary to maintain confidentiality of information if you don't want anyone on the network to access your machine or information liberally. There are several tools available that allow intruders to eavesdrop on network traffic and capture valuable proprietary information. Cryptography provides mechanisms and techniques that ensure confidentiality of information on networks.

◆ **Authentication**. Implies verifying the identity of entities communicating over the network. Think of a network that does not authenticate entities or communication. The result will be intruders forging Internet Protocol

(IP) addresses and posing as others. Cryptography not only authenticates the originator of the message, it also verifies the identity of the recipient of the message.

◆ **Integrity**. Implies verifying whether or not the original content of the information is not manipulated or tainted during transmission. If integrity of information is not maintained, someone may alter or corrupt it, and such manipulations may go undetected. Cryptographic systems use techniques and mechanisms that help in verifying the integrity of information being exchanged on a network. An example of a breach of integrity of information would be an intruder secretly tampering with the digital signature attached to a document.

◆ **Nonrepudiation**. Implies that a party in communication cannot refute a part or all of the communication that has taken place earlier. If nonrepudiation of transactions over a network is not maintained, anyone can communicate and then later deny the occurrence of communication completely or claim that communication occurred at some other time. An example of revocation of nonrepudiation is an originator of information disclaiming that it is the originator. A similar example is that the receiver of the information denies that he or she has received information.

Types of Encryption

As stated earlier, traditionally, ciphers were used to encrypt plain text message into cipher text message. Based on these ciphers, secret decoding keys were shared to encrypt and decrypt messages. However, modern cryptography has moved from simple ciphers (that involve rearranging and transformation of letters) to complex ciphers that involve using digital keys (bit strings) and mathematical algorithms (encryption algorithms) to encrypt and decrypt messages.

Before I discuss encryption algorithms, let us explore the various types of encryption mechanisms. Based on these, various algorithms are derived. The two types of encryption mechanisms are

◆ Symmetric key encryption
◆ Asymmetric key encryption

Symmetric Key Encryption

Symmetric key encryption uses the same key for encrypting and decrypting a message. This type of encryption mechanism is also called a secret key encryption mechanism because the key is shared between the sender and the receiver of the message. Sharing the key is done in a secure and secret manner to maintain confidentiality.

Consider the following example to understand the symmetric key encryption mechanism. Alice wants to send a message to Bob. She sends the encrypted message by performing the following steps (see Figure 6.2):

1. First, Alice and Bob share a copy of the secret key.

2. Then, Alice encrypts the message with the key and sends the encrypted message to Bob.

3. Finally, Bob decrypts the message with the shared key.

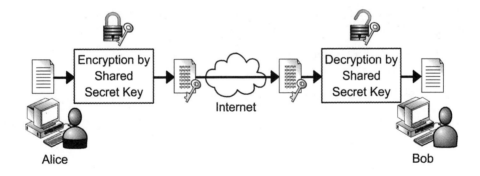

FIGURE 6.2 *Symmetric key encryption*

A common use of symmetric key encryption is security protocols. Security protocols use symmetric keys as session keys for maintaining the confidentiality of messages in online communication. For instance, Transport Layer Security (TLS) and Internet Protocol Security (IPSec) protocols use the symmetric key mechanism to generate session keys with standard algorithms to encrypt and decrypt messages. Each session maintains a different session key and these keys are renewed at specified intervals.

Another use of symmetric key encryption is technologies that provide encryption of bulk data, such as e-mail messages and document files. Secure/Multipurpose Internet Mail Extensions (S/MIME) using symmetric keys to encrypt messages for confidential e-mail and Encrypting File System (EFS) using symmetric keys to encrypt files for confidentiality are examples of these technologies.

When compared to asymmetric key encryption, symmetric key encryption is faster by 100 to 1000 times and places less load on the processors. This is because asymmetric key encryption uses heavy algorithms compared to symmetric key encryption. Due to these reasons, symmetric key encryption is used to provide secrecy where massive encryption or decryption is required.

Having discussed the use and advantages of symmetric key encryption, let me also acquaint you with a few drawbacks. The following are a few disadvantages of using symmetric key encryption:

◆ The key needs to be shared between the parties who want to interact. This may weaken the security as more than one person knows about the key.

◆ The process of sharing the key involves the risk of a third party intercepting the key over the network.

◆ The risk recurs each time the key is changed and exchanged between parties.

Asymmetric Key Encryption

Unlike symmetric key encryption, asymmetric key encryption uses different keys for encrypting and decrypting messages. Asymmetric key encryption is more commonly known as public key encryption. Therefore, from now on I'll address asymmetric key encryption as public key encryption.

Public key encryption requires two keys, a private key and a public key. A private key is known only to the owner. A public key is shared and made available to all the parties that would like to interact with the owner of the private key. Public key encryption operates by publishing the user's public key in a directory (usually in an LDAP or X.500 compatible directory). This directory is accessible to all users who are interested in exchanging the message.

The algorithms used in public key encryption involve complex mathematical functions that ensure that the encryption process, once performed, cannot be reversed easily. These algorithms are designed in such a manner that the message encrypted with the public key can only be decrypted with the corresponding private key. Similarly, the message that is encrypted with the private key can only be decrypted with the corresponding public key of the set. In addition, keys are generated such that it is not possible to determine one key even if you know the other.

 NOTE

Asymmetric encryption's main principle: It is computationally infeasible to determine the decryption key given only the knowledge of the cryptographic algorithm and the encryption key.

Consider the following example to understand the asymmetric key encryption mechanism. Alice wants to send a message to Bob. She sends the encrypted message by performing the following steps:

1. Alice obtains a copy of Bob's public key that is published by Bob in a directory on the network.
2. Alice encrypts the message with Bob's public key and sends the message to Bob.
3. Finally, Bob decrypts the message with his private key.

In the preceding example, Bob is the only person who can decrypt the message, as long as he is the only person who can access his private key.

Figure 6.3 is the graphical representation of the preceding example. The figure shows Bob's interaction with several users.

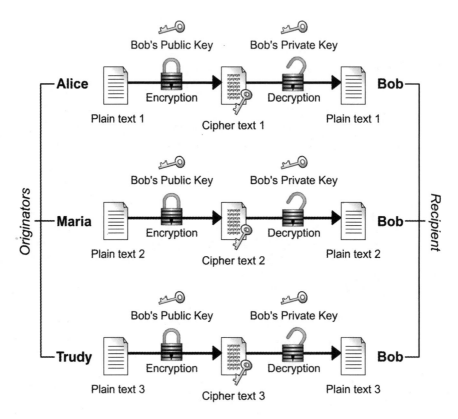

FIGURE 6.3 *Asymmetric key encryption*

A common implementation of this mechanism is RSA public key encryption. The following are functions that RSA public key encryption can perform:

◆ Encrypt the symmetric secret keys to protect these while they are exchanged over the network or are being used, stored, or cached in systems.

◆ Create digital signatures to provide authentication and nonrepudiation for resources and data integrity for electronic e-mail and documents.

 NOTE

RSA public key encryption is covered later in the chapter. For details on RSA, you can refer to the section "RSA Encryption Algorithm."

Encryption Algorithms

Modern encryption algorithms are based on the same basic design (substitution and transposition) as traditional algorithms; however, the area of emphasis is not the same. Traditional algorithms were simple but used long keys to develop an encryption mechanism. Modern algorithms work on a totally opposite theory. Algorithms used nowadays are made so complex that even if a cryptanalyst manages to obtain the encrypted text, it will be difficult for him to decrypt it or make any sense out of it due to its complexity. We should remember that no code is unbreakable or impenetrable. Governments employ cryptanalysts to break such complex secret codes.

There are several encryption algorithms available. However, I'll only discuss the ones most commonly used. For secret key encryption, I'll discuss *DES* and *IDEA*. For public key encryption, I'll discuss the *Diffie-Hellman* cryptosystem and *RSA* algorithms.

  NOTE

Notice that the description of each algorithm is precise. This is to acquaint you with the algorithms available.

Data Encryption Standard (DES)

In the 1970s, the National Bureau of Standards in association with the National Security Agency identified the *Data Encryption Standard* (DES) as a standard for protecting sensitive commercial and unclassified information. IBM created the first outline of this algorithm and named it *LUCIFER*. It became an official centralized standard only in November, 1976.

DES basically performs two operations on the input data, bit shifting (permutation) and bit substitution (combination). These operations are performed repeatedly and in a nonlinear manner so that the resultant cipher text cannot be reversed to its original form without a key. This algorithm works on chaos theory where simple operations are performed repeatedly and randomly so that ultimately there is a state of chaos.

DES encrypts plain text data into chunks of 64 bits (although effectively only 56 bits) at a time. The complete cycle of DES is divided into 19 distinct stages. The first stage involves independent key transposition on the 64-bit plain text. The last stage performs the exact inverse of transposition performed in the first stage. The second but last stage swaps the left-most 32 bits with the right-most 32 bits. The remaining 16 stages (most important stages) perform the same function. However, each of these stages is parameterized by different set of keys. Each 64 bits of plain text is iterated from stages 1 to 16. The algorithms in these stages are designed in such a manner that the same key is used to encrypt and decrypt data. In the case of decryption, the steps are executed in the reverse order. Figure 6.4 depicts DES work model with its 19 stages.

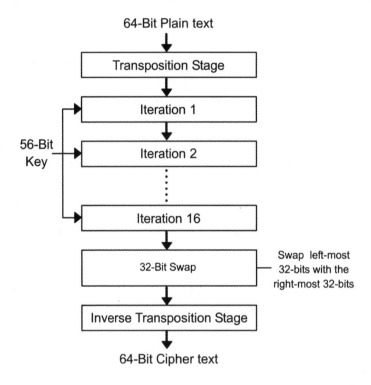

FIGURE 6.4 *The DES work model*

 NOTE

The length of the input key in DES is 64 bits. However, the actual effective key used by DES is only 56 bits in length. The least significant (right-most) bit in each byte is a parity bit. In every byte, these bits are set as an odd number of 1s. These parity bits are ignored while computation takes place. Therefore, the seven most significant bits of each byte are used, resulting in a key length of 56 bits.

International Data Encryption Algorithm (IDEA)

There have been several algorithms introduced after DES. For example, BLOW-FISH introduced by Schneier in 1994, Crab by Kaliski and Robshaw in 1994, and SAFER K64 by Massey in 1994. However, of these algorithms, the most popular block cipher (after DES) was the IDEA. IDEA stands for *International Data Encryption Algorithm* and was designed by two researchers, Lai and Massey in 1990, in Switzerland.

The structure of IDEA is based on the DEA model only. In IDEA, 64-bit plain text data blocks are jumbled in a sequence of iterations that produce 64-bit cipher text output blocks. The mangling of bits in iteration is so extensive that eight iterations are more than sufficient. IDEA uses a 128-bit key to encrypt and decrypt data. Figure 6.5 depicts the IDEA model with its 8 stages.

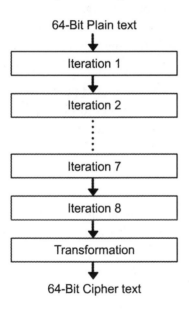

FIGURE 6.5 *The IDEA model*

IDEA is available as both software and hardware implementation. The first software implementation of IDEA was executed on a 33-MHz 386 and produced an encryption rate of 0.88 Mbps. Current machines execute at least 10 times faster than a 33-MHz 386 and produce an encryption rate of at least 9 Mbps. An experimental 25-MHz VLSI chip was built at ETH Zurich (Swiss Federal Institute of Technology, Zurich) and encrypted at a rate of 177 Mbps.

Diffie-Hellman Encryption Algorithm

In the secret key encryption mechanism, sharing the key has been the weakest link that makes encrypted data vulnerable to attacks. Regardless of the fact that the cryptosystems devised for encrypting data are strong, it becomes worthless if the intruder somehow gets hold of the key. Initially (at the time of secret key encryption), all cryptologists assumed that the encryption and decryption key were the same and had to be distributed to all users. They never thought of having different encryption and decryption keys.

In 1975, two researchers at Stanford University, Whitefield Diffie and Martin Hellman, proposed an encryption mechanism that used two different keys for encryption and decryption. The core purpose of proposing the mechanism was to provide a secure method for exchanging secret keys between communication parties over an insecure network. In other words, the purpose was to provide another mechanism for securing the secret key encryption that was already deployed and used by several technologies at that time. Later, this mechanism was popularly known as public key encryption.

In the earlier sections, I have already discussed the working of public key encryption. In this section, I'll basically concentrate on how Diffie-Hellman provides security to the secret keys on the network. This is popularly known as the Diffie-Hellman key agreement.

Diffie-Hellman Key Agreement

The Diffie-Hellman key agreement is not an encryption mechanism. Instead, it is based on mathematical functions that allow parties that intend to communicate to generate a shared secret key. The shared key then encrypts the symmetric key, which may be data encryption keys developed in DES, Triple DES, or IDEA. The following steps explain the process of the Diffie-Hellman key agreement:

1. Each party agrees on a public value, g, and a large prime number, p.
2. Next, each party chooses a secret number, say x and y. Only the respective parties know these numbers.
3. Then, both parties use their secret numbers (x and y respectively) to derive public values. For example, one party generates the public value, g^x mod p, and the other generates the public value, g^y mod p. These public values are then exchanged between the parties.

4. Each party then uses the other party's public key to generate a shared key that will help both the parties to communicate confidentially.

In the preceding process, it is very difficult for a party with malicious intent to generate the shared key because they are not aware of the secret values used.

Consider the following example, which will add more clarity to the process explained above. Alice and Bob want to confidentially generate and share a secret key. They perform the following steps after agreeing upon public number, g, and prime number, p:

1. Alice chooses a secret number, x, and generates a public value, $g^x \bmod p$. She sends this public value to Bob.

2. Bob chooses a secret number, y, and generates a public value, $g^y \bmod p$. He sends this public value to Alice.

3. Alice uses $g^y \bmod p$ as her secret key to communicate with Bob.

4. Bob uses $g^x \bmod p$ as his secret key to communicate with Alice.

Figure 6.6 depicts the Diffie-Hellman key agreement with Alice and Bob as the interacting parties.

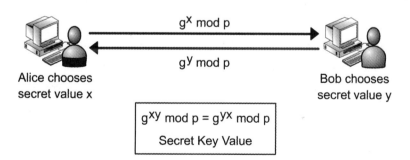

Alice and Bob agree on public number g
and prime number p

$g^x \bmod p$

$g^y \bmod p$

Alice chooses
secret value x

Bob chooses
secret value y

$g^{xy} \bmod p = g^{yx} \bmod p$
Secret Key Value

FIGURE 6.6 *The Diffie-Hellman key agreement*

In the preceding process, $g^{xy} \bmod p$ is equal to $g^{yx} \bmod p$. Therefore, Alice and Bob can use these secret keys with symmetric algorithms to confidentially communicate with each other. The process uses the mod function to generate the secret key. The mod function ensures that both parties generate the same secret key. In addition, the mod function ensures that the intruder cannot easily generate the secret key. An intruder can obtain the values of public number g and prime number p. But because the mathematical functions used (in conjunction with the large prime number) are very complex, the intruder cannot very easily determine the secret values, x and y. The secret values, as you already know, are only known to the owners and are not visible on the network.

The Diffie-Hellman key exchange is used by security protocols, such as Secure Socket Layer (SSL), Secure Shell (SSH), Internet Protocol Security (IPSec), and Transport Layer Security (TLS), to provide secret key exchange while communicating on a network.

RSA Encryption Algorithm

The RSA encryption algorithm takes its name from the initials of its three discoverers Rivest, Shamir, Adelman. This method uses numbers and functions to generate public and private keys. I'll very briefly summarize the working of this algorithm.

Before the encryption process begins, there are certain values that need to be computed:

1. Each party agrees on two large prime numbers, a and b. These numbers are generally greater than 10^{100}.
2. A value n is computed as: n = a x b.
3. A value x is computed as: x = (a-1) x (b-1).
4. A number is chosen is relatively prime to x and named d.
5. A value e is determined such that (e x d) = (1 mod x).

After computing the above values, the encryption process begins. The plain text message P is divided into blocks, such that P falls in the interval 0 < P < n. This is achieved by grouping plain text into blocks of k bits, where k is the largest integer for which the condition 2^k < n is true.

Now, the following notation encrypts the plain text message, P:

C = Pe (mod n)

Now, the following notation decrypts the plaintext message, P:

P = Cd (mod n)

RSA Key Exchange

RSA is also used as a mechanism for securely exchanging a secret key between the interested parties over a secure network. This mechanism operates by encrypting the secret key with the intended recipient's public key. This secret key can be decrypted only by the recipient's private key. It is difficult to capture or deduce the encrypted secret key because it requires the private key for decryption.

Consider the following example to better understand the above explanation. Alice and Bob want to share a secret key securely over the network. Alice sends the encrypted secret key by performing the following steps:

1. Alice obtains a copy of Bob's public key that is published in a directory on the network.

2. Alice encrypts the secret key with Bob's public key and sends the encrypted secret key to Bob.

3. Finally, Bob decrypts the secret key with his private key.

Figure 6.7 depicts the exchange of the secret key between Alice and Bob using the RSA key exchange mechanism.

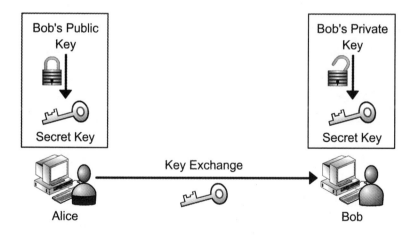

FIGURE 6.7 *The RSA key exchange mechanism*

Authentication Mechanisms

There are several mechanisms available that help to authenticate the validity of a user at the time he logs on to a system. We have already discussed two such authentication mechanisms in earlier sections: the Diffie-Hellman key exchange and the RSA key exchange mechanism. In this section, I'll introduce you to a few other authentication mechanisms.

The following are a few protocols that provide authentication services:

◆ Challenge-response protocols

◆ KDC authentication mechanism

◆ Kerberos V5

◆ Digital Signatures

Challenge-Response Protocols

Challenge-response protocols are based on the principle that one party sends a random number (as a challenge) to the other, who converts it into a special number and returns the result. To explain the challenge-response protocol, I'll again take the example of Alice and Bob. It is assumed that a secret key is already shared between them.

To depict the communication between Alice and Bob, the following notations will be used:

◆ A and B signify Alice and Bob.

◆ X_i signifies the challenge, where the subscript i indicates the challenger (i is replaced by A or B).

◆ K_i signifies the secret key, where the subscript i indicates the owner (i will be replaced by A or B).

◆ K_s signifies the session key.

The following steps summarize the communication between Alice and Bob in a challenge-response protocol. As you read these steps, refer to Figure 6.8 for the message sequence.

1. Alice sends her identity, A, to Bob in message 1. The message is sent in the manner agreed upon between Alice and Bob.

2. At this point, Bob is not sure of Alice's identity. To ensure that the message has come from Alice and not from any other person, Bob sends a challenge with a large random number, R_B. This forms message 2 and is delivered in plain text.

3. To prove her identity, Alice encrypts the random number, R_B, with the shared secret key, K_{AB}. She sends the encrypted cipher text, $K_{AB}(R_B)$, in message 3 to Bob. At this point, Bob is sure that the message has come from Alice because only Alice knows about the secret key, K_{AB}. In addition, the random number, R_B, is chosen from a large range (for example, a 128-bit random number). Therefore, it is implausible that any other person would have seen this message in the session.

4. Now, Bob is sure about the authenticity of Alice's identity. However, Alice still does not have any proof of Bob's identity. To check if Bob is who he claims to be, Alice also sends a random number, R_A, in plain text to Bob in message 4.

5. To provide a proof of his identity, Bob encrypts the random number, R_A, with the shared secret key, K_{AB}. He sends the encrypted cipher text, $K_{AB}(R_A)$, in message 5 to Alice. When Alice receives the encrypted message, $K_{AB}(R_A)$, she is sure that she is interacting with Bob.

After authenticating their identities, if Alice wishes to continue the interaction with Bob, she can send the session key, K_s, encrypted in secret key, K_{AB}.

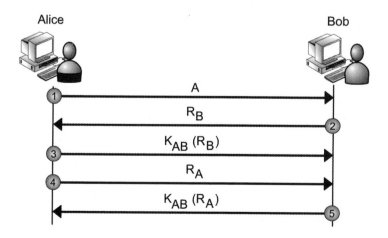

FIGURE 6.8 *Authentication using the challenge-response protocol*

The above process is quite long and contains some extra messages that can be eliminated. Figure 6.9 illustrates the authentication process using the challenge-response protocol with only three messages. For instance, Alice initiates the challenge-response protocol by sending her identity, A, and random number, R_A, to Bob. Bob, in response to Alice, sends the encrypted random number, $K_{AB}(R_A)$, along with his random number, R_B. Finally, Alice responds by sending the encrypted random number, $K_{AB}(R_B)$. The earlier process of five steps is reduced to three steps.

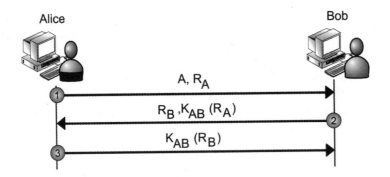

FIGURE 6.9 *Authentication using a three-step challenge-response protocol*

The three-step authentication challenge-response protocol is an improvement over the original protocol. However, it has several loopholes. This type of protocol is prone to *reflection attacks*. Consider the following example to understand how a reflection attack can be initiated in challenge-response protocols. Let us assume that Bob is a machine in a bank that allows multiple simultaneous sessions with outside teller machines. An intruder named Maria initiates a reflection attack on Bob. Maria poses as Alice and sends the identity, A (which is originally Alice's identity), and the random number, R_M, to Bob. Bob, as usual, responds by sending his own challenge, R_B, and encrypted cipher text, $K_{AB}(R_M)$. At this point, Maria is in a fix because she does not know about the shared secret key, R_{AB}.

Now, Maria initiates another session with Bob by sending R_B (taken from message 2) as her challenge. Bob, as usual, sends back a reply that contains the cipher text, $K_{AB}(R_B)$, and his own challenge. Maria gets the missing information and aborts the second session. She completes the first session by sending the message with the encrypted message, $K_{AB}(R_B)$. Because Bob is convinced that it is Alice interacting with him, he gives the bank account details to Maria.

Learning from the flaws in the three-step challenge-response protocol, there are certain rules that should be followed while designing any authentication protocol:

◆ Let the initiator prove his identity before the responder proves his. In the three-step challenge-response protocol, Bob makes the mistake of providing the valuable information before he is convinced about the identity of Alice. Note that the five-step challenge-response protocol requires the initiator Alice to prove her identity first.

◆ Use different shared secret keys for providing a proof of identity. This may mean using two shared secret keys.

◆ Let the initiator and responder use different sets of challenge numbers. For instance, one party may use even numbers and the other may use odd numbers.

KDC Authentication Mechanism

Sharing a secret key with another party worked quite well, but probably was not a complete success. It meant sharing n keys to interact with n people. This might lead to a key management problem because there will be several keys.

Another approach adopted is the use of a trusted *key distribution center* (KDC). In this approach, each user stores his or her secret key in the KDC. The KDC is responsible for authentication and session key management.

To explain how KDC operates, I'll discuss the simplest KDC authentication protocol, *wide-mouth frog*. This protocol derives its name from the nickname of its inventor, Michael Burrows.

I will again take the example of Alice and Bob to explain the idea behind the wide-mouth frog protocol (see Figure 6.10). The following steps depict the communication between Alice and Bob through KDC:

1. Alice sends a session key, K_s, to KDC requesting to initiate a connection with Bob. Alice sends this message as a cipher text message that is encrypted with the secret key, K_A, which she has already shared with KDC.

2. KDC decrypts the message with Alice's secret key, K_A, to extract Bob's identity and session key.

3. KDC then creates a new message with Alice's identity and session key and sends it to Bob. The message sent is encrypted with Bob's secret key, K_B, which he has already shared with the KDC.

4. When Bob decrypts the message with his secret key, K_B, he knows that Alice wants to communicate with him, and he also knows the session key she wants to use during communication.

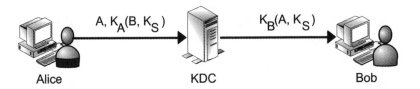

Alice   KDC   Bob

FIGURE 6.10 *The wide-mouth frog authentication protocol*

In the above process, you will notice that the task of authentication is managed by the KDC. KDC knows that the message has come from Alice because she encrypts her identity and session key with the secret key that she has already shared with KDC. Similarly, Bob knows that the message has come from KDC because a secret key that he has shared with KDC encrypts the message he has received.

However, the wide-mouth frog protocol is vulnerable to replay attacks, in which a valid data transmission is maliciously or fraudulently repeated, either by the originator or by an intruder who intercepts the data and retransmits it.

To explain the replay attack, I will again take the example of Alice, Bob, and Maria. In this example, Bob is a banker and Maria tries to snoop into the network with malicious intentions. Maria, with the intention of stealing some money from the bank, first strikes a deal with Alice. She does some work for Alice, then asks Alice to transfer the amount owed to her account.

Meanwhile, Maria intercepts the message that KDC sends to Bob. She also captures Alice's request to transfer money to Maria's account. Some time later, Maria again sends both the messages to Bob. This time Bob thinks that Alice has again struck a deal with Maria and, therefore, transfers money in Maria's account. Using replay messages, Maria manages to fetch money from Bob.

There are several other KDC protocols that are more sophisticated than wide-mouth frog protocols. To name a few, the Needham-Schroeder protocol and Otway-Rees authentication protocol. However, we will not go into details of these protocols because they are out of the scope of our chapter.

Kerberos V5

Kerberos is a network authentication protocol that enables users interacting on a network to prove their identity. In this section, I'll introduce you to Kerberos as a network authentication service in general, discuss version 5 of Kerberos specifically, discuss important terms and components related to Kerberos, and describe the authentication process.

Background of Kerberos

Kerberos is a network authentication protocol that provides third-party authentication services. Systems installed with Kerberos require the user to type the password only once. Other authentication services (including encryption) for the user are handled by Kerberos itself.

Kerberos was originally designed at MIT in 1987. Since then, this product has seen several changes and has matured into a committed product with support from commonly used operating systems and applications. Kerberos still undergoes positive developments with new releases, occurring approximately twice a year. The commonly used versions of Kerberos are 4 and 5. Version 4 is used at Fermilab as a part of AFS (Andrew File System), a distributed network file system that enables files from any AFS machine to be accessed across the country as easily as files stored locally. Version 5 is used by Microsoft for authentication in Windows 2000. Both these versions are widely used by several other mechanisms, laboratories, and universities.

Usually, Kerberos is implemented in application-level programs, such as telnet, FTP, rsh, rcp, rlogin, and ssh. It can be built into other programs as well. For example, it can be installed on a machine to enforce Kerberos authentication features. Programs implementing Kerberos, or machines installed with Kerberos software are referred to as *strengthened* or *Kerberized* programs or machines.

Kerberos Services

Kerberos validates the identity of a user or network service using the shared secret key concept. It allows clients and servers on a network to mutually establish identities without revealing passwords. By using cryptographic methods, it also ensures that the privacy and secrecy of information being exchanged is maintained.

Kerberos basically operates by issuing tickets. A ticket is a sequence of a few hundred bytes that can be easily exchanged on virtually all network protocols. Tickets ensure that the process implementing the protocol (using Kerberos) can validate the identity of users and resources on the network.

 NOTE

In network terminology, users and services on a network are referred to as *principals*.

In Kerberos V5, password authentication occurs in a central place for all machines in the strengthened realm. It does not take place on end-user systems. End-user systems are not involved in the password authentication and maintenance process.

Before going into details of the complete Kerberos authentication process, let me summarize the above discussion into the following two points:

◆ Kerberos provides authentication and secure communication services to principals on a network.

◆ It generates secret keys for requestors and provides a mechanism to safely transfer keys over a network.

KERBEROS REALMS

Kerberos divides the network into security domains, which are known as *realms*. Each realm has its own authentication server that implements its own authentication policy. Due to the presence of different realms on the network, organizations implementing Kerberos can maintain different levels of security with different security policies for various departments of the organization. A realm can accept authentication from other realms if the security policy defined in it allows that. However, it can reject authentication if the policy requires a re-authentication process.

Realms defined in Kerberos are hierarchical. This implies that a realm can have "child" realms under it. The hierarchical arrangement allows child realms that do not have direct authentication permissions to share authentication information with parent realms. For instance, a user in an organization in one realm may want to connect to a computer in another realm. The user, in this case, need not to go through the re-authentication process if the computer to which he or she wants to connect lies in the parent realm.

Components Involved in Kerberos V5

Kerberos involves three services in its process in addition to client work stations:

- **Authentication Service (AS)**. Authenticates users during log in.
- **Ticket-Granting Service (TGS)**. Issues tickets that are proof of the identity.
- **Application Server**. Provides services to the client.

These key components work together to provide authentication services to the client. Kerberos V5 uses another important component in addition to the ones listed above. It primarily implements authentication through the key distribution center (KDC). In the previous section, I discussed the basic functions of KDC in an authentication process. KDC's main role in Kerberos is to jointly implement the authentication services and ticket-granting services for all the machines in the realm. It shares a permanent secret key for each principal (users and services on the network). It maintains a database that stores the details of all principals in a realm. Due to this, KDC is also referred to as the *Kerberos database*.

 NOTE

For users on a network, the shared secret key is the hash of the user's password. For services, the key is the random bit string.

To understand how authentication takes place in Kerberos, you need to know certain terms:

- **Session key**. KDC generates, at random, a temporary secret session key that needs to be shared between the KDC and client. The session key exists until the time the accompanying ticket is alive. The basic purpose of a session key is to authenticate principals several times during the ticket lifetime. Its main aim is to limit the use of a shared secret key (that is actually the hash value of the password) over a network.
- **Ticket**. Kerberos employs tickets to authenticate principals on a network. Tickets are encrypted records that contain the session key, the user and service IDs, and the client's IP address. Some of the information contained in the ticket is encrypted with the shared secret key that is only known to the KDC and the principal. A ticket is also accompanied

by a copy of the session key, which is encrypted by the shared secret key. The ability of principals correctly decrypting the relevant parts of the tickets determines the authenticity of the principals on the network.

◆ **Credential**. A session key and a ticket together are known as a *credential*.

The authentication service issues secret session keys and credentials based on a user's password or encryption key. It can also issue ticket-granting tickets, even though that is actually a function of the ticket-granting service. Each of the tickets issued to clients is a ticket for individual Kerberized service that the client would like to use.

Authentication Process in Kerberos

I'll explain the authentication process with the help of the example of Alice and Bob. Following are the steps that take place when Alice (a user using the strengthened machine) wants to communicate with Bob (an application server). (Please refer to Figure 6.11.):

1. Alice, using the strengthened machine, types her name for authentication. The machine sends her identity A to the KDC in plain text. Note that the machine does not ask for the password at this time.

2. KDC's authentication service responds back with credentials encrypted in Alice's secret key. The encrypted credentials include a session key, K_S, and a ticket, $K_{TGS}(A, K_S)$ that is actually meant for the ticket-granting service of the KDC. (Alice has already shared her secret key with KDC.) At this point, with the help of Alice's secret key, the message is again decrypted to obtain the session key and TGS ticket. Since Alice can decrypt the message with her secret key, the system is sure about Alice's identity. Therefore, only after successful decryption, does the work station ask for Alice's password.

3. After Alice successfully logs in to the system, she sends a message to the KDC again requesting to grant the TGS ticket for Bob, the application server. The components of this message request are $K_{TGS}(A, K_S), B, K_S(t)$. In these components, t represents the time stamp. The KDC tries to decrypt this message with the copy it has of Alice's secret key. If it can do so, and if the time stamp t is recent, the KDC is sure that Alice is the same person whom she claims to be.

4. The ticket-granting service of the KDC then responds by creating a session key, K_{AB}, that Alice can use with Bob. TGS sends two versions of the session key, $K_S(A, K_{AB})$ and $K_B(A, K_{AB})$. The first key is encrypted with the session key that the KDC had granted to Alice so that Alice can read the message. The second is encrypted with Bob's secret key, so that Bob can decrypt it. Alice cannot understand the second version because she is not aware of Bob's secret key that is shared with KDC.

5. Now, Alice sends a copy of the session key, K_{AB}, encrypted in Bob's secret key to Bob. This message is accompanied by a time stamp, t, again.

6. The response from Bob, $K_{AB}(t+1)$, is proof from Bob that Alice is actually talking to Bob and not anybody else.

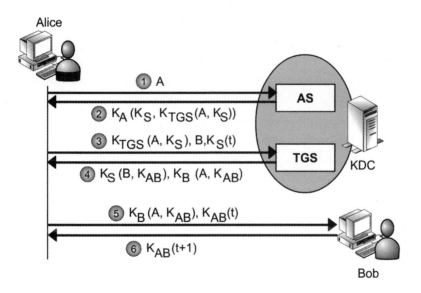

FIGURE 6.11 *The authentication process in Kerberos V5*

Digital Signatures

The legitimacy of legal, financial, and other documents is judged by the presence of handwritten signatures of authorized parties on documents. In most cases, documents need to be presented in their original form. Photocopies of documents are usually not accepted.

Nowadays, most business communications take place online. Computerized message systems have mostly replaced the exchange of physical documents. But how can one be sure of the authenticity of documents being exchanged online?

It is not easy to devise a substitute for handwritten signatures. Essentially, such a system needs to be devised by which one user can send a "digitally signed message" to another user. Such a system should fulfill the following requirements:

◆ **The receiver should be able to verify the identity of the sender**. Institutions that provide financial services would not be able to work online if this requirement is not fulfilled. For instance, a customer may direct his bank to debit his account with a certain amount of money because he has made purchases. At this point, before the bank proceeds with any transaction, it needs to be sure of the customer's identity.

◆ **The sender should not be able to disclaim the message he has sent**. Consider the example of a bank again. A customer may direct the bank to buy shares as a part of the bank's investment program. Soon after, the share price falls sharply. A dishonest customer might disclaim his consent by saying that he never sent such message.

◆ **The receiver should not be able to change the message later**. Going back to the bank example, let us assume that soon after the deal between the customer and the bank is finalized, the price of shares shoots up. The bank may try to create a signed contract that displays the consent of purchasing one share rather than one hundred.

There are several approaches to creating digital signatures. A couple approaches are to use secret keys or public keys. Creating digital signatures using secret keys is a bit obsolete approach now. However, because there are still several organizations that use this approach, I'll discuss it. In the next section, I'll explore the two mechanisms for creating digital signatures.

Secret Key Signatures

In this approach, a central authority that everybody knows and trusts plays an important role. From now on, while explaining secret key signatures, I'll address the central authority as CA. Each party shares a secret key with the CA so that it can use digital signatures in the documents being transmitted. These secret keys are a secret between the concerned party and the CA.

When a party wants to send a message to another party, it contacts the CA. I am again coming back to the example of Alice and Bob. Let us assume that Alice wants to send a message with a digital signature to Bob. Therefore, Alice sends a message to the CA that contains details, such as the name of the party to which she wants to send the message (in our case it is Bob), a random number, the time stamp, and the message. All these details are encrypted with Alice's secret key. The CA knows that the message is coming from Alice, since it is encrypted with the same secret key that Alice has shared with it. The CA decrypts the message and sends a message to Bob. The message sent to Bob by the CA contains an encrypted digital signature that also contains the time stamp.

This approach is not used that often nowadays due to controversies it has faced in the past. Though the controversies were resolved later, it still has not been a sought-after choice. Let me discuss some controversies that had a negative effect on this approach. What if Alice disclaims the message she sent to the CA? In most cases, all the parties would sue each other. The court asks the CA to prove that Alice sent the message. The CA displays the message that Alice sent. This message is encrypted with the secret key that is only shared between Alice and the CA, proves that Alice is at fault.

Public Key Signatures

One drawback of using secret key digital signatures is that each party has to trust the CA. Moreover, each message has to pass through the CA, even if the party does not desire to do so. The CA gets to read all confidential interaction between the two parties. Mostly, the centralized trusted authority is the government, the banks, or the lawyers. However, they also do not draw total confidence from people. Rather, it is difficult for any person to trust an authority unconditionally. Therefore, a combined understanding between communication parties concluded that it is best to not involve outside authorities in the digital signing of documents.

Fortunately, another approach was identified for creating digital signatures. It involved the use of public key cryptography. This has, indeed, been a sought-after choice. The simplest approach to creating digital signatures by using public key cryptography may involve the originator of message encrypting the signature with his private key and enclosing the signature in the original message. Anyone with the originator's public key can decrypt message to the original message. The authenticity of the signature is verified when the decrypted message matches the original one because only someone with the private key can create the signature.

However, this approach also has some flaws. Encrypting data to provide digital signatures is not feasible due of the following reasons:

♦ The encrypted signature contained in the message is usually the same size (if not larger) as the message itself. Therefore, the complete message (message + digital signature) is double its size, consumes large storage space, and consumes large bandwidth. Transferring the message over the network would involve unnecessary overhead.

♦ Public key encryption is complex and therefore a bit slow. It also exerts a heavy computational load on the processors. Therefore, while messages with such digital signatures are transmitted, the network, as well as computer performance, is notably degraded.

♦ Such messages are prone to cryptanalysis attacks because the attackers know certain portions of the plain text messages in advance. An example of the known portion of the message is the subject of the e-mail that is accompanied in the header of the message.

Looking at the overhead attached to digital signatures created using simple public key cryptography, it seems digital signatures algorithms are a better option. These algorithms are also based on public key cryptography, but they use more efficient methods, such as message digests. Messages that enclose digital signatures based on algorithms use the originator's private key to create a digital thumbprint of the data. Because of the message digest mechanism, the signature size is usually smaller than the digital signatures created earlier. In addition, digital signatures using message digests put relatively less load on the processors, consume less bandwidth, and also generate encrypted text that is relatively smaller in size.

The most widely used digital signature algorithms are the RSA digital signature process and the Digital Signature Algorithm (DSA). However, before I acquaint you with these mechanisms, let me first introduce you to the concept of the message digest.

Message Digests

Message digests generate digital summaries of information (documents and files transmitted online). Message digests are for the most part based on hash functions. A hash function is the mathematical computation applied to a message to generate a small string, called a digest. This digest represents the complete file or document.

A message digest length usually varies between 128 to 160 bits. For each document, a unique message digest is created. Identical documents can have the same message digests, but if even one bit of text is changed, the resultant message digest is different. The uniqueness of a message digest depends upon the creator. That means, an identical document may also have different message digests. It all depends on the message digest functions used to create it.

It is also impossible to create identical message digests for two different messages. Every message digest created by a private key is unique to the creator and can only be decrypted using the corresponding public key.

As you are already aware, message digests are usually used in conjunction with public key technology to create digital signatures. These are also used as digital thumbprints to maintain authenticity, integrity, and nonrepudiation of messages. Another important function of message digests is to verify the integrity of digitally signed electronic files and documents. I have explained this concept in detail in the section on RSA digital signatures.

Two most commonly used message digest algorithms are MD5, a 128-bit digest developed by RSA Data Security, Inc., and SHA–, a 160-bit message digest developed by the National Security Agency.

Message digests with a Hashed Message Authentication Code (HMAC) function is another mechanism for ensuring data integrity of documents. Let us look at HMAC in detail.

Hashed Message Authentication Code (HMAC) Function

A *Hashed Message Authentication Code* (HMAC) function is used to authenticate messages transmitted over a network. HMAC is described in RFC 2104 of the Network Working Group of the Internet Engineering Task force (IETF). HMAC MD5 also uses the standard message digest functions, MD5 and SHA–.

HMAC is extensively used by Internet technologies, such as the TLS and IPSec protocols, as a means of verifying the integrity of data transmitted over insecure networks. HMAC operates by creating a message digest for each block of data. It uses a random symmetric key to encrypt the message digests. The secret key is shared between the concerned parties as in the case of symmetric key encryption. The encrypted data is decrypted using the shared secret key.

The effectiveness of HMAC encrypted data depends on the strength of the message digest used in data encryption and also on how securely data is exchanged over the network. It is difficult for an intruder to tamper with the HMAC data being transmitted because he does not have the knowledge contained in the secret key. Unlike digital signatures, HMAC does not require communicating parties to have public and private keys.

Having gone through the message digest, let us look at algorithms that use message digests to create digital signatures.

RSA Digital Signatures

RSA digital signatures use a private key to encrypt the message digest, which forms the digital signature. This digital signature is then attached with the original message. Figure 6.12 depicts the RSA digital signature process on a basic level.

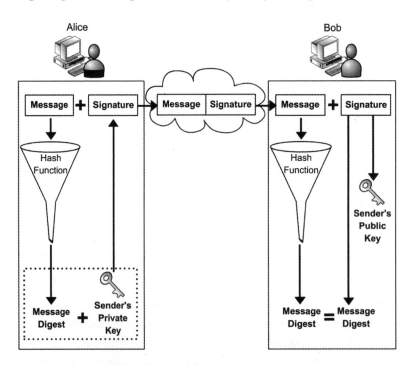

FIGURE 6.12 *RSA digital signature process*

We have discussed how digital signatures are encrypted and attached with a message. But how can the recipient be sure of the integrity of the digital signature attached? There is a possibility that the message has been spoofed on the network and an alteration made in the digital signature itself. To verify the contents of the digitally signed message, the recipient generates a new message digest from the message he has received. He does this by decrypting the message received with the originator's public key. Then, he compares the decrypted digest with the newly generated digest. If the two versions match, the integrity of the message is verified. The originator's authenticity is also verified because the public key can decrypt only that message which is encrypted with the corresponding private key of the set.

Digital Signature Algorithm (DSA)

Another mechanism for creating digital signatures is the Digital Signature Algorithm (DSA). DSA is a mechanism defined in the Digital Signature Security Standard (DSS) introduced by the National Security Agency. DSS is accepted as a digital signature standard by the United States government.

DSA functionality is similar to RSA. However, unlike RSA, DSA does not encrypt message digests with private keys or decrypt the message digest with the public key. Instead, DSA uses mathematical functions to generate a digital signature. These digital signatures are created using two 160-bit numbers derived by the message digest and the private key. DSA uses the public key to verify the signature. But this verification process is much more complex than the RSA process.

If both the technologies, RSA digital signatures and the digital signature algorithm, are available, which technology should be chosen and why? Both, digital signatures created using RSA and DSA, provide an equal level of security. However, each has its own strengths and weaknesses. DSA signatures use the SHA– message digest function only for creating a message digest. This function assures strong digital signatures. On the other hand, RSA allows the use other message digest functions (in addition to SHA– message digest function) to create a message digest. Due to this, RSA digital signatures may prove to be weaker in some cases. Because DSA signatures use SHA– message digest functions, it puts a heavy load on the processor and is, therefore, slower compared to RSA signatures. RSA digital signatures are generally faster to process.

DSA was defined to create digital signatures only. Therefore, no provisions were made to accommodate the data encryption functionality. Due to this, DSA is not subject to any restrictions from export or import policy rules. On the other hand, RSA is imposed with such restrictions. Therefore, DSA digital signatures are most commonly used when RSA digital signatures cannot be used because of government policy or any other restriction.

Summary

In this chapter, you studied a few of the commonly used authentication mechanisms that validate users on insecure computer networks. The chapter began by clarifying a common confusion related to authentication and authorization. It discussed how authentication is different from authorization and how each works at a different level of security. Authentication verifies whether or not a user is the person who he or she claims to be. Authentication is the first step toward enabling a user to access resources. Authorization verifies whether the user's attempt to access a particular application or file is permitted or not. Authorization is the next step after authentication.

Cryptography is the foundation for most authentication mechanisms. Therefore, the first section of the chapter gave an overview of cryptography. The section covered the goal of cryptography in terms of the four basic functions that it provides: confidentiality, authentication, integrity, and nonrepudiation. This section also compared traditional cryptography with modern cryptography. It discussed how modern cryptography has broken the barriers of mere encryption and decryption functions and has provided mechanisms to bind documents to their creation at a particular time, to access shared disk drives, and to create high-security mechanisms.

This section also discussed the two types of encryption mechanisms available: secret key encryption and public key encryption. It also discussed the most commonly used encryption algorithms. For secret key encryption, DES and IDEA were covered. For public key encryption, Diffie-Hellman cryptosystem and RSA algorithms were covered.

The last section of the chapter discussed various authentication methods deployed to implement authentication features in systems and networks. As a part of this discussion, the challenge-response protocols, the KDC authentication mechanism, the complete architecture and working of Kerberos V5, message digest functions, and digital signatures were covered.

Check Your Understanding

Multiple Choice Questions

1. Consider the following situation. Bob is a banker and Trudy tries to snoop into the network with malicious intentions. Trudy, with the inten-

tion of stealing some money from the bank, first strikes a deal with Alice. Trudy does some work for Alice, then asks Alice to transfer the amount owed to her account.

Meanwhile, Trudy intercepts the message that KDC sends to Bob, who also captures Alice's request to transfer money to Trudy's account. Some time later, Trudy again sends both messages to Bob. This time Bob thinks that Alice has again struck a deal with Trudy and, therefore, transfers money to Trudy's account.

Identify the type of attack that has occurred in this situation.

a. Reflection attack

b. Replay attack

c. Reflex attack

d. None of the above.

2. An authentication protocol is based on the principle that one party sends a random number to the other. The other person converts the random number into a special number and returns the result. Identify the authentication mechanism.

a. KDC authentication mechanism

b. Kerberos V5

c. Digital signatures

d. Challenge-response protocol

3. Consider the following two statements:

Statement A: *Integrity* in cryptography implies verifying whether or not the original content of information has been manipulated or tainted during transmission.

Statement B: *Nonrepudiation* in cryptography implies that only authorized users can view or use classified information.

Which one is TRUE about the statements written above?

a. Statement A is TRUE but statement B is FALSE.

b. Statement B is TRUE but statement A is FALSE.

c. Both the statements are TRUE.

d. Both the statements are FALSE.

4. State whether the following statement is TRUE or FALSE:

   Symmetric key encryption uses the same key for encrypting and decrypting a message.

5. Consider the following situation and identify the attack.

   Bob is a machine in a bank that allows multiple simultaneous sessions with outside teller machines. An intruder named Maria initiates a reflection attack on Bob. Maria poses as Alice and sends the identity, A (which is originally Alice's identity), and the random number, R_M, to Bob. Bob, as usual, responds by sending his own challenge, R_B, and the encrypted cipher text, $K_{AB}(R_M)$. At this point, Maria is in a fix because she does not know about the shared secret key, R_{AB}.

   Now, Maria initiates another session with Bob by sending R_B (taken from message 2) as her challenge. Bob, as usual, sends back a reply that contains the cipher text, $K_{AB}(R_B)$, and his own challenge. Maria gets the missing information and aborts the second session. She completes the first session by sending the message with the encrypted message, $K_{AB}(R_B)$. Because Bob is convinced that it is Alice interacting with him, he gives bank account details to Maria.

   a. Reflection attack

   b. Replay attack

   c. Reflex attack

   d. None of the above.

Short Questions

1. Consider the following situation. Alice sends her identity, A, and random number, R_A, to Bob. Bob, in response to Alice, sends the encrypted random number, $K_{AB}(R_A)$, along with his random number, R_B, to Alice. Finally, Alice responds by sending the encrypted random number, $K_{AB}(R_B)$. Identify the mechanism used to verify the authenticity of entities involved in the communication. Also, state if this is the most appropriate manner of communication over the network.

2. Is the Kerberos network authentication mechanism prone to any types of attacks? If the answer is yes, what countermeasures does the mechanism provide to avoid such attacks?

3. RSA digital signatures use a private key to encrypt the message digest, which forms the digital signature. This digital signature is then attached with the original message. But how do RSA digital signatures ensure the recipient about the integrity of the digital signature one has received?

4. Briefly list the rules that should be followed while designing any authentication protocol.

5. Briefly explain the communication process between parties through the key distribution center.

Answers

Multiple Choice Answers

1. b.

2. d.

3. a. Nonrepudiation does not imply that only authorized users can view or use classified information. This is actually defining confidentiality. Nonrepudiation implies that a party in communication cannot refute some or all communication that has previously taken place.

4. TRUE.

5. a.

Short Answers

1. Alice and Bob are trying to authenticate with each other using the three-step challenge-response protocol. This is not the most appropriate mode of communication because it has a major flaw in it. Bob makes the mistake of providing valuable information before he is convinced of Alice's identity.

2. The Kerberos network authentication mechanism is prone to replay attacks. These attacks can be avoided by using a time stamp in the messages being passed. Time stamps indicate how recently a user has accessed his or her machine.

3. RSA verifies the contents of the digitally signed message by generating a new message digest from the message that has been received. The receiver does this by decrypting the message with the originator's public key. Then, he compares the decrypted digest with the newly generated digest. If the two versions match, the integrity of the message is verified. The authenticity of the originator is also verified because the public key can decrypt only that message which is encrypted with the corresponding private key of the set.

4. The following are rules that should be followed while designing any authentication protocol:

   • Let the initiator prove his identity before the responder proves his.

   • Use different shared secret keys for providing proof of identity. This may mean using two shared secret keys.

   • Let the initiator and responder use different sets of challenge numbers. For instance, one party may use even numbers and the other may use odd numbers.

5. The following steps depict the communication between Alice and Bob through the key distribution center (KDC):

   1. Alice sends a session key, K_S, to the KDC requesting to initiate a connection with Bob. Alice sends this as a cipher text message encrypted with the secret key, K_A, which she has already shared with the KDC.

   2. KDC decrypts the message with Alice's secret key, K_A, to extract Bob's identity and session key.

   3. KDC then creates a new message with Alice's identity and session key and sends it to Bob. The message sent is encrypted with Bob's secret key, K_B, which he has already shared with the KDC.

   4. When Bob decrypts the message with his secret key, K_B

Chapter 7

*Understanding
Public Key
Infrastructure*

Digital certificates are intended to provide assurance for transactions on the Internet. Efficacy of digital certificates is achieved with the combination of Public Key Infrastructure (PKI) and the legal support provided by networks.

Public key infrastructure, as the name suggests, is the infrastructure that lays a foundation for managing security policies, encryption keys, and applications that generate, store, and mange keys on the Internet. It provides a mechanism to generate, distribute, and utilize keys and digital certificates.

As an extension of the previous chapter, this chapter will introduce you to the basics of PKI. The first section discusses various components of PKI and its different authorities. Then, the chapter describes how digital certificates work and help to establish the identity and assure the authenticity of information that is exchanged over the Internet. The next section discusses the life cycle of a transaction in PKI. The last section discusses the processes that are implemented in a PKI solution.

What Is PKI?

PKI tries to bring the security of the physical world to the electronic world. For example, you are usually only asked to provide a driver's license to prove your identity when you write a check. The ease with which you prove your identity through a driver's license in the physical world is also available in the electronic world through PKI. It tackles the problems of trust, authentication, and security over the Internet.

In addition, cryptography and PKI are closely linked. In the previous chapter, I mentioned that cryptography is the foundation of every type of mechanism that provides authentication functions. The benefits of cryptography can be reaped only when it is properly implemented through an infrastructure provided by PKI. In fact, PKI is a set of components that provides public key–based security to applications and users.

The core security goals of cryptography are confidentiality, authentication, integrity, and nonrepudiation. In addition to these goals, PKI intends to provide the following:

◆ Policies that indicate rules for the working of cryptographic systems

◆ Mechanisms for creating, storing, and managing keys and certificates

◆ Strategy for creating, storing, managing, and distributing keys and certificates

Let me summarize the preceding discussion by this statement: PKI is an infrastructure that is a combination of products, services, facilities, policies, procedures, agreements, and people that provide for and sustain secure interactions on open networks (the Internet).

The following section discusses the components of PKI that integrate all the entities mentioned above.

Components of PKI

As stated in the preceding section, PKI is a frame comprised of hardware, software, policies, and procedures. For this framework to become functional, PKI provides the following components:

◆ Certification authority (CA)

◆ Registration authority (RA)

◆ PKI clients

◆ Digital certificates

◆ Certificate Distribution System or repository

I'll take each of these components separately and explain their functions in PKI deployment.

Certification Authority (CA)

A certification authority, commonly addressed as CA, is a trusted authority that authenticates the identity of entities involved in electronic transactions. To authenticate the identity, CA issues digital certificates. These certificates are digital documents signed by the private key of the certification authority. They contain information such as the name of the subscriber, the subscriber's public key, a serial number, and other information. The certificates basically confirm that a particular public key belongs to a particular individual or organization.

A certification authority can be of several different types. A few of the types are listed below.

Internal CA

A certification authority acting as an internal CA certifies an organization's employees, their positions, and their level of authority. Such certificates enable an organization to define the access control rules to its internal resources or the flow of information. For instance, for every employee in an organization, the CA can create a key and issue a certificate that is directly related to the computer systems to which the employees have an access. The computers can decide whether or not to grant an individual employee access based on the certification on the key. This is an effective mechanism deployed by organizations to maintain authenticity and access control. It also avoids the need to distribute the access control list and a password file to computers that may even be placed around the world.

Outsourced Employee CA

An organization might sign an agreement with an outside firm to provide certification services for its own employees. This is similar to an organization hiring another firm that creates identification cards.

Outsourced Customer CA

An organization might sign an agreement with an outside firm that hires a CA to take care of the organization's current or potential customers. This type of outsourcing saves the organization expenses on creating its own procedures for certificates. However, it also involves risks in trusting the outside firm's certification practices.

Trusted Third-Party CA

A trusted organization or government can take the role of a CA that binds public keys with the legal names of individuals and businesses. Such a CA allows individuals with no prior relationship to establish each other's identity and engage in legal transactions.

To use a certificate issued by a CA, you need to have a copy of the CA's public key. Presently, public keys are being distributed as a part of the software package, such as Web browsers and operating systems. However, if a CA's public key is missing from the list offered by these packages, these can easily be added at the user's end.

Revocation of Certificates

In certain cases, a certification authority can also revoke certificates it issues. The following are a few of those cases:

- ◆ If the private key of the key holder has been compromised.
- ◆ If the CA ascertains that it has issued the certificate to the wrong person or organization.
- ◆ If the individual has lost his authorization rights for the particular service for which the certificate was issued.
- ◆ If the CA finds that its system has been compromised and, as a result, the certificates issued might be falsified.

A mechanism to manage this is to maintain a certificate revocation list (CRL). A CRL is a comprehensive list of all certificates that have already been revoked by the CA as well as the ones that are due for revocation on a specific date. It clearly specifies the period that the certificate will be valid. This list is then published for clients to check each certificate before proceeding with any transaction. You can compare the CRL mechanism operated by the CA to the list that credit card companies make of stolen credit cards or cards that have already expired. Just as any retailer verifies credit card credibility by checking the list issued by the credit card company, in the same manner clients can check the credibility of certificates.

CRLs theoretically manage the revocations and help in authentications quite well. However, they also have certain drawbacks:

- ◆ A CRL document tends to grow quite quickly because of items added to it every now and then.
- ◆ There is a period of time that a certificate is revoked and the time the new CRL is distributed in which a certificate appears to be a valid but is not.
- ◆ Information contained in CRLs can be used for traffic analysis.

Due to the preceding drawbacks, CAs prefer to use real-time verification through online database management systems placed on the Internet. Though these systems also require reliable networks, they do dispense with CRL drawbacks.

Before the CA issues a digital certificate, it verifies the certificate request with a registration authority (RA). When applying for the validation of certificate requests, a CA follows its own rules and procedures. These procedures depend on an organization's policy and the infrastructure available to validate the request. If the request is validated, the CA then issues the request.

Registration Authority (RA)

An RA is an intermediary authority that coordinates the interaction between clients and CAs. The role of an RA was designed to ease the CA from the load of bulk certification requests. Whenever the CA feels that it cannot handle the load of accepting and validating requests or issue bulk certificates, it contacts the RA to at least handle the interaction between the CA and the client. The following are a few functions that an RA performs:

◆ Receive and validate requests from organizations

◆ Forward these requests to the CA

◆ Receive the processed certificate from the CA

◆ Send the certificate to the organization that requested it

The benefit of the RA is reaped the most when it is used for scaling PKI applications across different geographical locations. For instance, each RA is allotted an area of operation, such as an RA for a northern region, southern region, eastern region, or western region. The CA delegates the work based on their respective regions.

PKI Clients

The entities and organizations that issue a request for digital certificates are generally referred to as PKI clients. A PKI client needs to follow certain steps to obtain a digital certificate from a CA:

◆ Send a request to generate a public and private key pair. The client or CA can generate this key pair, which contains information about the client.

◆ After the key pair is generated, a request is sent to the CA for the digital certificate. This request is generally routed through the RA.

◆ After the client receives the digital certificate, it uses this certificate to authenticate itself in interactions over the Internet.

To ensure security over the Internet, a client also needs to share some responsibility. First and foremost, a client needs to ensure the safety of its private key. If the private key is lost, then the security of messages exchanged can be easily compromised as the unauthorized entities over the net can decrypt messages. You can ensure the safety of the private key by using several hardware components, such as tokens and smart cards. A token is a physical device that users carry to authenticate themselves over the Internet. Similarly, a smart card, as already discussed, is a physical device (like a credit card) that is also used to authenticate users over the Internet. A smart card contains a microprocessor that stores the security information, such as a user's personal identification number. In this way, a user's private key is secured.

Having discussed the basic components of PKI, let me now take up the most important component of PKI, which are digital certificates.

Digital Certificates

Securing a public key against imitation and key modification is a major concern. Data integrity mechanisms are usually used to ensure that a modified public key does not go undetected. However, data integrity mechanisms alone are not enough to prove that the public key belongs to the authorized person. A mechanism is required that binds the public key with a global trusted authority that ensures identity and authenticity. One such mechanism deployed by PKI is the digital certificate. Digital certificates work on the following two goals:

◆ To establish the integrity of the public key

◆ To bind the public key and its associated information to the owner in a trusted manner

Digital certificates ensure that the public key for a certificate, which is authenticated by the CA, works well with the private key owned by the PKI client.

A digital certificate includes the following elements:

◆ Serial number

◆ Digital signature of the CA

◆ Public key of the user to whom the certificate has been issued

◆ Date of expiration

◆ Name of the CA that issued the certificate

After the digital certificate is obtained, an organization or an individual performs the following steps to use the certificate:

1. The sender sends a digitally signed message with his or her private key to ensure the integrity and authenticity of the message.

2. After receiving the message, the receiver verifies the digital signature with the sender's public key.

3. The receiver then checks the validity of sender's digital certificate against the global directory database, which returns the status of the certificate to the recipient. The transaction is considered complete only if the certificate is valid.

After a certificate has been issued, it needs to be distributed to users and organizations. This role is performed by a Certificate Distribution System Repository.

Certification Distribution System (CDS) Repository

The Certification Distribution System Repository distributes the certificates to users and organizations. Depending on the implementation of PKI in the organization, certificates may be distributed by either of the following two mechanisms:

◆ By the users themselves

◆ By a directory server that uses LDAP to extract information stored in an X.500 compliant database

The CDS performs the following tasks:

◆ Generates and issues key pairs

◆ Validates public keys by signing them

◆ Revokes expired or lost keys

◆ Publishes public keys in the directory service server

You are now familiar with the components of PKI. Let me now brief you on its functions.

Functions of PKI

In order to provide secure communication over a network, PKI provides the following functions:

- Generates public and private key pairs for creating and authenticating digital signatures
- Provides endorsement to ensure that the private key is accessed only by authorized people
- Creates and issues certificates to authenticate users
- Registers new users to validate their identity
- Revokes certificates that have expired or are not valid
- Updates and recovers keys in case of key compromise
- Provides a mechanism to validate keys
- Maintains a history of keys for future reference

The above functions are a summary of what PKI does. The following section explains the complete life cycle of a PKI transaction.

Life Cycle of an Electronic Transaction in PKI

The following steps are involved in the life cycle of an electronic transaction in PKI:

- Generating key pairs
- Applying digital signatures to identify the sender
- Encrypting the message
- Transmitting the symmetric key
- Verifying the sender's identity
- Decrypting the message and verifying its contents

Generating Key Pairs

Generating key pairs is the first step in the PKI framework. In this step, the user who wishes to send an encrypted message over the network first generates a key pair. This key pair comprises a private key and a public key, which are unique to each user of PKI. First, the private key is generated, and then, by applying some hash value, the corresponding public key is generated. The private key is used for signing the message and the corresponding public key is used to authenticate the validity of the signature. When a user wants to encrypt any message, he or she uses the public key. To decrypt this message, the corresponding private key is used.

Applying Digital Signatures

As discussed in the previous chapter, a digital signature attached to an encrypted message authenticates the sender's identity. Let me reiterate how a digital signature is derived and attached to an encrypted message through the following steps:

1. The original message is converted to a fixed length by applying a hash function on the message.

2. This message is then encrypted with the sender's private key. The resultant message is called a message digest.

3. Finally, this digital signature is attached with the original message.

Encrypting the Message

After the digital signature is attached to the message, the complete message is encrypted again, this time with a symmetric key. This symmetric key is common between the sender and the receiver and is used for encryption and decryption.

Transmitting the Symmetric Key

After the message and the digital signature are successfully encrypted, the symmetric key needs to be transmitted to the receiver. This is because this key is used to decrypt the message also. You need to ensure that the symmetric key is transmitted in a secure manner because if this key is compromised, the authenticity of the entire message is lost. To maintain the safety of the symmetric key, it is also encrypted with the receiver's public key. Encrypting the symmetric key with the receiver's public key ensures that only the receiver can decrypt the encrypted symmetric key by his or her corresponding private key. The encrypted message and symmetric key are then transmitted to the receiver over a secure channel.

Verifying the Sender's Identity

Until now the messages were encrypted. However, how can the receiver be sure of the sender's identity? The CA plays a role here. As discussed earlier, the CA acts as a trusted third party to authenticate the identity if the those participating in the transaction. Now, when a receiver receives a message, it contacts the CA to authenticate the sender's identity. Upon receiving the request, the CA verifies the digital signature attached with the message that verifies the identity of the sender.

Decrypting the Message

After the receiver takes delivery of the encrypted message, he or she needs to decrypt it. This can be done by using the encrypted symmetric key that was sent along with the message. However, before decrypting the message, the encrypted symmetric key needs to be decrypted by using the receiver's private key. After the symmetric key is decrypted, it can be used to the decrypt the message.

The digital signature attached with the message is decrypted by using the sender's public key. The result is a message digest. To verify that the message digest is not tampered with during transit, the decrypted message is again hashed to obtain a second message digest. The resulting message digest is compared with the message digest received from the user. If both the digests match, it indicates that the message has not been tampered with.

Processes in PKI

As already discussed, PKI ensures authenticity and integrity and also maintains the trust and legal status of electronic transactions. The following processes ensure the authenticity and integrity of information:

Certificate Requests

To obtain digital certificates from the CA, the user sends a request for the certificate. There are various standards set for sending a certificate request. The most commonly used one is the PKCS#10.

A certificate request comprises the following details:

◆ Distinguished name (commonly called DN) of the CA.

◆ Public key of the user

◆ Algorithm identifier

◆ Digital signature of the user

The user sends the PKCS request through a secure channel on the network. If it cannot find a secure channel, it usually downloads the CA's public key and uses that to make the certificate secure.

Medium of Sending Requests

Usually, the certificate request is sent to the CA by an e-mail that needs to be in PEM (Privacy Enhanced Mail) format. This is because the original certificate request is in binary format, which cannot be transmitted through e-mail. Therefore, the binary message sent using PEM format converts the message to ASCII format.

A client can also send a certificate request through a Web browser. In such a transmission, PKCS#10 is used with SSL. The client makes an SSL connection with the certification server, and then transmits the certificate request through a secure channel.

Policies (Certification Practice Statement)

The security policy of an organization defines how it will maintain confidentiality, integrity, authenticity, and nonrepudiation of information. A security policy lays certain principals for securing information; for instance, it defines the usage of cryptography and how organizations need to manage their public and private keys.

As stated earlier, a PKI framework may be operated though an internal CA or a trusted third party. In the case of a trusted third party, which is also called a Commercial Certificate Authority, the PKI system needs a Certification Practice Statement (CPS). The CPS outlines operational procedures that an organization needs to follow. It defines how these procedures and policies need to be implemented, how certificates would be issued, accepted, and revoked, and how the keys will be generated, registered, and certified. The CPS also defines the location of the keys and how they should be made available for a user's request.

Certificate Revocation

You are already aware that each certificate has a validity period associated with it, which begins from the time the certificate is issued and lasts until the time it expires. During this period, the certificate can be used to authenticate users. However, a certificate may lose its validity before the period comes to an end, and it cannot be used to authenticate users. A certificate losses its validity in the following situations:

◆ When certificate security has been compromised

◆ When the person holding the certificate is not authorized to perform tasks related to the certificate

A situation in which the certificate loses is validity before it expires is called *certificate revocation*. A certificate that has been revoked can be used to validate information that was encrypted at the time when the certificate was still valid.

Communicating Certificate Revocation

When a certificate is revoked, information about this needs to be posted on a certificate server so that users are warned not to use those certificates. Information can also be published in a Certificate Revocation List (CRL). A CRL is a list of certificates that have been revoked. To prevent the CRL list from becoming too long, the certificate entry should be removed as soon as the revoked certificate reaches its expiration date. This ensures that revoked certificates are not used for malicious purposes.

A CA distributes CRLs at regular intervals, which need to be short enough to prevent revoked certificates being used before they are published in the CRL.

Client-to-Client Interaction through PKI

If two or more clients need to interact with each other through PKI, they need to first validate each other and decide upon the various encryption, authentication, and data integration mechanisms. The following protocols are used between the communicating parties in a PKI framework:

◆ Internet Security Association and Key Management Protocol (ISAKMP)

◆ Internet Key Exchange (IKE)

- Oakley
- Skeme

The ISAKMP and IKE protocols need Security Associations (SAs) to define their connection rules. SAs basically describe how security services need to be utilized optimally for secure communication. SAs ensure all this for ISAKMP and IKE protocols by defining their connection parameters. IKE is a hybrid protocol that implements the Oakley key exchange and Skeme key exchange in the ISAKMP protocol. The Oakley and Skeme protocols are basically used to derive authenticated keys.

The following two sections discuss the ISAKMP and IKE protocols in more detail.

Internet Security Associations and Key Management Protocol (ISAKMP)

The ISAKMP defines the procedures and packet formats for security associations. They are mechanisms used to establish, modify, and delete SAs. SAs contain information required to perform network-related activities in an organization. It defines payloads for exchanging key generation and for authenticating data.

The ISAKMP protocol is independent of the following factors:

- The key management protocol used
- The encryption algorithm used
- The authentication mechanism used

Therefore, ISAKMP is independent of IPSec and is compatible with IPv4 and IPv6.

Internet Key Exchange Protocol (IKE)

The IKE protocol is used with the IPSec standard. It automatically manages the IPSec SAs and facilitates secure communication through IPSec. It also indicates the validity of IPSec SAs. IKE gives CA support for building manageable and scalable IPSec implementation.

When you use IKE, you do not need to manually specify the IPSec SAs parameters for the peer devices. Also, when no policy is specified, the default policy is applied, and it contains the default value for each parameter.

Phases of IKE Protocol

IKE operates in two modes: main mode and quick mode. The following sections examine the modes in detail.

Main Mode

In the main mode, also called phase 1 of SAs, clients present their digital certificate to prove their identity. Digital certificates contain the signature of the CA to facilitate the authenticity of the client. Now, if one client does not trust the CA of the other client, then exchanging digital certificates proves futile and the communication is discontinued. If the clients trust each other's CA, authentication is completed, and the clients form a secure channel for phase 2 by encrypting the information with the receiver's public key. The purpose of phase 1 is to protect a network from eaves dropping.

Quick Mode

In the quick mode, clients negotiate the IPSec SAs. Once the two clients agree and trust each other on the CA, the quick mode (also called the second phase of SAs) negotiations start. In this phase, the following parameters are agreed between the parties:

- Key type
- Key length
- Symmetric key algorithm
- Encryption algorithm
- Hash functions

The quick mode is faster compared to the main mode. In fact, this mode does not accentuate the need to set up a secure channel for information exchange. However, due to this reason, it is prone to threats from hackers if they manage to discover the source of the SAs.

Summary

This chapter introduced you to the basics of PKI, which is the infrastructure that lays a foundation for managing security policies, encryption keys, and applications that generate, store, and mange keys on the Internet.

The first section of the chapter covered various PKI components that integrate the PKI framework, which primarily consists of hardware, software, policies, and procedures. The components discussed were as follows:

- Certification authority (CA)
- Registration authority (RA)
- PKI clients
- Digital certificates
- Certificate Distribution System (CDS) Repository

The second section of the chapter talked about the life cycle of a transaction in the PKI framework:

- Generating key pairs
- Applying digital signatures
- Encrypting the message
- Transmitting the symmetric key
- Verifying the sender's identity by using a CA
- Decrypting the message

The last section discussed the processes that are implemented in a PKI solution:

- Certificate issuance
- Certificate revocation
- Client-to-client interaction

Check Your Understanding

Multiple Choice Questions

1. Which one of the following is not a type of certification authority?

   a. Internal CA

   b. Outsourced employee CA

   c. Outsourced customer CA

   d. None of the above

2. To use a certificate issued by a CA, you need to have a copy of which of the following?

   a. CA's public key

   b. RA's public key

   c. RA's private key

   d. CA's private key

3. Consider the following two statements:

   Statement A: A CRL is a comprehensive list of all the certificates that have already been revoked by the CA as well as the ones that are due for revocation on a specific date.

   Statement B: An RA is an intermediary authority that coordinates the interaction between clients and CAs.

   Which of the following is TRUE about the statements written above?

   a. Statement A is TRUE but statement B is FALSE.

   b. Statement B is TRUE but statement A is FALSE.

   c. Both the statements are TRUE.

   d. Both the statements are FALSE.

4. State whether the following statement is TRUE or FALSE:

   A CRL is a comprehensive list of certificates that never needs to be updated. You can add more certificates without worrying about the overflow in it.

5. Which of the following is not a part of the certification request?

a. Public key of the user

b. Private key of the user

c. Algorithm identifier

d. Digital signature of the user

Short Questions

1. List the cases in which a CA can revoke the certificates it issues?

2. What does a PKI client need to do to obtain a digital certificate?

3. What are the essential components of digital certificates?

4. Briefly list the functions of a certification distribution system.

5. Explain the process of transmission of the symmetric key in PKI.

Answers

Multiple Choice Answers

1. d.

2. a.

3. c.

4. FALSE. It is difficult to manage CRLs that are large in size. Therefore, CAs usually delete the certificate entries that have reached their expiration date.

5. b.

Short Answers

1. The following are a few of cases in which a CA may revoke its certificates:

   - If the private key of the key holder has been compromised.
   - If the CA ascertains that it has issued the certificate to a wrong person or organization.
   - If the individual has lost his authorization rights for the particular service for which the certificate was issued.
   - If the CA finds that its system has been compromised, and, as a result, the issuance of certificates might be falsified.

2. A PKI client needs to perform the following steps to obtain a digital certificate from a CA:

   - Send a request to generate a public and private key pair. Either the client or CA can generate this key pair, which contains information about the client.
   - After the key pair is generated, a request is sent to the CA for the CA certificate. This request is generally routed through the RA.
   - After the client receives the digital certificate from the CA, it uses this certificate to authenticate itself in interactions over the Internet.

3. A digital certificate includes the following elements:

   - Serial number of the certificate
   - Digital signature of the CA
   - Public key of the user to whom the certificate has been issued
   - Date of expiration of the certificate
   - Name of the CA that issued the certificate

4. The CDS performs the following functions:

   - Generates and issues key pairs
   - Validates public keys by signing them
   - Revokes expired or lost keys
   - Publishes public keys in the directory service server

5. After the message and the digital signature are successfully encrypted, the symmetric key needs to be transmitted to the receiver. This is because this key is used to decrypt the message also. You need to ensure that the symmetric key is transmitted in a secure manner because, if this key is compromised, the authenticity of the entire message is lost. To maintain the safety of the symmetric key, it is also encrypted with the receiver's public key. Encrypting the symmetric key with the receiver's public key ensures that only the receiver can decrypt the encrypted symmetric key by his or her corresponding private key. The encrypted message and symmetric key are then transmitted to the receiver over a secure channel.

Chapter 8

Firewall Solutions

Nations ensure the security and safety of their people by controlling their boundaries. In the same manner, networks ensure the security and privacy of their users and information by controlling access to those networks.

The need to access information over the Internet has caused a scurry to connect private networks. Private networks that connect to the Internet provide hackers the opportunity to exploit the resources of these networks. Before the Internet, the only way a hacker could connect to private networks was by directly dialing through a modem or by a public telephony network from home. At this point, remote access security was a comparatively minor issue.

However, with the Internet, a network is directly connected to every other network on the Internet. At this point, there is no intrinsic central security control for private networks.

Firewalls are the security mechanism employed at the boundaries of a private network and serve as a security checkpoint. Firewalls look over all the communication that takes place between two networks. While scrutinizing, if required, they drop the communication packets that don't match the policy rules defined in them.

There are several firewall products available, and different experts provide different theories on how firewalls should be used. This chapter is a generic introduction to firewalls as a solution, covering their different types, their architectures, and topologies. The chapter also covers a discussion on selecting appropriate firewall solutions.

Firewalls: An Overview

Let me begin explaining firewalls with a very basic example. An office of an organization has several people visiting it. However, only employees or customers of the organization are allowed entry onto the office premises. Perhaps security personnel check the credentials of each person visiting the office before allowing him entry. In some cases, a check is also made to verify that employees are not carrying in any material that they are not allowed (such as pets or alcohol). However, these restrictions do not prevent employees from mixing with people outside the office. Employees are allowed to go outside, but not everyone is allowed to come inside. So, security or any other entity responsible for restricting or controlling access to the office building can be compared to a firewall.

What is a firewall in the context of networks? A network firewall is very well defined in the *NSA Glossary of Terms Used in Security and Intrusion Detection* as a "system or combination of systems that enforces a boundary between two or more networks." Simply stated, a firewall implements security rules that separate networks from unwanted communication.

Network firewalls keep crucial information away from danger while at the same time allowing information to pass. Firewalls keep hackers and attacks, such as denial of service and ping of death, away from networks and also allow HTTP packets and e-mail to pass through.

On Which Layer Does a Firewall Operate?

A firewall may operate at different levels of the layered network architecture of the OSI and TCP/IP models. The lowest layer at which a firewall can operate is the Network layer. At the Network layer, a firewall can determine if a packet is from an authenticated source. However, at this layer a firewall cannot authenticate the sanctity of the information being transmitted.

Firewalls deployed at the next layer, the Transport layer, provide more sophisticated functions than Network layer firewalls. Transport layer firewalls can validate connections before deciding on whether to allow or disallow the packet. This validity is checked by looking at a certain set of rules, which are configured at the firewall.

Firewalls deployed at the Application layer can perform more sophisticated functions such as filtering traffic based on the content of the data packets or, rather, the application types. These firewalls also log the activities of the data packets being rejected. Firewalls can also reconstruct the packets being rejected on the basis of the records being maintained.

Functionality of Firewalls

Having identified the layers at which a firewall may operate, let us look at some network firewall functions that ensure data security and integrity:

◆ **Packet filtering**. This refers to the filtering of incoming and outgoing packets based on protocol and address information, though the content of the packets are not checked. This is the most basic feature of a firewall.

◆ **Network address translation**. This feature hides hosts on the internal network from hosts on the external network by translating the IP addresses and ports of internal hosts to a common external IP address of the firewall. Firewalls operating with this feature prevent internal hosts from being monitored by malicious hosts on the public network.

◆ **Proxy services**. These perform data exchange on behalf of the client applications with the remote systems. This hides the client computer behind the firewall, and to the remote system it appears as if the proxy is interacting with it.

◆ **User authentication**. This feature is handy when remote users (on a public network) use dynamic IPs to connect to private networks. For instance, a user who connects to the Internet using a modem to gain access to a private network. In this case, restriction based on IP addresses is not practical because the user will get a different IP address when he connects. Therefore, the firewall will ask for authentication before allowing entry to the private network. As you can see this is regardless of the source.

◆ **Tunneling**. By creating a virtual tunnel, this feature enables physically separate networks to use the Internet as a medium of communication. Such an implementation of firewalls help in deploying Virtual Private Networking (VPN).

Based on the functionalities that a firewall may be providing, firewalls can be classified as packet-filtering firewalls, Network Address Translation (NAT) firewalls, circuit relay firewalls, and application proxy firewalls. Let us look at each of these in detail.

Packet-Filtering Firewalls

Packet-filtering firewalls are the most basic firewalls that operate on the Network layer of the OSI and TCP/IP model. These firewalls filter packets based on rules that are defined in the firewall. If packets don't conform to the criteria specified, they are simply dropped. Packet filtering can be implemented in routers or on a Network Operating System (NOS) with routing capabilities.

Packet-filtering firewalls have some inherent problems because they do not provide total security for an internal network. To counter this drawback, packet filters are usually combined with proxy servers and network address translators. I'll explain how packet filtering is merged with application proxy firewalls and network address translator firewalls a little later in the chapter. Let me first brief you on how packet-filtering firewalls are implemented.

Standard packet filters determine the sanctity of packets based on the information contained in the headers of individual packets. Theoretically, filters can be configured to sort packets based on any part of the information in the protocol header data fields. However, most only filter data based on the following protocol header data fields:

- ◆ **IP protocol field**. There are four protocols, UDP, TCP, ICMP, and IGMP, against which the IP protocol field can be used to filter data packets. However, these protocols are so general that most servers and routers need to leave these open for interaction. Therefore, filtering on the basis of an IP protocol field is generally not successful. An example of IP protocol filtering is a server, whose sole purpose is to serve a TCP-based service, such as HTTP, blocking all UDP and ICMP services.

 NOTE

If you disable the ICMP port, you will not be able to ping your server. However, your server can send and receive TCP/IP packets.

- ◆ **IP address filtering**. This restricts connections to (or from) specific hosts and networks based on their IP addresses. Most firewalls operate by specifying rules, such as "allow packets from 172.17.10.11 through 172.17.10.30 but block all other packets," "packets coming from 128.162.11.14 are not permitted to pass," or "allow all packets except packets with IP address 172.17.10.11 through 172.17.10.30."
- ◆ **TCP/UDP port**. This is the most commonly used information to filter data packets. This type of filtering is also based on the information contained in IP protocol data header fields because the information about TCP or UDP port numbers is specified there. Common protocols that can be filtered based on the TCP or UDP port field are Echo, Quote, FTP, telnet, SMTP, DNS, HTTP, Gopher, NetBIOS Session, SNMP, POP, NFS, and X Windows. Some of these protocols are sensitive to

attacks because of the high-level of operational control that they give to attackers. Therefore, it is important to block the ports of these protocols.

- **Telnet**. If the telnet port is left open on a host, it will give hackers an open door into the command prompt of the machine, which is like giving access to the complete machine.

- **NetBIOS session**. If the NetBIOS session port is left open to the Internet on Windows hosts, hackers can connect to the file servers as if they are local clients. Ideally, NetBIOS should not be enabled on the external interface (NIC that has an external IP).

- **POP**. The POP protocol can be a threat to remote clients who need to access their e-mail. This is because POP uses plain text passwords to allow access to e-mail accounts. If hackers find this port open, they can easily sniff passwords off the network without the user's knowledge.

- **NFS**. If the NetBIOS session port is left open to the Internet on UNIX hosts, hackers can connect to the file servers as if they are local clients.

Figure 8.1 displays a packet-filter firewall rejecting undesired traffic based on the TCP port rule "All ports denied except TCP Port 80, TCP Port 25, and TCP Port 21."

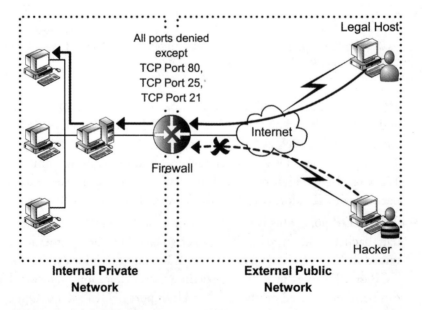

FIGURE 8.1 *Packet-filtering firewall*

There are two types of packet-filtering firewalls, *stateless* packet-filtering firewalls and *stateful* inspection packet-filtering firewalls. I'll examine each of these firewalls separately.

Stateless Packet-Filtering Firewalls

Original packet filters are called stateless packet filters because they cannot retain "session setup" information between two hosts on private and public networks. These filters do not have the capability to determine if a return socket connection is established between the hosts. For example, a host on a private network sends a request to access a site at the address 10.0.0.1 through port 80. The request packets delivered to the host on the public network also contain information about the return socket (IP address and port number) on which the host on the private network would like to listen. A stateless packet filter cannot retain this information. For example, it isn't possible to permit HTTP responses to pass through the firewall only in response to HTTP requests.

Stateful Packet-Filtering Firewalls

Stateful packet filters retain the state of connections by recording the session establishment information between two hosts across networks. Based on this information, filters decide whether or not the packets returned from a public network are from trusted hosts.

Stateful firewalls are handy when you have to filter connectionless traffic, such as DNS that are based on UDP. Stateful firewalls check the response to a request by checking the packets awaiting a response in the state table.

A stateful packet-filtering firewall examines the network traffic that passes through it. This type of firewall has the ability to check the contents of the packet by allowing certain types of commands within an application while disallowing other commands. For instance, a stateful packet-filtering firewall allows the FTP GET command on the other hand disallows the PUT command.

A stateful packet-filtering firewall also has the ability to secure the stateless protocols. For instance, in the case of UDP protocol–based applications (DNS, RPC, NFS), with static packet filtering, it is difficult to filter data packets because there is no concept of request and response. These applications are also called "stateless" applications. Therefore, in the case of static packet filtering, it is best to disallow UDP-based packets. With stateful packet filtering, UDP-based applications can be secured by creating virtual connections over and above the UDP connections. Each UDP packet request allowed to pass the firewall is recorded in the state table of the firewall. UDP packets traveling in the opposite direction are verified against the ones awaiting a response in state table. A packet that is an authentic response to a request packet is passed on, and all others are dropped. If a response does not arrive in a specified period of time, the connection is timed out. In this way, even UDP applications can be secured.

Stateful packet-filtering firewalls do not allow any services to pass through them except those they are programmed to allow and connections that are maintained in their state tables.

When a host on a private network wants to connect to a host on a public network, it transmits, with the connection synchronization packet (SYN packet), the socket (that is the IP address and port) on which it expects to receive a response. When the SYN packet is routed through the stateful packet-filtering firewall, the firewall makes an entry of the session in its state table. The session entry contains details, such as destination socket (IP address and port number) and source socket (IP address and port number). When the host on the public network sends a response back, the filter checks the entry in its table to verify the packet's source and destination socket information. If no entry is found, the packet is dropped. Figure 8.2 illustrates how the stateful packet-filtering firewall allows data to pass through it.

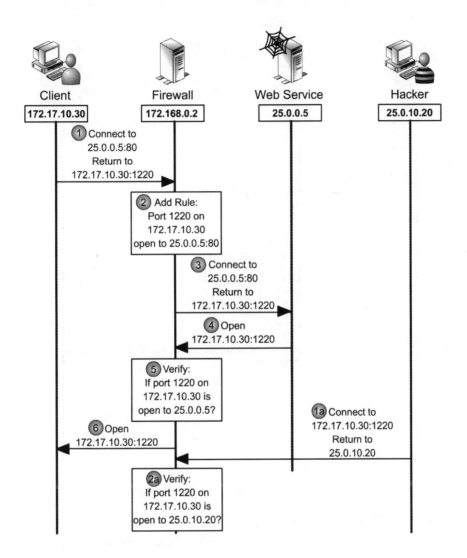

FIGURE 8.2 *Stateful packet-filtering firewall*

When a TCP session is closed, or if TCP close session packets are not received after a period of delay, the stateful packet-filtering firewall removes the entries of the TCP session from its table. This ensures that hackers don't use the information about the dropped connections to again create connections with the internal network. Figure 8.3 illustrates how the stateful packet filter removes state entries from its database and, as a result, rejects a connection from a malicious hacker using a spoofed IP address.

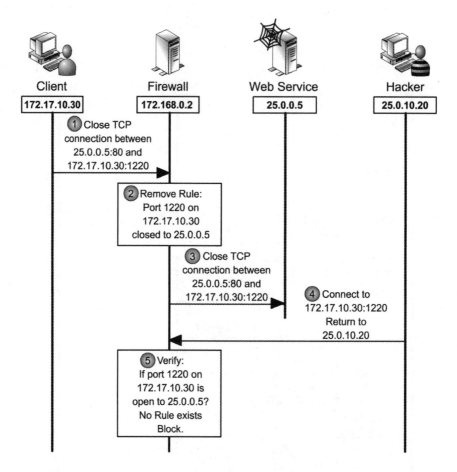

FIGURE 8.3 *Stateful packet-filtering firewall removing entries from its database*

Constraints of Packet Filters

As stated earlier, there are constraints in packet-filtering firewalls. Due to this, they are not commonly used. One of these constraints is that packet filters cannot check the content of packets for the presence of malicious data before passing them to an internal network. They rely on the header information to make pass or drop decisions on the data packets. Due to this constraint, packet filters alone do not represent an effective security measure for networks. They need to be combined with application-level proxy servers or circuit-level firewalls to provide effective security.

Network Address Translation (NAT)

Network address translation was originally implemented as a solution to the scarcity of IP addresses for hosts on private networks. It converts IP addresses in a private network to globally unique IP addresses that can be used on the Internet. The serendipitous capability of NAT to provide security has proved that NAT is a means of effective internal host hiding.

NAT hides all network-related information about internal hosts on private networks from public networks by making all traffic appear to originate from a single IP address. It allows you to use any range of IP addresses for your internal network, regardless of the fact that they are already being used elsewhere on the Internet. This implies that you don't need to register IP addresses or reassign IP addresses for private networks (in case they are already used) before you connect your private network to the Internet.

NAT hides hosts on a private network by translating the IP addresses of internal hosts to a common firewall address when packets are passed through. The firewall then forwards the packets to an external host on a public network from its own IP address. To the host on the public network, it appears as if the request is coming from a busy computer on the Internet.

 TIP

One of the reasons for introducing IP version 6 was to solve the scarcity of IP addresses over the Internet. However, NAT's unanticipated capability of reusing IP addresses and providing security to hosts on private networks (by hiding all IP addresses behind a single IP address) has superseded this purpose of IP version 6.

 NOTE

Windows NT does not provide NAT functions. To implement NAT functions on Windows NT, you need to use a third-party software firewall. Windows 2000 supports NAT. Several versions of UNIX use publicly available IP masquerade software to implement NAT. Linux supports NAT out of the box.

Firewalls Implementing NAT

A firewall performs NAT functions by maintaining a translation table that contains the mapping of internal sockets (IP addresses and port number of hosts on a private network) with external firewall sockets (IP address and port number of the firewall). When a host on a private network wants to establish a connection with the hosts on a public network, the firewall swaps the internal socket with the external socket and makes an entry in its translation table. This entry indicates the actual internal socket (socket of the host on the private network), the destination socket (socket of the host on the public network), and the external firewall socket.

After creating an entry in its table, the firewall sends a request to the external host on behalf of the internal client. To the external client, it appears that the request is coming from another computer on the Internet.

In response to the request, when the host on the public network sends data packets back to the firewall, the firewall runs the reverse translation process. It tries to map the external host's socket with the entries it has made in the translation table. If no entry is found for the external socket or if the IP address of the source (the host on the private network) is different than the address the firewall expects to see, the packet is dropped.

An example with a diagram will add more clarity to the preceding translation process. A host on a private network with the IP address 25.0.10.20 wants to access a site on the Internet with the IP address 172.17.10.30. The host transmits the request through the available port 25.0.10.20:1234 and the destination address 172.17.10.30:80 to the firewall whose external IP address is 127.110.121.1.

The firewall receives the request packet and makes the following entry in its translation table:

Source   25.0.10.20:1234

Destination   172.17.10.30:80

Translation   127.110.121.1:15485

It then transmits packets using the translated IP address and port number to the host on the public network. In other words, destination 172.17.10.30:80 receives a request from 127.110.121.1:15485. The host on the public network sends back the packets with the source IP address 127.110.121.1:15485.

After receiving the packet, the firewall searches its table for a matching socket entry. If the entry is found, it confirms that the packet is for the internal host. If the entry is not found, the packet is dropped and an entry is logged about it.

The firewall then modifies the packet by replacing the external firewall address with the internal address of the host and passes the packet to the private network. Figure 8.4 illustrates the process of translation.

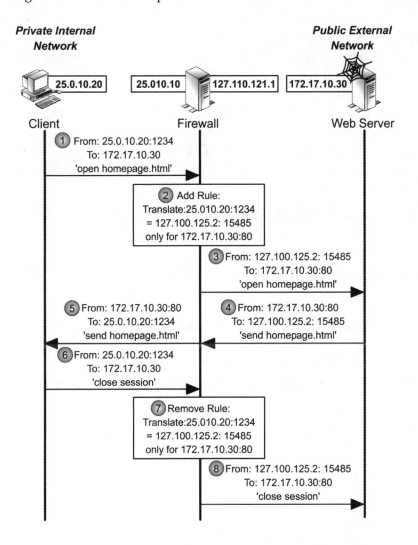

FIGURE 8.4 *A firewall with the network address translation feature*

CAUTION

NAT should use at least one valid authorized IP address to perform IP address translation functions.

The Downside of NAT

NAT solves several problems associated with direct Internet connections made through packet-filtering firewalls. However, because NAT operates on the Transport layer, it does not completely restrict the flow of malicious data packets. This is because it is not capable of checking the content of the data packets being transmitted. It is possible for higher-level protocols to exploit the weaknesses in higher-level traffic. Hackers can deploy network monitors to spy on the traffic coming out of a firewall to determine whether address translation is occurring. After gaining such information, the hacker can hijack TCP sessions or spoof IP addresses from the firewall. To prevent this, you need to merge firewalls with proxy services that operate on the Application layer.

Let me now brief you on application circuit relay firewalls and how they improve the security of the data packets being transmitted on a network.

Circuit Relay Firewalls

Circuit relay, also called a *circuit-level gateway*, is a firewall methodology in which data connections are validated before the data is actually exchanged. This implies that the firewall not only performs the pass/reject function on data packets but also determines whether the connection between both ends is valid according to configurable rules. A firewall may validate a connection on the following:

- Destination IP address and/or port
- Source IP address and/or port
- Time of day
- Protocol
- User
- Password

After verifying the connection, the firewall then opens a session and permits traffic to pass. However, several times, the firewall also places restrictions on the time limit for the data to pass.

Every session of data exchange is authenticated and monitored, and all traffic is allowed to pass during the time the connection is open. One advantage of a circuit relay firewall is that it covers up the limitations of the unreliable UDP protocol in which the source address is not validated as a function of the protocol.

A circuit-level firewall operates on the Transport layer. This sometimes becomes a disadvantage for a circuit-level firewall because it may require substantial modification of the programming that normally provides transport functions, such as Winsock.

Application Proxy Firewalls

The word *proxy* actually means one thing substituting for another. Proxy servers substitute the direct communication link between a client and a server with their services. Like NAT, proxy servers hide the client from the server without disturbing the communication link between the two. However, this is not what proxy servers were originally designed for.

Proxy servers were originally developed to cache Web pages. *Caching* a Web page means storing a copy of it on the server. In the early days of the Internet, speed was slow, the Web was relatively small, and Web pages were static. Since the speed was slow, repeated access to sites by a number of people would make the network traffic even slower. Therefore, proxy servers were used to cache Web pages so that organizations could eliminate repeated access to the same Web page.

However, when the Internet expanded, its speed improved, Web pages became dynamic, and, as a result, caching became less effective. Web pages began to change at such a fast pace that caching them was no longer important. However, the caching process highlighted a brighter side of proxy servers: they can be used to hide hosts on a network behind a single machine, they can filter URLs, and they can verify the content of data packets being transferred. Proxy servers evolved from mere caching machines to firewalls.

When a host on an internal network attempts to connect to a Web site on the Internet, a proxy server receives the request from the host. If the proxy server is also functioning as a cache server, it looks for the Web page requested in its memory. If the Web page exists in the cache memory, it sends the page back to the host. However, if the Web page does not exist, it forwards the request on behalf of its host.

How do clients on the network interact with the proxy? Clients access Web pages through browsers. Now, browsers are set up with the address of the proxy server. This implies that whenever a client sends a request through a browser, the browser automatically sends all Web page requests to the proxy server rather than resolving the IP address and processing the request directly.

It is not necessary that a proxy server runs on a firewall. Any server, placed either inside or outside a network, can perform the role of a proxy. Both a firewall without proxy services and a stand-alone proxy server cannot provide security services. A proxy server should have some sort of packet filtering to protect itself from network attacks, such as denial-of-service attacks. Similarly, a firewall should perform proxy services if it wants to provide true security features (see Figure 8.5).

Let us explore some functions of a proxy firewall:

◆ **Proxy firewall with the IP filtering and masquerading feature**. These firewalls can block direct outbound connection attempts to remote hosts. The proxy firewall then connects to the remote server and requests data on behalf of the client by IP masquerading (NAT functionality).

◆ **Proxy firewalls with application-level filtering for specific content**. Some proxy firewalls can be set with rules to look for content in HTML pages that refer to Java or ActiveX-embedded applets and drop these packets. This prevents the applets from executing and, therefore, avoids the accidental download of viruses and Trojan horses.

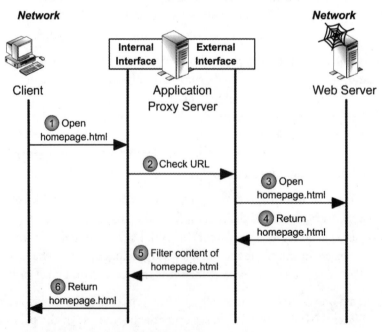

FIGURE 8.5 *An application proxy firewall*

Application Gateway

The application gateway is a type of application proxy firewall that goes a step further in controlling traffic on a network. It acts as a proxy for applications by performing all data exchanges with the remote system on their behalf.

An application gateway makes pass or reject decisions based on specific rules, such as permitting some commands to a specific server (but not others), restricting file access to certain types, and changing rules according to authenticated users. This type of firewall also logs traffic details and monitors events on the host system. It can also be programmed to sound alarms or notify an operator under defined conditions.

Application-level gateways are generally regarded as the most secure type of firewall. They are normally implemented on a separate computer on the network whose primary function is to provide proxy service.

A disadvantage of an application gateway is that its setup is very complex, and, therefore, may require detailed attention to the individual applications that use the gateway.

Caution While Implementing Application Proxy Firewalls

Proxies can only work for specific applications. For instance, you need a separate proxy module for HTTP services, another module for FTP, and a separate module for telnet. As these protocols evolve, the modules of proxies also need to be upgraded.

In addition to this, several protocols are either proprietary or are so rare that they don't have corresponding security proxies available. For example, proxies don't exist for applications like Lotus Notes. For such applications, protocols must either communicate through Network layer firewalls, or data packets should be sent through general TCP proxies that regenerate content and simply transfer packets. An example of a generic proxy is the SOCKS proxy that regenerates content and flushes the malicious content that might be detected by a firewall.

In view of these shortcomings, it is suggested to not use proxy servers for all application protocols. In addition, it is advised you use higher-level proxies that can inspect executable content, such as ActiveX and Java, in Web pages.

Firewall Layouts

Once you set up a firewall on the borders of your private network and the Internet, you think that your network is secure. However, such a setup restricts the flow of traffic from the external network to your private network. What if you want to provide public services to your customers? Is it possible for a private network to be secure and provide public services to its customers and simultaneously secure its own network? There can be several answers to this question. However, which answer is right depends upon the kind of security an organization is looking for and the level of services it wants to provide to its customers.

There are several layouts that organizations use to protect their networks. Here are a few of the most commonly used layouts:

◆ ISP filtered packet services

◆ Single firewall

◆ Demilitarized zone (DMZ)

◆ Screened host firewall

◆ Screened subnet firewall

The following section discusses each one of these layouts in detail.

ISP Filtered Packet Services Layout

Most Internet service providers offer the packet-filtering feature as an additional service for its customers. ISPs set up their own firewalls to filter traffic to and from private networks. In addition to providing the packet-filtering feature, a few ISPs also provide the services of proxy servers and network address translation. Figure 8.6 illustrates how an ISP's packet-filtering firewall operate.

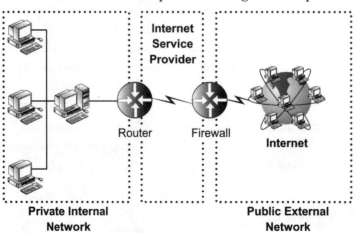

FIGURE 8.6 *An ISP's packet-filtering firewall*

The only advantage of getting a packet-filtering firewall from an ISP is that an organization doesn't need to make a heavy capital expenditure on setting it up. However, such a setup brings security risks. Even if the Internet service provider assures a complete security solution, an organization is still not safe because its network is in the hands of another organization. There can never be a surety of the intentions of the other organization and its employees, especially, in the case of any dispute between the organization and the ISP.

Apart from these risks, configuration is another administrative problem. It is difficult to rely on an ISP's customer support team for changing security rules and, consequently, reconfiguring the firewall. In addition, a private network is also vulnerable to the ISP's other subscribers who are usually inside the same firewall.

Single Firewall Layout

A single firewall is the most fundamental firewall layout. In this type of layout, the two networks are simply separated from each other by a firewall in between. A single firewall is configured to not only secure the private network from the Internet, but also to allow the private network users to access the Internet. Since there is only one firewall and a single connection to the Internet, there is a single point of control and management in such a layout. Figure 8.7 illustrates a single firewall layout separating a private network from the Internet.

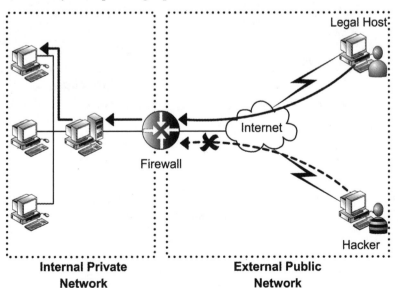

FIGURE 8.7 *A single firewall layout*

All is fine until an organization wants to separate its network from the external public network, that is, the Internet. However, organizations may need to provide public services, such as Web and FTP, to customers or may intend to operate mail servers. In such situations, organizations have several options. First, an organization can place its public servers behind a firewall and thus open a connection to the external network for accessing the public servers of other organizations. This method is also termed as a dual-homed gateway firewall. The firewall has two interface cards, one for the trusted network and the other for the untrusted network (see Figure 8.8).

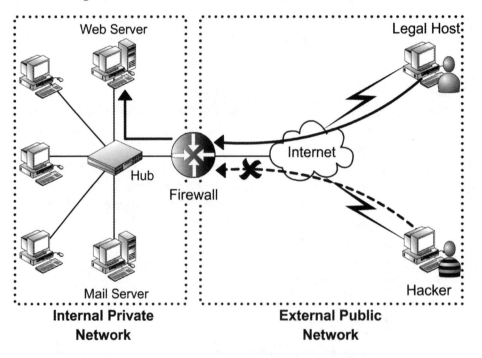

FIGURE 8.8 *A single firewall with servers protected behind the firewall*

In the second option, the organization can place its public servers outside the firewall scope, exposed to the public network. Figure 8.9 illustrates the placement of the public servers of the organization after the firewall.

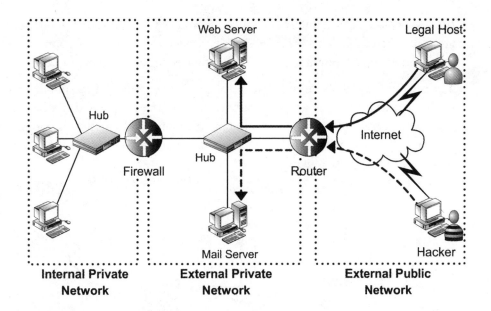

FIGURE 8.9 *A single firewall with servers exposed to the Internet*

This layout, where the public servers of organizations are placed either behind the firewall or after the firewall and are exposed to the world, is also termed an untrustworthy host layout. Here, *untrustworthy* refers to the public servers because they may allow intrusion into the private network of an organization.

The problem with placing the public servers of organizations outside the firewall is that they are open to unrestricted hacking attempts. This type of layout is only suitable if these servers don't contain much useful information.

The problem with opening a connection through the firewall for the external network to access organizations public servers is that any packet may enter the private network if it appears to confirm to the rules of your packet filter firewall. This implies that hackers who manage to exploit higher-level service software might gain access to the private network.

Demilitarized Zone (DMZ) Layout

In the earlier section, I discussed layouts where the organization was hosting public services to its customers. You can see that such layouts involve potential risk to the internal network. The risk of having exposed public servers can be reduced using two firewalls and two levels of firewall security. In such a setup, the first firewall is placed at the Internet connection and the organization's public servers are placed behind it. This provides security as well as allows connection attempts to customers in the external network for public services of the organization.

The second firewall is placed between the private network and the public servers of the organization. This setup provides security to the private network because it is now not connected with any external connections, and its setup is completely hidden from the outside world. The area between the two firewalls is termed the demilitarized zone (see Figure 8.10).

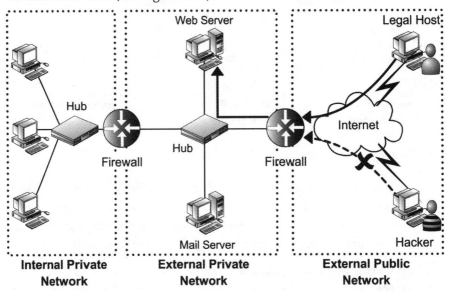

FIGURE 8.10 *A demilitarized zone layout*

In a demilitarized zone layout, when a hacker tries to intrude into the network of an organization, he is blocked at two levels. If he manages to cross the first hurdle, he is stopped at the second level of security. The DMZ layout is considered to be the safest security mechanism for organizations.

Firewalls also allow the use of the virtual DMZ layout. Figure 8.11 illustrates a virtual demilitarized zone created by a single firewall setup. In this setup, a firewall contains three interfaces connected to an external network (i.e., the external network, the internal network, and the public server network) with three different security policies. The security policies can be customized to block connection attempts to your internal network but bypass your public server network. This way you are making use of two firewalls through a single product. This type of firewall is also referred to as a trihomed firewall.

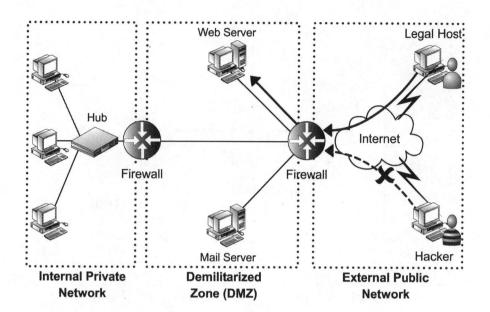

FIGURE 8.11 *A virtual demilitarized zone layout*

In addition to the layouts discussed above, there are two other kinds of layouts that organizations use. These layouts are appropriate when organizations want to provide both packet filtering and proxy services to their networks.

Screened Host Firewall Layout

A screened host firewall layout consists of a *bastion host* and a *screening router*. A bastion host is a hardened server dedicated to hosts services that is accessible from the Internet, like Web, mail, and DNS services.

A screening router is the first stop between the Internet and the internal network (see Figure 8.12). The main role of a screening router is to analyze the data packets that attempt to connect to a private network based on rules specified in the router. The data packets are rejected if they don't pass the security policy rules. If data packets pass the rule, they are screened the second time at the bastion host on the private network.

This kind of a firewall is more secure than a packet-filtering dual-homed firewall but less secure than a screened host firewall and dual-homed firewall bastion setup.

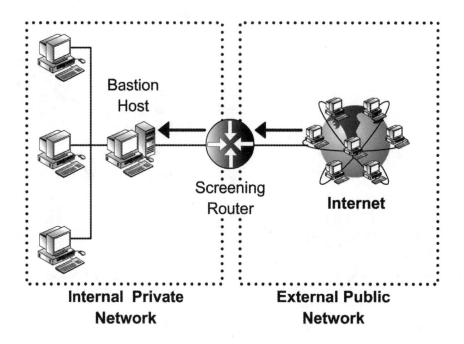

FIGURE 8.12 *A screened host firewall layout*

Screened Subnet Firewall Layout

A screened subnet host firewall layout is also nothing but a demilitarized zone layout. Like the demilitarized zone, this layout also contains two firewalls. However, in addition it also contains a bastion host on the network.

 NOTE

Actually, in the case of a screened subnet firewall layout, you are just hardening the machines in the DMZ, that is, all machines in the DMZ are bastion hosts. You are basically securing the computers in the DMZ.

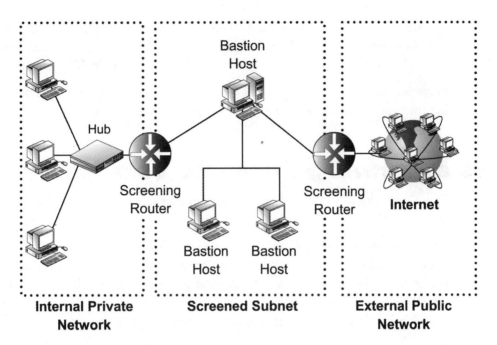

FIGURE 8.13 *A screened subnet firewall layout*

In Figure 8.13, notice that a bastion host and some other host computers form a *subnet*. A subnet is ideally a part of a private network consisting of computers that have the initial part of their IP addresses in common. A subnet is placed between two screening routers.

One screening router is placed between the Internet and the screened subnet. The second screening router is placed between the screened subnet and the private network. The subnet is referred to as screened subnet because traffic is screened from both ends of the routers. The screened subnet contains a bastion host, a Web server, and an FTP server. This screened subnet is also referred to as a demilitarized zone.

When a customer wants to access resources from the Web server of an organization, it sends a request through the screening router to the screened subnet. In the screened subnet, the request passes through the bastion host that performs proxy operations on the data packets before finally responding to the host on the external network. Similarly, if a host in the private network wants to access certain resources from its public services, the request is first screened through the router and then passes through the bastion host.

A screened subnet firewall is used when a high level of security is required for computers on a LAN. In addition to providing security, a screened subnet firewall also hides the internal network of the organization from the public network.

However, there are a few downsides of using such a complex network. Configuring the routers and bastion host in such a layout is complicated.

Is a Firewall a Complete Solution?

In earlier sections, we looked at the different types of firewalls and their layouts in organizations. But is a firewall a complete security solution for an organization?

The answer is, No. No mechanism developed to date can completely secure a network. Firewalls are effective in protecting private internal networks from external public networks, but they are not foolproof solutions that can keep all types of attacks at bay. Administrators who install firewalls assume that their networks cannot be hacked. However, they are completely mistaken.

There are so many methods in which to exploit a network that no mechanism can be completely secure. For example, take the case of an organization that allows only SMTP mail to be passed through a firewall. An employee receives an e-mail from the boss asking for some important documents. The employee clicks the Reply button, attaches the documents to the return e-mail, and sends it. However, the hacker who forged the e-mail request and manipulated the Reply column to contain his address, receives the e-mail. A firewall is not capable of checking this type of exploitation because many users have different From and Reply addresses. Some users send mail from multiple e-mail addresses but like to receive mail at only one address.

Another example of a serious security threat to the network of an organization is employees (with the help of a modem) dialing out to their Internet service providers and evading the network. Modems are the easiest and cheapest means available to evade a network. In fact, all computers are sold with internal modems or most of the operating systems contain software for setting up modems to connect to a dial-up Internet service provider. Most employees have their own dial-up network accounts that they can use from the workplace. Since employees face several restrictions in offices (such as no file downloads from FTP, blockage of pornography sites, blockage of Internet Relay Chat), they dial out so that they can evade their organizations' security policies.

Employees don't understand the high risk of using dial-up networks. Modem connections are bi-directional. If employees have a file shared on their machines, this offers a good chance for hackers to gain entry into the system through the dial-up network.

To avoid such issues in an office, organizations need to implement certain precautionary measures:

- ◆ The number of connections to the Internet should be reduced to a minimum. Organizations should create a network that is dedicated to Internet access. A private network should be completely separated from this network. Any employee who needs to access the Internet should access it from the network dedicated to the Internet.

- ◆ Restrictions should be placed on dial-up connections to the Internet. Organizations should remove modems and uncontrolled network devices that may provide access to the Internet.

- ◆ Free COM ports in the BIOS settings of client computers should be disabled. In addition, entry to the BIOS should be restricted by adding a password so that employees cannot override its security settings.

- ◆ Restrictions should be placed on unrestricted file sharing. File sharing should be allowed only on user-based authentication methods. File sharing and print sharing should be installed on the client computers only for unavoidable reasons.

- ◆ Users should be encouraged to store all files on network file servers.

- ◆ Internal clients should be configured with IP addresses in the 10 domains that are not routed by most Internet routers. Network address translation should be used to masquerade internal addresses to routable external addresses.

Selecting a Firewall Solution

There are several firewall solutions available on the market. Choosing between these solutions is a difficult and an analytical job. In fact, choosing and implementing a security solution is a vital and expensive affair. An organization may either choose to select, deploy, and manage a firewall solution itself, or it may assign the job to security solution experts. In either case, certain factors need be considered before selecting an appropriate firewall solution. The following are a few factors that need to be considered:

- ◆ Identify vulnerable points in the network.
- ◆ Estimate the cost of implementing a firewall.
- ◆ Identify prerequisites for installing a firewall.
- ◆ Select a suitable type of firewall solution.
- ◆ Select a suitable firewall layout.
- ◆ Evaluate the features of the firewall.
- ◆ Match requirements with features.
- ◆ Evaluate the firewall solution.

Identifying Vulnerable Points in the Network

The first step in choosing an appropriate firewall solution is identifying vulnerable points in the network that can pose a security threat to your organization. The vulnerable points not only include network resources, such as gateway equipment, servers, workstations, and networking equipment, but also include services, such as the Internet, FTP, e-mail, and critical business applications. An administrator of the organization should identify the common threats by studying the trends of attacks occurring in the market and also analyzing the organization's past experience with respect to any attacks it has suffered. In addition, the administrator needs to identify specific applications used in the organization that have their own security requirements. For instance, the application that the Human Resource Department uses to hide crucial information from employees has specific security requirements.

Identifying the vulnerable points of an organization gives the administrator a broad perspective. The administrator can focus on primary security areas of the organization. In addition, it helps the administrator to devise substitutes for these vulnerable points and provide a viable security solution.

Estimating the Cost of Implementing a Firewall

While selecting a security solution for its network, an organization should evaluate the cost of implementing the solution against the benefits that can be reaped from it. Estimating its cost is like estimating the cost of any other component. It mainly involves calculating the costs of purchasing and maintaining the solution. The cost of implementing a firewall includes the following:

◆ **Purchase**. The cost of purchasing a firewall is the market price of a firewall product. Before purchasing a firewall solution, the administrator should take quotes from various vendors and search the Internet for the various firewall solutions available. There are firewall products available as integrated hardware and software solutions. These solutions are costly but easy to implement. Freely downloadable firewall solutions are also available, but they might not provide the desired solution because they are generic.

◆ **Installation**. The cost of installation includes the cost that the vendor charges to deploy (install and configure) the product and the product-specific training that the organization's personnel may require as a precautionary measure to rectify problems in the firewall.

◆ **Administration**. The cost of administration includes costs incurred in changing the security policy of the organization based on the current nature of the threats, the cost incurred in interpreting logged information, and the cost for subsequent corrective actions.

◆ **Maintenance**. Most large organizations outsource firewall maintenance tasks to network security firms. These security firms charge the organization annual or monthly fees for their services, which constitutes the cost of maintaining of the firewall. Maintenance tasks may vary from amendments and customizations in firewall policies to fixing bugs and troubleshooting problems on a daily basis.

Identifying Prerequisites for Installing a Firewall

The next step is to identify the basic requirements essential for installing a firewall. An organization should have a clear understanding of the following issues because these lay the foundation for firewall setup and installation:

◆ Organizations should have a clear understanding about the level of security that they want to provide in their network.

◆ A basic firewall security policy should be prepared that clearly defines the access area of network services to users. The policy should also layout the rules for enabling services, such as e-mail and FTP.

◆ A detailed report of event logs and audit documents should be prepared because these facilitate in defining a security policy.

◆ The requirements of the network should be clearly laid down. For example, will the network require network address translation and routing functions? If the network requires this functionality, its design should be prepared accordingly.

◆ A document should be prepared that clearly lists the operating system and hardware and software resources that the organization is currently using. This facilitates network administrators in deciding if any software or hardware needs to be upgraded before the firewall is installed.

◆ A detailed analysis report should be prepared that defines the types of attacks and loopholes that lead to an attack in the organization. This report should also define the current security checkpoints used and the reasons for the failure of these checkpoints to counter attacks.

Selecting a Suitable Type of Firewall Solution

An organization should select the appropriate firewall solution depending upon the prerequisites and requirements identified, the cost of the product evaluated, and performance considerations. An organization might choose to implement an application-level firewall solution or a network-level firewall solution. The following discussion lists the situations when an application-level or network-level firewall should be chosen. You can choose an application-level firewall if

◆ the organization needs to implement a robust packet-filtering tool.

◆ high network speed is not the main concern.

◆ the organization's network has high-end hardware systems that can support the high processing requirements of the firewall software.

◆ the organization needs to monitor both network- and application-based communication.

◆ the organization wants to include additional security features, such as intrusion detection.

You can choose a network-level firewall if

◆ the organization wants to use a firewall device or router that is preconfigured with firewall software and can be easily attached to its network setup, regardless of the operating systems being used on the network.

◆ network speed and performance are the main concerns.

◆ the organization is looking for a cost-effective firewall solution.

◆ the organization wants to implement features, such as IP filtering and reporting, without installing additional features.

After deciding the level at which the firewall will be implemented, the organization needs to choose a firewall technology.

◆ An organization may choose to use application proxy services if it plans to provide application-level security. Application proxies also provide an IP masquerading facility that hides an internal network from an external network. Also, as I have already discussed, proxy applications can include additional security features, such as an intrusion detection system.

◆ An organization may choose a stateful packet-filtering firewall if it wants data packets to be examined and validated before they enter its network.

◆ An organization may go for a hybrid system because it offers both packet filtering and a proxy firewall.

After deciding the level of firewall security and the type, an organization needs to decide the mode of acquiring the firewall solution. There are several firewall products available that are freely downloadable as well as available from vendors for a price. Proprietary firewalls are mostly hardware-based and are appropriate for organizations with large setups. This is because vendors not only install the firewall solution on a network, but also provide maintenance support if there is a problem. Software-based proprietary firewalls also exist, such as Gauntlet, and MS-ISA server

Selecting a Suitable Firewall Layout

Another important decision that organizations need to make is which type of layout of firewall to use. The following are a few situations that brief you about layout patterns:

◆ A single firewall layout is most appropriate when an organization needs to implement an economical firewall solution. This implies that if the organization plans to use only one router for implementing firewall functions, the single firewall layout is the best and most cost-effective solution.

◆ The untrustworthy host layout, where the public servers of organizations are either placed behind the firewall or after the firewall and are exposed to the world, is appropriate when the public servers of the internal network do not require high security and also do not disrupt the services of the internal network.

◆ The demilitarized zone layout is the most appropriate when an organization wishes to protect its public servers as well as its internal network.

Evaluating Features of the Firewall

Until now, we looked at an organization's requirements while selecting a firewall solution. However, we also need to look features of the firewall product before finally deciding on a solution. A few features that need to be considered are scalability, complexity level, performance, and additional features.

Scalability

A firewall solution is *scalable* if it can integrate other new applications and firewalls. For instance, even after deploying a firewall solution, an organization might need to upgrade its system with antivirus updates or may need to deploy an intrusion detection system to strengthen its security. The firewall should be flexible enough to integrate these changes with minimal or no changes in its deployment. If it is not scalable, the organization might need to purchase a new solution every time it wants to add some new features.

Complexity

A firewall should not be so complex that it is difficult to understand, install, configure, and maintain. Easy installation steps eliminate the risk of erroneous configuration settings. In addition to offering ease in installation, the firewall interface should also be simple and consistent so that it is easy to administer. However, easing the complexity of a firewall does not mean making it is so simple that any outsider can hack into the network.

Performance

The performance of a firewall solution should strengthen the speed and performance of the organization's entire network instead of hampering it. The firewall should be secure enough to manage heavy data traffic. It should provide authentication features to validate the entry of users and data packets into the network. In addition, ideally, a firewall should be configured to download and install product updates regularly. It should also be able to revive a network quickly in case of any breakdown.

Additional Features

The features discussed above are basic features that are mandatory for any firewall solution. However, there are certain additional features that can make a firewall solution complete:

◆ Firewall solutions should preferably contain tunneling functionality to implement a site-to-site encryption solution.

◆ Firewalls should log the activities of the network so that administrators can track events of the day.

◆ Firewalls should have built-in high-availability to handle network risks that may arise due to unforeseen breakdowns. This feature enables firewalls to transfer their operations to backup firewalls if there is a breakdown.

◆ Some firewalls also provide mechanisms that can trap intruders. One such mechanism is the honeypot mechanism, which entices intruders by displaying data that is not genuine.

Matching Requirements with Features

Once an organization has evaluated the features of a firewall solution, the next important step is to match network security requirements with the features of the various firewall solutions available in the market. Only that solution should be chosen that fulfills most of the network's requirements. Care should be taken while evaluating firewall features. Quotes for a firewall solution should be taken from different vendors. In addition, before finalizing the deal, organizations should also check the after-sales support that vendors propose to provide. After-sales support (troubleshooting) is a vital aspect of the firewall implementation process.

Evaluating the Firewall Solution

Once you have matched firewall features with network security requirements and before you finally select a firewall solution, it is recommended that you assess the firewall solution again with the following factors:

◆ **After-sales technical support.** Vendors should provide efficient technical support, not only during the installation of the firewall but also after its sale. This will ensure that regular support is available in case of any breakdown or whenever maintenance is required.

◆ **Maintenance costs.** Maintaining a firewall product is part of its total cost. Many organizations make the mistake of not adding the cost of maintenance in the total cost of the product, and when such maintenance costs are incurred (which are usually very heavy), they blame the vendor for not informing them earlier. Therefore, when signing a contract with the vendor, organizations should also check the warranty period and warranty clause offered. This will help the organization to evaluate the type and extent of support that the vendor will provide.

◆ **Product documentation**. Organizations should check if the product they wish to buy contains detailed documentation about installing, configuring, and troubleshooting the firewall.

◆ **Prototype of a firewall**. Before an organization finally buys a firewall product, it must ask for a prototype to test and evaluate its functioning. This helps to evaluate both the shortcomings and strengths of the product. In addition, the organization gets a chance to verify that the firewall solution is providing complete security to its network.

Summary

This chapter was a general introduction to firewalls as a solution to securing networks. It was basically divided into four sections. The first section covered an overview of firewalls and the layers on which they operates.

The second section discussed the functionality of firewalls. Here, the section, very briefly, listed the various functions that a firewall is capable of performing. Based on these, firewalls have been classified into four categories: packet-filtering firewalls, network address translation, circuit relay firewalls, and application gateway firewalls. Each type of firewall was discussed in detail.

The third section of the chapter discussed the five main layouts of a firewall: ISP filtered packet service layout, single firewall layout, demilitarized zone layout, screened host firewall layout, and screened subnet firewall layout. Each layout was discussed with explicit diagrams that added clarity to the content.

The fourth section of the chapter discussed factors that need to be considered when selecting a firewall solution. The section identified eight areas where stress should be laid before the organization finally buys a firewall solution:

◆ Identify vulnerable points in the network.

◆ Estimate the cost of implementing a firewall.

◆ Identify prerequisites for installing a firewall.

◆ Select a suitable type of firewall solution.

◆ Select a suitable firewall layout.

◆ Evaluate the features of the firewall.

◆ Match requirements with features.

◆ Evaluate the firewall solution.

Check Your Understanding

Multiple Choice Questions

1. Which protocol header data field restricts connections to specific hosts and networks based on IP addresses?

   a. IP protocol field

   b. TCP/UDP port

   c. IP address filtering

   d. TCP protocol field

2. Consider the following two statements:

   Statement A: A bastion host is a hardened server that is dedicated to host services that are accessible from the Internet, like Web, mail, and DNS services

Statement B: A screening router analyzes data packets that attempt to connect to a private network based on the rules specified in the router.

Which one is TRUE about the statements written above?

a. Statement A is TRUE but statement B is FALSE.

b. Statement B is TRUE but statement A is FALSE.

c. Both the statements are TRUE.

d. Both the statements are FALSE.

3. Consider the following two statements:

Statement A: Network layer firewalls cannot authenticate the sanctity of the information being transmitted over the network.

Statement B: Transport layer firewalls have the capability of reconstructing the data packets being rejected on the basis of the records maintained.

Which one is TRUE about the statements written above?

a. Statement A is TRUE but statement B is FALSE.

b. Statement B is TRUE but statement A is FALSE.

c. Both the statements are TRUE.

d. Both the statements are FALSE.

4. What is the lowest layer at which a firewall can operate?

a. Application

b. Transport

c. Network

d. Session

5. An organization plans to use only one router for implementing firewall functions. Their budget is also very limited. Which of the following layouts would be most appropriate for the organization?

a. Single firewall layout

b. Untrustworthy host layout

c. Demilitarized zone

Short Questions

1. Describe tunneling in the context of firewalls.

2. What are the differences between stateless and stateful firewalls?

3. Describe packet filtering very briefly.

4. What considerations should you keep in mind while evaluating features of a firewall?

5. What are the components of a dual-homed gateway firewall?

Answers

Multiple Choice Answers

1. c.

2. c.

3. a. Reconstructing the rejected data packets is not a function of Transport layer firewalls. Instead, it is a function of Application layer firewalls.

4. c.

5. a.

Short Answers

1. Firewalls provide a mechanism by which to establish a secure connection between two private networks operating on the Internet. Tunneling enables physically separate networks to use the Internet as a medium of communication.

2. Stateless packet-filtering firewalls cannot retain session setup information between two hosts on private and public networks. In contrast, stateful packet-filtering firewalls retain session setup information by recording the session establishment information between hosts across networks.

3. Packet filtering refers to the filtering of incoming and outgoing packets based on protocol and address information. The contents of the packets are not checked. This is the most basic feature of a firewall.

4. Features of a firewall product that need to be considered are scalability, complexity level, performance, and additional features.

5. A dual-homed gateway firewall has two interface cards, one for the trusted network and another for the untrusted network.

Chapter 9

Let me begin this chapter by sharing with you the traditional way in which most organizations respond to intrusions. Organizations generally protect their systems and networks by operating on the *fortress mentality*, also referred to as a *perimeter defense*. The fortress mentality involves using a myriad of preventive measures to keep out unauthorized access to information. To explain the fortress mentality, consider the example of an organization that protects its systems by deploying several preventive measures. For instance, the organization installs theft-prevention devices, such as tagging devices, hardware locks, and drive locks. When you move towards the network of this organization, you will encounter firewalls.

To gain entry into the network of this organization, you need to take access permissions from a single sign-on authority. Then, you get the rights to use your user name and password for access control to log in. After you are inside the network, there are other role-based authentications that give rights and permissions to selected files and folders. Finally, each file is further protected from unauthorized disclosure by decryption.

A typical response of an organization to protect itself is to add another layer of security. An organization can continue adding security preventive measures like layers of an onion. However, this approach has its own limitations. Unfortunately, such layers sometimes stand in the way of smooth information flow.

Another hurdle to securing the boundaries of an organization is that there is no control over internal intrusions. A computer crime and security survey conducted by Computer Security Institute/Federal Bureau of Investigation (CSI/FBI) in 1999 indicated that at least 82 percent of losses to organizations were due to attacks from inside the organization. Perimeter defense designed to keep intruders at bay does not prove effective here because insiders have keys to all the locks, so to speak. Almost all access control mechanisms, in this case, may prove insignificant against insider threats.

Now, imagine that in spite of so many layers of security, an intrusion (let's assume it's an external attack) takes place in the organization. How would the organization know? Like an imprudent house burglar, the intruder wouldn't leave muddy footprints or evidence of his visit. Security systems, such as a firewall with logging capabilities, would probably detect the intrusion. However, a smart hacker may manage to bypass that also.

Therefore, an organization needs to deploy a solution that not only protects it from external threats but also protects it from threats that may arise from within the organization. In addition, the solution should be a perfect balance of access and access controls that will allow information to flow freely.

Let me take another example of a jewelry store that deploys a mechanism that not only allows customers to view and buy jewels but also keeps armed robbers at a distance. This proves to be an ideal prevention mechanism for the store, but how does this store manage to keep such tight security? It uses video cameras. In case of loss or while the attack is being performed, video cameras are a method to identify criminals, evaluate the extent of the damage, and assist in prosecution.

The parallel capability in computer security is *intrusion detection*. Intrusion-detection tools, like video cameras, are not prevention devices or techniques, but they are superb deterrents. They allow you to detect threats and evaluate damage just like video cameras in the physical world.

This chapter is a discussion on how you can secure your network from attacks that may go undetected even after security technologies are installed on the network. The chapter begins by defining an intrusion-detection system. Next, the chapter clarifies the confusion related to the need for intrusion-detection systems and firewalls. Then, the chapter discusses models on which intrusion-detection systems are based. The next section of the chapter identifies the types of intrusion-detection systems that are available. It covers, in detail, the architecture and working of network-based, host-based, and hybrid intrusion-detection systems. The chapter also gives tips that should be kept in mind while selecting an intrusion-detection system. Finally, the last section of the chapter discusses honeypot, a tool complementing intrusion-detection systems.

What Is Intrusion Detection?

Intrusion detection is the art of detecting and responding to computer exploitations and attacks. Its functions broadly include prevention, deterrence, detection, response, damage appraisal, attack anticipation, and tribunal support.

There are various intrusion-detection techniques available, and each technique provides different benefits depending upon the environment. A technique that is uitable in one environment may not be suitable in the other environment. Therefore, you would find that there are several definitions of intrusion detection floating around. The most commonly used ones (but not necessarily accurate) are the following:

- ◆ **Intrusion detection** implies detecting unauthorized access to a computer network.

- ◆ **Misuse detection** implies detecting activity that matches explicit patterns of misuse.

- ◆ **Anomaly detection** implies detecting deviations from acceptable behavior profiles.

- ◆ **False-positive** is an alarm of some irregular activity that is not misuse. It is a false alarm.

- ◆ **False-negative** is misuse that is not detected or alarmed.

 NOTE

The terms *false-positive* and *false-negative* are related to errors (false alarms) raised in an attempt to detect intrusion. I will discuss these terms again a little later in this section.

The preceding are specific definitions that emphasize various aspects of intrusion detection. More generic definitions that explain the broad capabilities of intrusion detection and intrusion-detection systems are given by the Intrusion Detection Sub-Group (IDSG) of the president's National Security Telecommunications Advisory.

Intrusion is unauthorized access to, and/or activity in, an information system.

Intrusion detection is the process of identifying that an intrusion has been attempted, is occurring, or has occurred.

An *indication* is information that suggests a threat. Indications include specific evidence that an intrusion has occurred and implicit evidence revealing the interests, intentions, and capabilities of the threat.

NOTE

The National Security Telecommunications Advisory Board (NSTAC) is a group chartered by the president of the United States to protect the nation's critical infrastructures. The preceding definitions were released by IDSG in its report in December 1997.

Intrusion-detection systems (IDS) provide several uses beyond detecting and responding to misuse and intruders. A few of these uses include assessment and prosecution support. There have been several attempts to define terms related to intrusion detection more clearly and precisely, but the name *intrusion detection* remains the common term for the broader set of capabilities. However, all the definitions are acceptable. You can focus attention on your specific requirements for detection, response, and escalation while matching them to a tool and capability set.

Having discussed definitions of intrusion and intrusion detection, let me now brief you on how an intrusion-detection system operates.

How Does an IDS Work?

Traditionally, to detect any intrusion attempt and to analyze data, administrators used to manually monitor logs generated by various security systems (such as firewalls). Nowadays, the process of monitoring resources, logging details about an intrusion attempt or an unusual pattern of using resources, and analyzing details are taken over by IDS. IDS also monitors CPU usage, disk I/O, memory, user activity, and the number of attempted logins. If the logs show a deviation from normal network usage, the IDS triggers an alarm.

How does IDS do that? IDS maintains a database of signature files that contain the known patterns of attacks. What is a signature? Every attack has its unique feature, pattern, and behavior. This is known as the *signature*. IDS recognizes an attack or intrusion by matching the signature of the attack by signature files in the database.

Several times, the IDS is also unable to detect an intrusion attempt or an attack, or it considers a normal activity as an intrusion attempt. This results in errors being generated. Errors can be classified as false-positive and false-negative.

A false-positive error is generated when the IDS considers a normal activity on the network as an intrusion attempt or a deviation, and then raises an alarm. If this type of alarm continues to occur, the administrator might start ignoring true alarms. This may result in actual intrusion attempts being missed.

A false-negative error occurs when the IDS ignores an intrusion attempt and considers it as normal behavior of the network system.

IDS and Firewalls

There is often confusion between the functions of IDS and firewalls. People generally misinterpret the functions of firewalls, which are actually the functions of an IDS. According to common understanding, firewalls recognize attacks and block them. However, this is not true.

Let me quickly recap the functionality of firewalls, and then compare the functionality of firewalls with IDS.

Firewalls operate by blocking everything and then programmatically allowing in only a few chosen items. In a perfect world, all the systems and networks would be locked down and secured, and a firewall would not be needed. The precise reason for having a firewall is to curb the security holes.

Therefore, when a firewall is installed, it first stops all communication. Then, the administrator adds rules that allow specific types of traffic to pass through and disallows other traffic. For instance, a firewall allowing access to the Internet blocks all UDP and ICMP datagram traffic, stops incoming TCP connections, but allows outgoing TCP connections. In other words, a firewall allows internal users of the organization to access the Internet; however, it rejects any external requests from the Internet to access the network.

A firewall is like a fence around your network that has a few gates allowing restricted entry. This fence has no capability to detect if somebody is trying to break in (such as somebody digging a hole underneath the fence) or if somebody coming through the gate is allowed entry. It simply restricts access to the designated points.

To summarize, a firewall is not a dynamic system that can sense an attack being performed.

In contrast, an IDS is a much more dynamic system. It has the capability of detecting and recognizing attacks against networks that firewalls are unable to see.

Consider the following example of intrusion. An organization employee receives an e-mail from another employee saying he has found a file that was missing for a long time. The employee opens the e-mail and clicks the executable attachment, which is zipped. The executable document has a Trojan horse installed in it. The Trojan horse then opens a connection to the hacker's computer. Now, the firewall installed on the network does not prevent the hacker from serving his attack software on a common port 80. This is because the firewall is programmed to disallow outbound connections through certain ports only. It considers any other outbound HTTP connection flowing out of the network to a Web server as just another connection.

If an intrusion-detection system would have been installed, it could have raised an alarm at any unusual activity on the network. For instance, in the preceding example in normal course, employees do not access the site with which the Trojan horse tries to open a connection. This is an unusual activity for the intrusion-detection system and, therefore, it raises an alarm.

 NOTE

The functionality defined in the preceding example is just one instance of the functionality of an intrusion-detection system. Each intrusion-detection system varies in the capability and functionality that it can provide.

IDS Techniques

To detect intrusive activities, an IDS can be based on one of the following two techniques:

- ◆ Anomaly-detection technique
- ◆ Misuse-detection technique

Anomaly-Detection Technique

The anomaly-detection technique is based on the assumption that all activities that do not match a set behavior pattern are anomalous activities. An anomaly is a behavior pattern that is not normal and is irregular. To differentiate anomalous activities from normal activities, the IDS identifies a normal activity profile on the network. If any activity does not match that profile, the IDS considers it an anomalous activity and thus raises an alarm.

An anomaly-based IDS operates by creating a baseline of normal activities on a network. This baseline is generally established on the statistics recorded from the behavior of I/O operations, CPU usage, memory, user activity, and number of attempted logins. An IDS monitors network activities by comparing the behavior of components on the network with the baseline generated. If even a slight deviation is observed (that is, deviation from the normal behavior defined on the baseline), an anomaly-based IDS raises an alarm.

Consider the following example. The CPU usage of a computer on a network has been 70 percent over the past month. However, on one particular day, its CPU usage is recorded as 100 percent. For the IDS, this is an unusual activity and, therefore, an alarm is raised (see Figure 9.1).

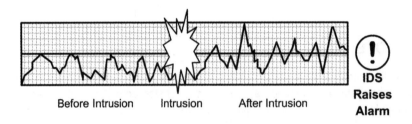

FIGURE 9.1 *Anomaly model of an IDS*

An anomaly-based IDS has a few disadvantages, however. One disadvantage is that *any* deviation from normal activity is treated as an intrusion. As a result, even a slight deviation raises an alarm, and most of the time it is false-positive. Another disadvantage is that this model does not have the capability to analyze the behavior pattern or identify the reason for an abnormal event.

Misuse-Detection Technique

The misuse-detection technique represents attacks in the form of a pattern or a signature. In this model, the IDS maintains a database of all the known signatures of attacks. An alarm is raised whenever the attack signature matches one that the IDS has in its database. The misuse-detection technique also has the capability to detect variations of the same attack (see Figure 9.2).

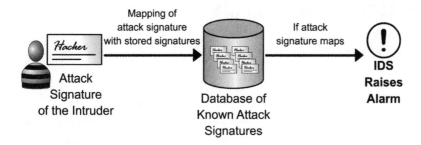

FIGURE 9.2 *Misuse model of an IDS*

The misuse model operates like antivirus software, which detects all virus attacks if it is updated regularly with the latest virus signature. Similarly, the misuse-based IDS model detects only those signatures that are already stored in the database.

In an IDS based on the misuse model, the false-positive alarm rate is nil. However, the drawback of this model is that the system is unable to detect any new types of attacks that have not been detected earlier.

Types of Intrusion-Detection Systems

Intrusion-detection systems based on an anomaly or misuse model can be classified as

◆ Network-based intrusion-detection systems

◆ Host-based intrusion-detection systems

◆ Hybrid intrusion-detection systems

These classifications are based on the manner in which each IDS is deployed on the network. Each IDS can be deployed outside the network, as a part of the network, or at both levels. The following sections will discuss each type of IDS separately. The discussion should give you insight on the architecture and the route of data (data packets or event logs) through each IDS type. It will also acquaint you with operational concepts and the benefits and issues attached to each IDS type.

However, before starting with the section, I would like you to get acquainted with certain terms that will be used quite often in our discussion.

Common Terms Related to IDS

The following terms are the components of any intrusion-detection system, whether it be network-based, host-based, or a hybrid system.

Command Console

The *command console* is the central authority that controls the entire IDS. It is usually a dedicated machine with tools for setting policy and dispensing alarms. The command console maintains contact with monitored machines and/or network sensors over an encrypted link.

A command console also performs the functions of an assessment manager, a target manager, and an alert manager. An IDS can have these functions installed in one console or deployed on separate components. Primarily, the assessment manager manages static configuration information, the target manager maintains connections with components on the network, and the alert manager collects and maintains alert data.

Mostly, vendors provide their own console with their product. However, now there is a trend of integrating the command console capabilities with network management systems, such as HP OpenView, and enterprise management systems, such as Tivoli.

Sensor

Sensors are software programs that can be installed on dedicated machines or network devices on mission-critical network segments. These are self-contained detection engines through which network data packets pass. The sensors' main role is to search network packets for patterns of misuse and, in case of deviation, report alarms to the central console on the network

Alert Notification

The *alert notification* component in an intrusion-detection system is responsible for contacting the security officer in case any deviation is noticed. They do so by sending onscreen alerts, audible alerts, paging, or e-mailing.

Response Subsystem

The *response subsystem*, as the name suggests, is responsible for taking action based on threats reported against the target systems. These subsystems can generate responses automatically or can also be initiated by the system operator. The most common responses generated by subsystems include reconfiguring a router or firewall and shutting down the target system.

Database

The *database* is the information storehouse for all the activities observed by the intrusion-detection system. The database includes both misuse and behavioral statistics. These statistics help to create a behavioral pattern of activities that can later be used to assess damage or investigate activities.

Network Tap

The *network tap* is a device or software program that congregates information from the network. It can be a software agent running on the sensor or hardware device, such as a router. Because the role of a network tap is to gather information from the network, it becomes a critical component in preventing packet loss in high-bandwidth networks.

Having discussed the terms, let me now begin with the network-based IDS.

A Network-Based IDS

A *network-based IDS* is used to monitor and analyze data packets that pass through the network. This type of IDS operates in contrast to a host-based IDS that evaluates data originating on computers (hosts), such as event log files. A network-based IDS is positioned to detect access attempts and various attacks that originate outside the network.

Most network-based attacks are aimed at exploiting operating system vulnerabilities, which can be subjugated through unauthorized access or logins, data or resource theft, password downloads, bandwidth thefts, packet flooding, malformed packets, denial-of-service, and distributed denial-of-service attacks. These types of attacks are only detectable by a network-based IDS. It is nearly impossible to detect these attacks by a host-based IDS. This is a key distinguishing factor between the two technologies.

Architecture of a Network-Based IDS

A network-based IDS consists of sensors deployed all over the network that report to the command console. A network-based IDS can be based on two architectures:

◆ Traditional sensor architecture
◆ Distributed network-node architecture

Traditional sensor-based architecture, also called a promiscuous-mode network IDS, aims at monitoring all segments of the network. In this case, the promiscuous-mode network sensors reside on a dedicated machine. Distributed network-node architecture monitors packets meant for a single destination computer. Unlike promiscuous mode, the distributed network-node IDS has a set of distributed agents deployed on mission-critical machines.

Traditional Sensor Architecture

A sensor in promiscuous mode is used to sniff packets off the network. Once off the network, data is fed into a detection engine to assess its sanctity. Detection engines are typically installed on the sensor machine itself, or they are separate components on the network. Taps are used in conjunction with sensors to take packets off the network, and they are distributed to the various mission-critical points. To understand how data packets travel through the traditional sensor architecture, study the following steps:

1. When one computer communicates with another computer, network packets are exchanged.
2. Packets are then sniffed from the network through a sensor that is placed on the network somewhere between the two communicating computers.
3. A sensor-detection engine is used to match predefined patterns with the current pattern of data packets. If the pattern matches, an alert is generated and forwarded to the central console.
4. Through the console, the security officer is notified through various methods, such as audible, visuals, pagers, e-mail, or SNMP.
5. A response is generated by the response subsystem automatically or as per the directions of the security officer.
6. The alert (containing details of misuse and behavioral patterns) is stored for later review, correlation, and assessment.

7. Reports are generated summarizing alert activity.

8. Data forensics are used for evaluating long-term trends. Few IDS also allow recording the original traffic so that the session can be replayed for reviewing later.

Figure 9.3 illustrates the traditional network intrusion-detection architecture.

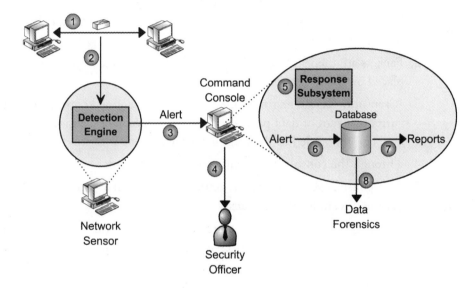

FIGURE 9.3 *The traditional network intrusion-detection architecture*

Distributed Network-Node Architecture

The promiscuous-mode network intrusion-detection systems resulted in data packets being lost on high-speed networks. As a solution to this, a distributed architecture for a network intrusion-detection system was suggested. This architecture has a sensor attached to every computer on the network. Each sensor is concerned only with packets that are coming to the target computer on which it is installed. The sensors then communicate with each other and the main console to collate and correlate alarms.

The network-node architecture has added confusion regarding the difference between the host- and network-based IDS. A network sensor running on a host does not make it a host-based sensor. Network packets going to and sniffed at a host are still a part of a network intrusion-detection system. The basic difference between network- and host-based intrusion detection is not the location of the sensor or mode of operation but the source of data. A network intrusion- detection system processes TCP/IP packets; whereas, the host-based intrusion-detection system processes event logs generated from an operating system and applications.

To understand how a data packet travels through the distributed network-node architecture, study the following steps:

1. When one computer communicates with another computer, network packets are exchanged.
2. Packets are then sniffed from the network through a sensor that is placed on the destination computer.
3. A sensor detection engine is used to match predefined patterns with the current pattern of data packets. If the pattern matches, an alert is generated and forwarded to the central console.
4. Through the console, the security officer is notified.
5. A response is generated by the response subsystem automatically or as per the directions of the security officer.
6. The alert (containing details of misuse and behavioral patterns) is stored for review, correlation, and assessment at a later stage.
7. Reports are generated summarizing alert activity.
8. Data forensics are used for evaluating long-term trends.

Figure 9.4 illustrates the distributed network-node architecture.

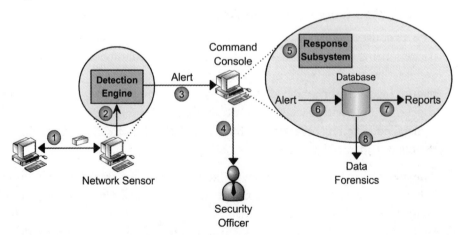

FIGURE 9.4 *The distributed network–node architecture*

Operational Mode of a Network-Based IDS

Operational mode implies the manner in which you plan to operate your intrusion-detection system based on your monitoring goals. A network-based intrusion-detection system can, in fact, be operated in a manner that requires few resources. The placement of a sensor in the network plays an important role in defining the operational mode of the IDS. A sensor placed outside the firewall recognizes source addresses attempting to connect your network. These sensors detect the attack attempts on the network from outside the organization. A sensor placed inside the firewall detects attacks that could successfully evade your firewall. These sensors are also helpful in detecting illicit traffic originating from within the network aimed at a source outside the firewall.

A network-based intrusion-detection system can use two operational modes, tip-off and surveillance.

Tip-Off

In the *tip-off* operational mode, the IDS is used to detect a network intrusion at the time it is being performed. This is the traditional approach of intrusion detection in which patterns are observed and any suspicious activity detected is tipped-off (warned) to the security officer stating that intrusion may be occurring. The tip-off operational mode is basically a warning indicating that the system is detecting abnormal activity that was previously undetected.

Surveillance

Surveillance, as the name suggests, scrutinizes the target machines closely for behavioral patterns of misuse. The main feature of surveillance is to observe the behavior of a small set of components on the network. Unlike the tip-off, surveillance takes place when intrusion has already occurred, been indicated, or is suspected.

Benefits of Network-Based Intrusion Detection

Network intrusion detection is a comprehensive security plan against threats originating outside the organization. If combined with host-based technologies, it can detect most threats and misuse activities. The following are the benefits of a network intrusion-detection system.

Deterrence

There are several laws governing computer crimes, which have made hacking from the outside a risky affair. The network intrusion-detection system can issue hackers a notice that their actions may lead to legal action. The deterrent value of an intrusion-detection system can be improved by taking measures, such as an e-mail from the system administrator requesting termination of the attack. The e-mail may also serve as a warning to other hackers, stating that entering an organization's network may lead to legal action. If the hacker is smart enough to spoof the source address, then deterrence may not be effective.

Detection

A network intrusion-detection system detects activities both deterministically and in a decision support context. Signatures serve as deterministic tools because they detect patterns and match them with predefined patterns. Expert operators perform effective analysis on these signatures by using a behavioral analysis tool. Statistical methods serve as decision support mechanisms. These methods may not be able to determine the attacker or the exact attack on the system; however, they provide enough information whose analysis, if done properly, can help in figuring out the problem.

Automated Response and Notification Mechanism

Most intrusion-detection systems can respond back when an intrusion is detected. The response can be automated or manual and can include both local and remote notification. Most commercial products provide the following options:

- **Pager**. The most commonly used medium because it notifies the administrator wherever he or she is. This is also a cost-effective method of notification.
- **SNMP trap**. Notifies the network operations center.
- **Onscreen**. Gives notification on the console. This method requires someone to be alert to a message being flashed on the console.
- **Audible**. This method is successful if the receiver is within hearing distance of the alarm.
- **E-mail**. This method is efficient only if the alarm is not critical and does not require immediate action; it can wait for a day or two.

The above means can be used to generate both automated and manual responses. Automated responses have inherent risks attached; therefore, they should be used conservatively. Most commercial products provide the following options for an automated response:

- ◆ **Reconfigure the router/firewall**. Reconfiguring the router or firewall includes rejecting or blocking the addresses that are attempting attacks on the network.

- ◆ **Counter attack**. Some IDS are configured to counter attack in case an intrusion is detected. However, such an option is not recommended because of the liabilities.

- ◆ **Close a connection**. Another automated response is to close the attacker's connection while he or she is midway through the attack.

Issues in Network-Based Intrusion Detection

As stated earlier, the traditional network-based technologies are facing problems, such as packet loss in high-speed networks, switched networks, and encryption. In addition, new technologies have come up that can detect sniffers deployed by an IDS to capture data. This makes the sniffing devices attack targets. The solution to a few of these problems is network-node technologies. However, they still pose a threat to the IDS system. Let us see how each one of these is an issue in a network-based IDS.

Packet Reassembly

Before transferring a message, TCP/IP breaks the message into small packets, which then need to be reassembled at the destination computer. Several network-based signatures make a search against the content of the complete message. Because the message is broken into small packets, packets may fudge the detection engine and prove harmful when they are reassembled at the destination computer. A solution to the packet reassembly problem is to use the network-node intrusion-detection system. Because each sensor is deployed on the target system, packets are reassembled on the system, and the signature is matched with the complete message on the target system.

High-Speed Networks

Network taps used in traditional technologies have been reported to drop packets on high-speed networks. If the network is heavy with traffic, the problem is intensified. For instance, a tap on a 10-MB TCP/IP network does not show any problem keeping pace with the data packets. However, a tap on a 100-MB network, which is heavily loaded, may drop many packets that are otherwise necessary for detection. Networks faster than 100 MB create more problems.

Packets being dropped on the network can provide a veil for hackers. Hackers intentionally flood the network to cause the system to drop packets. However, a network flooded with packets is an indication of a detectable behavior.

Network-node architecture is an effective solution to this problem. Sensors placed on target machines can easily handle data packets.

Sniffer-Detection Programs

Nowadays, programs are available that can detect sniffers deployed on the network. For instance, there is a program called AntiSniff that sends packets of various forms to each computer on the network. These packets use latency and other techniques to determine if a machine has a sniffer installed, for example in case of a network-based IDS, to find if there is a network tap installed.

Programs like AntiSniff promise to detect network taps used by an intrusion-detection system. When the network tap is detected, the attacker has enough valuable information to evade the detection system.

Switched Networks

Asynchronous Transfer Mode (ATM) networks, also called switched networks, transmit data in small fixed-length packets. These packets offer some key advantages over earlier packet technologies, such as packets that can be switched swiftly and efficiently in hardware. However, there is one disadvantage—switched networks do not support traditional network taps and, as a result, do not allow networks to be monitored.

Due to the varied benefits that ATM provides, the most widely used networks are based on ATM. In addition, many advantages of a network intrusion-detection system are directly related to the distributed network taps. This implies that the advantages of an intrusion-detection system are lost on ATM networks.

The capabilities of ATM networks can be achieved by bridging most ATM switches through an administration port. However, this solution also leads to the performance problem in the network. Also, the selection of intrusion-detection tools is significantly dependent on the type of switch to be bridged.

A work-around for ATM networks is, once again, a network-node architecture where each sensor is deployed on the system to be monitored. The sensor can then read the data packets from the stack at a layer where it can be converted into a protocol that the intrusion-detection system can understand.

Encryption

Most intrusion-detection systems depend on signature mapping for detecting intrusions. If the data packets being transmitted are encrypted, then the purpose of detection is defeated because it is not possible to match the patterns then.

However, encryption is becoming common at most levels of networks. For example, it is used in virtual private networks (VPN), secure shell (ssh), and secure socket layer (SSL). This implies that such trends would lead to intrusion-detection deployment in most networks.

Work-arounds are also available for circumventing encryption. However, none of these are a complete solution to these limitations.

The following are a few work-arounds for evading encryption while detecting intrusions:

- ◆ Placing the network sensors inside of the VPN device where data is decrypted. However, this solution also only works up to a point because most of the time data is encrypted to the session and application level. This implies there is no room left for intrusion-detection systems to pick up the data in decrypted form from the network.
- ◆ Saving the encryption keys on the router or any other network devices. However, this also does not work too well. Managing encryption keys to decrypt data is not a very easy job, and it is a major security threat.

A Host-Based IDS

A host-based intrusion-detection system uses data that originates on computers (hosts), such as application and operating system event logs, for analysis. This system is unlike a network-based intrusion-detection system that uses data originating on the network, such as TCP/IP packets.

Data sources on a host include operating system event logs (such as kernel, Basic Security Model, and security) and application logs (such as syslog, relational databases, and Web server). Host-based technologies are effective in detecting misuse inside a network because the data that is used for analysis resides on the machine of authenticated users. Event logs from these machines provide information about files accessed and programs used by the authenticated users. This closeness to authenticated users gives administrators an opportunity to analyze trends and perform data damage assessment. Because event logs are on authenticated machines and are protected, they can be presented in court as support documentation while prosecuting computer criminals.

The cost of deploying a host-based intrusion-detection system is higher than a traditional network intrusion system. However, costs are minimized if host-based monitoring is managed properly.

Attacks Detected by Host-Based Intrusion Detection

As stated earlier, attacks detected by host-based intrusion detection are those specific to the host. If you have been a security officer, you will be familiar with these attacks. Each of these attacks denotes a quantifiable loss and would not be possible to detect with a network-based intrusion-detection system. However, they can be detected by host-based intrusion-detection systems. Let me give you a few examples:

◆ **Misuse of privileged rights**. This occurs when a user is granted root, administrative, or some other privileges, and he or she uses them for illicit purposes. Host-based intrusion detection is successful in these situations because monitoring takes place on the same system where rights are granted.

◆ **Abuse of elevated privileges**. Administrators usually give elevated privileges to users for the purposes of installing special applications, speeding up the work process, or accessing a particular file on the network or a particular machine. Most security policies restrict root or administrator privileges, but situations often arise when administrators need to give these permissions. So the administrator elevates privileges for users, thinking that he will reduce them later. However, many times the administrator forgets to remove such privileges, which may lead to their misuse. In addition, the request for elevated privileges might have social engineering intentions to gain access to other resources on the systems and the network.

◆ **Utilization of accounts by ex-employees**. The moment an employee is not a part of the organization, most organizations have a policy of deleting or seizing his or her account. However, the deletion or seizure of an account may take some time, and that may mean doors are open for employees to exploit the situation to their advantage.

◆ **Creation of back-door accounts**. Situations may arise when an administrator creates accounts about which only he is aware. For instance, while installing a software package, for successful execution, the software may require the creation of an account. In normal course, to create an account, a formal request is received and, after creation of the account, proper documentation is done. But in the course of installing this software, the administrator, using his privileges, may create an account without following the formal procedure. Now, there may come a time when the administrator is asked to leave the organization, and thus privileges related to all his accounts are taken away from him. But, because there was no documentation for one account, the administrator has rights to an account about which the organization is not aware. This leaves an open hole.

Architecture of Host-Based Intrusion-Detection Systems

There are two architectures possible for host-based intrusion detection: centralized host-based architecture and distributed real-time architecture. These architectures are based on distributed target agents. Therefore, before I discuss these architectures, it is necessary to discuss target agents. This term will be repeated time and again in our discussion on the two architectures.

Target Agent

Target agents are small executable programs that run on target systems. A target agent allows the target system to perform privileged activities locally that might not otherwise be possible. A few of these activities include capturing TCP/IP packets from the network, processing event log data, centralizing raw event log data, checking file integrity, verifying system configuration, detecting misuse and forwarding alerts, and executing responses locally on the target.

Agents usually run in the background as demons in UNIX or services in Windows NT/2000. UNIX and Windows NT/2000 hosts have communication programs, such as application programming interfaces (APIs), for remote administration that provide capabilities of agents. These hosts alone can perform the functions of agents (though not very effectively, unless the agents' small executable programs are installed). However, once a host has an agent executable program installed, its ability to perform as an authenticated local user is not degraded. The end-user capabilities of a host with an agent installed are not affected if the agent is managed and configured properly.

It is possible to have either a single agent or multiple agents on one target system. A single agent may provide multiple capabilities, and at the same time, multiple agents might perform a single task on a host.

Having discussed target agents, let me now give you the details of the two architectures.

Centralized Host-Based Architecture

In the centralized host-based architecture, the raw event log data is sent to a central location (on a machine different from the target) before it is analyzed. To understand how event logs travel through this architecture, study the following steps:

1. When an action takes place in the system, such as a file being accessed or a program being executed such as Microsoft Word, an event record is created. The record is written to a file that is usually confined by the operating system trusted computing base.

2. The target agent sends the file to the centralized command console at predetermined time intervals and over a secure communication channel.

3. The detection engine (on the console) matches the behavior patterns of this file with predefined behavior patterns. The data records are matched in their raw format, which is the original format.

4. Simultaneously, an event log is created. This log acts as a data archive for the organization in case of legal prosecution.

5. If the pattern in the file matches the predefined pattern, an alert is generated and forwarded to various subsystems for notification, response, and storage.

6. The security officer is notified through audible or visual methods, such as a pager, e-mail, SNMP trap, or various other methods.

7. A response is generated. The response subsystem matches alerts to predefined responses or takes direction from the security officer to execute a response.

8. The alert is stored in a relational database. The database may also store statistical data in addition to alerts.

9. The raw data is transferred to a raw data archive. The backup of this archive is taken periodically to reduce the amount of disk space used.

10. Reports are generated, summarizing the alert and the event logs. The report also has details of the involved target system and the attack method.

11. Data forensics are used for evaluating long-term trends. Behavior is analyzed using both the stored data in the database and the raw event log archive.

Figure 9.5 illustrates the centralized host-based architecture.

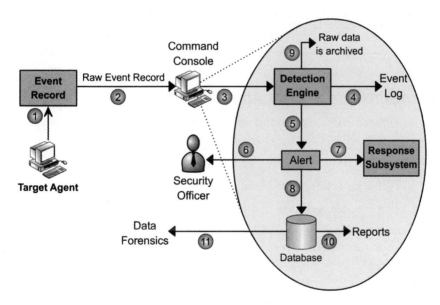

FIGURE 9.5 *The centralized host-based architecture*

Table 9.1 summarizes the advantages and disadvantages of a centralized detection architecture. This architecture puts little or no load on the target system, as all the analysis takes place in the console. There is no effect on the performance of the target system. In addition, this allows detection on a large scale because there are fewer performance concerns. Matching multiple host signatures is also possible because the detection engine residing on the centralized host has access to data from all targets. Lastly, the centralized raw data can be used for prosecution purposes and data forensics for evaluating long-term trends.

The disadvantages of this system include no real-time detection or responses generated. Network traffic is generated as the data is centralized on the console. If the bandwidth of the network is already used to its limit, the network may get clogged after a while.

Table 9.1 Advantages and Disadvantages of a Centralized Detection Architecture

Advantages	Disadvantages
No effect on performance of the target system	No real-time detection possible
Provides statistical behavioral information	No real-time response
Matching multiple host signatures is possible	Generates load on the network
Provides support of raw data archives in legal prosecution	

Distributed Real-Time Architecture

In a centralized host-based architecture, the raw event log data is analyzed on the target agent machine. To understand how event logs travel through this architecture, study the following steps:

1. When an action takes place in the system, an event record is generated.

2. The event is recorded in a file in real time and is processed on the target system only, as the detection engine is residing on the target system. (The processing of files is limited to target systems only in this architecture.)

3. The security officer is notified. The officer is informed through audible or visual methods, such as a pager, e-mail, SNMP trap, or various other methods.

4. A response is generated.

5. An alert is generated and sent to the central console.

6. The alert is stored in a relational database. Statistical behavioral data is not available in this architecture, as the data is limited to the single system.

7. Reports are generated summarizing the alert and event logs. The report also has details of the involved target system and the attack method.

8. Data forensics are used for evaluating long-term trends. Behavior is analyzed using only the stored data in the database because no raw data archive is generated.

Figure 9.6 illustrates the distributed real-time architecture.

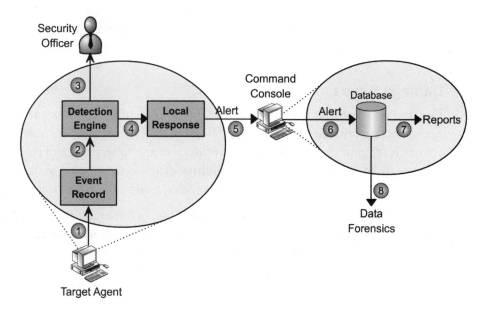

FIGURE 9.6 *The distributed real-time architecture*

Table 9.2 summarizes the advantages and disadvantages of distributed real-time architecture. The main advantage of this architecture is the real-time processing of data. The main disadvantage is that the performance of the host machine may be affected if the agent is not properly managed and deployed.

Table 9.2 Advantages and Disadvantages of Real-Time Architecture

Advantages	Disadvantages
Real-time alerts	Performance may be affected on the target system
Real-time response	No statistical behavioral information available
	Generates load on the network
	Matching multiple host signatures is not possible
	No support of raw data archives

Operational Modes of Host-Based Intrusion-Detection Systems

A host-based intrusion-detection system can be used in four operational modes: tip-off, surveillance, damage assessment, and compliance. The following section discusses two of these modes: damage assessment and compliance. I will not discuss the first two modes because they are the same as what we discussed in the network-based intrusion-detection system.

Damage Assessment

Damage assessment, as the name suggests, involves identifying the extent of damage caused after misuse has taken place. Because the event records are maintained, actions leading to the misuse, area of misuse, damage to security, and its residual effects can be derived easily. The capabilities of the system being used, such as reporting, raw data archiving, and data forensics, assist in damage assessment.

This mode of operation is particularly useful if human resources are scarce. Therefore, host-based systems may be exclusively used for damage assessment purposes if you want to reduce operational overhead.

Compliance

Compliance mode confirms that users are following security policies. Behavioral monitoring is used as a complementary tool to keep a check on users' activity. Compliance mode brings certain issues to the surface that otherwise may go undetected. For example, a user logging in at night and trying to access restricted files or the improper use of applications or processes.

Benefits of Host-Based Intrusion Detection

The benefits of host-based intrusion detection include misuse detection, deterrence, misuse anticipation, response mechanism, and damage assessment. I have already talked about these benefits in previous discussions, and they are not very different from network-based intrusion detection. Therefore, I will not discuss all the benefits again. However, there is one unique benefit that is not present in network-based intrusion detection but prevents misuse from inside a network, commonly known as *insider deterrence*.

Insider deterrence is similar to security provided by a video camera in a jewelry shop. The effect of deterrence is similar to the principle that people are more vigilant if they know they are being monitored. Insider deterrence is in fact one of the supreme benefits of host-based intrusion detection because it avoids misuse of resources, as employees are aware that they are being watched all the time.

An organization can augment the effect of deterrence in several ways. One of the methods is to publicize its existence. As when people put warnings on their lawn that the house is protected by a security alarm, in the same manner, organizations can put logon banners on employees' machines so that they are reminded they are being monitored continuously. This method would also eliminate the effect of monitoring every machine at every moment because employees will already be watchful. Another way to increase deterrence is to let people know that you are there. For example, in case of any misuse, send a warning so that the employee is aware someone is monitoring.

Another way of increasing deterrence is prosecution. Host-based intrusion detection provides proof of misuse by means of event log archives and statistical data. This evidence is generally enough to take legal action against the offender, in additon to probation and/or termination from the organization.

Continuous monitoring is obviously a viable security measure. In some organizations, such as sensitive government jobs, such security could be warranted. However, this type of continuous monitoring in an average organization may have a negative impact on employees (unlike other security measures that "run in the background," so to speak). Administrators who will potentially put these methods into action should remember that such "in your face" and borderline-accusatory methods could adversely affect employees (and possibly their performance) overall.

Issues in Host-Based Intrusion Detection

The benefits provided by a host-based intrusion-detection system are also accompanied by some costs. Most of these costs can be lessened with a fine system, a well-laid policy, and a carefully planned operational setup. However, in view of a host-based intrusion-detection system, considerations should be made in context of performance, deployment, and other compromise issues.

Performance

As you are already aware, host-based intrusion-detection systems are distributed mechanisms that process data originating from the host machine. Due to the architecture of host-based detection, host performance may be compromised. Performance degradation is something that cannot be avoided but is controllable through proper deployment, architecture choice, and policies.

A Windows NT workstation generates about 1 MB of event log data per day, a Windows NT server about 10 MB, a UNIX workstation about 8 MB, and a UNIX server about 20 MB. Now, let's assume that a relatively small network consists of 10 Windows NT servers, 5 UNIX servers, 200 Windows NT workstations, and 50 UNIX workstations. The total figure of data generated comes down to 800 MB of data per day. This amount of data is manageable if it is parsed, centralized, run through a detection system deployed on some other machine (probably the console itself), responded to when required, and archived on a regular basis.

Deployment and Maintenance

Deploying a host-based intrusion-detection system is difficult because the hosts are extensively distributed. Every target machine needs to be deployed with agents. The initial deployment and maintenance is a time-consuming job and, therefore, requires distributed deployment and a remote update mechanism.

Compromise

The very purpose of installing an intrusion-detection system can be defeated if a hacker gains access to the monitored target system and shuts down the agent. This would mean a compromise on the detection system.

Intrusion-detection systems are not very effective at detecting first-time misuse or intrusion activities. However, they are effective at identifying behaviors that have already been defined. A good system should be able to determine that an agent has been shut down. A log indicating a systematic pattern of shutdowns may signify that a set of systems are under attack.

Manipulating the Records of Agents

Hackers may gain access into agents to manipulate records on the system. They may insert records into the audit stream to indicate phony activity or remove records to erase an unauthorized activity. The best guard against such manipulations is to use trusted and protected event logs, for example, a binary kernel log. Syslog is not a very trusted data source; it is said that it can be spoofed easily.

We have looked at the benefits and issues of both network- and host-based systems. Therefore, before I close the discussion on the two systems, let me give a quick comparison.

Comparison of Network- and Host-Based Technologies

Table 9.3 compares network- and host-based intrusion-detection systems based on the benefits of each.

Table 9.3 Comparing Network- and Host-Based Technologies

Benefits	Network-Based	Host-Based
Deterrence	Weak deterrence for outsiders	Robust deterrence for insiders
Detection	Robust detection for outsiders	Robust detection for insiders
	Weak detection for insiders	Weak detection for outsiders
Response	Strong real-time response for outsiders	Strong real-time processing and response for insiders
Damage assessment	Weak damage assessment capabilities	Strong damage assessment capabilities
Prosecution support	Weak prosecution support	Strong prosecution support

Hybrid IDS

Both network- and host-based technologies are necessary for comprehensive detection. However, as discussed earlier, each one has its advantages and disadvantages that need to be considered against the requirements for the target environment. The best intrusion-detection system is one that provides the best features of the two systems. Hybrid systems include both network- and host-based features in a single management console.

Selecting the Right Intrusion-Detection System

There are a myriad of tools and techniques available for intrusion detection. However, the key to selecting an appropriate intrusion-detection system depends upon your environment-specific requirements and not relying on the industry hype. That is, the best system is one that best suits your needs. Following are steps that will help you assemble the latest information about vendors, evaluate the tools, and select the most appropriate solution:

1. Define your requirements
2. Perform research
3. Send a request to selected vendors for information
4. Establish selection criteria
5. Conduct an evaluation
6. Select a final vendor
7. Initiate a pilot project
8. Consult references
9. Send a request for a quote
10. Evaluate proposals and make a selection(s)

Defining Your Requirements

As already stated, while selecting any tool, your environment-specific needs should steer the selection process. Each intrusion-detection system has its unique features, and it is not necessary that these features fit the requirements of all organizations. Therefore, before even thinking of selecting a tool, the organization should be crystal clear about its requirements. In addition, you should also remember that the requirements should not be so rigid that if later you need new capabilities in the selected system it is not possible. Flexibility throughout the process will help the organization take advantage of new capabilities of the selected system that may arise during the information-gathering process.

While establishing requirements, another important thing to keep in mind is the wisdom check of the requirements set. It is quite possible that you've established requirements that are mutually exclusive and, therefore, are a failure. Consider the following example. An organization establishes the following two requirements:

◆ The system should monitor the systems in real time.

◆ The system should not cause any performance degradation on mission-critical systems.

In the previous sections, we have already established that these are mutually exclusive capabilities that a system cannot posses. Looking for such capabilities is not realistic.

Performing Research

After having a broad idea of your requirements, the acquisition process should start by learning as much as possible about intrusion-detection systems. Research is an important mechanism that will help you understand intrusion-detection technologies and formulate such requirements. Becoming aware of the capabilities of the technology selected, testing those expected capabilities will be easier in the later stages of acquisition process.

While conducting research, you need to cast as broad a net as possible. You need to make yourself acquainted with various vendor companies and tools as well as third-party information. The following are the three types of information you should look for while researching:

◆ **Vendor information**. This is probably the most important information you'll gather while selecting an intrusion-detection system. However, you need to be careful that the information you collect is from known and authenticated magazine articles and reviews. Vendors, in a bid to sell their product, may say several things that are probably not true, so you need to be watchful and thoughtful. When you purchase from a vendor, you are creating a relationship that is long-term. It is not just a one-time affair that will end after the purchase is complete. There are several other services that need to be considered after the purchase, such as maintenance of the system. Therefore, you need to know your vendor well before making your selection and that it will be able to provide all the after-sales services.

◆ **Third-party information**. Third-party vendors are vendors that operate independently. You should also consider and gather information about third-party vendors because they may provide features that other vendors don't.

◆ **Other research information**. Research communities also provide information about security and security tools, such as intrusion-detection systems and firewalls. While reading such articles, you need to always keep intrusion-detection research information in perspective.

Research Mechanisms

The usual approach to online research is to type the words **intrusion detection** in one of your favorite search engines. However, this is the poor way to make a search, as it may return large amounts of varied information. While making a search, it is best to look for key words and capabilities that match your requirements. In addition, there are several newsgroups, mail lists, consortiums, and independent Web sites that provide information about intrusion detection. The following links may help you get more details:

◆ **Michael Sobirey's Intrusion Detection Systems Page (http://www-rnks.informatik.tu-cottbus.de/~sobirey/ids.html)**. This page lists all intrusion-detection systems ever invented. However, it does not provide details about them.

◆ **ICSA.net (http://www.icsa.net/services/consortis/intrusion/)**. ICSA runs the intrusion-detection consortium, and their site provides valuable information about intrusion-detection systems.

◆ **SANS site (http://www.sans.org)**. The SANS site provides information on security as well as details on intrusion detection.

Requesting Specific Information

Having gathered information from research, the next step is to gather vendor-specific information regarding your requirements and assumptions. You do this by sending a request to selected vendors asking for more information about them. This is usually the first formal communication between vendors and the organization, which gives vendors an opportunity to have a quick look at your requirements. While sending requests, it is important to give vendors complete details about your requirements (as much as you understand your needs) and encourage them to write a response addressing your needs.

Establishing Selection Criteria

After you receive details from selected vendors, you need to set selection criteria, which help to rate proposed systems and steer your selection decision. You need to keep the selection criteria precise, clearly defined, and objective so that they give a clear picture of system features and justifty the selection to upper management.

While setting the selection criteria, you can work on the following suggestions.

Translating Requirements into Specific Criteria

The requirements specified in the requests sent to vendors should be formulated into specific criteria so that they can be used to evaluate proposed systems. In addition, features presented by vendors might not match your environment-specific requirements. Therefore, you need to properly and carefully map those features to your requirements before you begin selection. While mapping, you may need to drop, modify, or combine your requirements to formulate distinct criteria.

Weighting the Criteria

All criteria may not hold equal importance. Therefore, you should weight each criterion and assign priorities that reflect the relative importance of each. The weighting range established should give sufficient space for more important criteria to reflect the total score appropriately. A good practice is to have a range, which is as wide as your criteria list. For instance, if you have 10 criteria, it would mean a range of 1–10. If your criteria are really good, you can prioritize them from top to bottom and use the priorities as weights.

Rating the Proposed Systems

Having weighed the criteria, the next step should be to assign them score values. These values should be direct indicators of how well a tool meets the requirements. Scores assigned may carry some subjective judgments. Therefore, it is important that the evaluators also write down their justifications for the scores assigned.

Conducting an Evaluation

The evaluation process should continue until the acquisition process is complete. After criteria have been established and weights are assigned, you should prepare an evaluation sheet for each product. Other administrators should also fill out this evaluation sheet.

In addition, during the evaluation process, you should once again share your assumptions regarding products with vendors so that there is no misunderstanding between the two parties.

Selecting a Final Vendor

Because the evaluation process with respect to your requirements and details sent by the vendors is complete, it is now time for sending those vendors requests for proposals. I am sure you must be wondering what the difference is between asking for information and a request for proposal. The main difference between them is that a request for proposal is more focused on the specific requirements identified in the previous evaluations. The request for proposal should detail your requirements with clarity so that vendors can be specific in their responses.

Requirements of an organization may not meet the capabilities offered by existing technologies. Therefore, an organization should also look at what products the vendor proposes for the future. The proposal sent by vendors is a chance for them to explain their product in totality and any future technology that may meet the organization's needs.

Initiating a Pilot Project

After selecting a vendor, the organization should initiate a pilot project to test the capabilities of the proposed tool in the organization's environment. This will not only ensure that the tool acquired is appropriate but also give the organization an opportunity to familiarize itself with the tool. This gives the organization a chance to confirm the assumptions it has made, verify the claims made by vendor, and test the performance of the tool itself.

The pilot project can be initiated from the first phase of the acquisition process and can end with the last stage of the acquisition process. In the initial stages, the pilot project can be used to learn more about the product's tools and also to formulate the organization's requirements. In the last stages of the process, the product should be tested in the production environment or the environment that closely matches such an environment in the organization. The product should be tested in the production environment because only then will you know if the product is really detecting intrusions taking place in your system.

Consulting References

After evaluating the pros and cons of the selected product and before finally sending a request for quotation from the vendor, the organization should consult other references. The organization should ask the vendor for other organizations that are using its product in a similar environment. However, references may not want to disclose their identity. In such cases, the vendor may need to mediate between the organization and the reference. It is quite possible that the organization finds a site that gives information about the product and where it is being used. The organization should find a lead to such information and try to find out more about how it is being implemented in other organizations.

While conversing with references about the product, it is necessary to be watchful of the type of questions being asked. There is often a tendency to ask open-ended questions, and one should avoid asking subjective questions. Also, if the reference's requirements for deploying the product do not match the organization's requirements, the probing may not give a conclusion that is appropriate. It is preferable to ask the following type of questions of the references:

 ◆ "Which products are you using in your organization?"
 ◆ "Why did you select these products?"
 ◆ "Did you evaluate other vendors/products?"
 ◆ "What problems did you face during deployment of the product?"
 ◆ "What were your expectations of the product and the vendor?"

The following are subjective questions that you should avoid asking:

 ◆ "What do you think about the vendor and their product?"
 ◆ "Do you like the product and the vendor?"

Asking such questions is considered inappropriate because they are based on the respondent's mindset, and answers to such questions can defeat the purpose of the conversation.

Honeypot: A Tool Complementing IDS

A *honeypot* is another tool used for detecting intrusion attempts. It is an additional level of security over an intrusion-detection system. A honeypot, as the name suggest, is a tool that operates on a deception principle. Its main purpose is to fool an intruder by simulating a vulnerable computer on a network. The system on which it is installed contains data enticing enough for an intruder to attack. However, it is not critical to the organization.

Honeypots are used by intrusion-detection systems to detect different intrusion mechanisms that hackers deploy to compromise a system. For instance, a system is deliberately installed with a honeypot and applications that may attract an intruder to attack the system. When the intruder attacks, his activities are recorded in the log files. Later, these log files are audited, and attack signatures are identified. These signatures are stored in a database and used by the intrusion-detection system to detect similar attacks that may happen in future.

There are two types of honeypots:

◆ Production honeypots

◆ Research honeypots

Production Honeypots

Production honeypots strengthen an organization's security system. Their main aim is not to prevent intrusion but to act as a support system to other security systems.

Production honeypots provide support by detecting intrusions that go undetected by an intrusion-detection system. But how do they detect intrusions that are missed by other security systems? Many times, systems on which intrusion-detection systems are installed generate large amounts of data, which makes it difficult for an IDS to detect intrusion and, as a result, false-negative errors occur. Now, here comes the role of the honeypots. Organizations deploy production honeypots on separate servers on the network that have no extra resource or applications installed on them. Their main role is to detect intrusions that may occur from outside the network. Because no extra applications are installed, the server generates event logs of only those activities that are occurring from outside the organization. It is also easy to analyze such data because there is no need to separate normal network usage log data from the log data that is generated by intrusive activities. In this manner, any intrusive activity is easily detectable by production honeypots.

Research Honeypots

A *research honeypot*, as its name suggests, is used for research purposes. The main aim of deploying a research honeypot is to study and analyze the log patterns of intrusions that have already taken place. That is, they are used to determine threats that organizations have already faced so that such attacks do not go undetected in the future. They operate by studying intrusion tolls, techniques, and patterns.

While using honeypots as a research tool, the intruder is allowed to continue the intrusion even after it has been detected. The intruder's attack patterns are monitored and, accordingly, new policies are formulated to protect other computers from such attacks in the future. However, using honeypots for research is not a safe activity because, once an intruder has access to a honeypot, the complete network of the organization is exposed.

Using Honeypots

A honeypot can be used as a port monitor, a deception system, a multi-protocol deception system, and a full system:

- ◆ **Port monitor**. This is a deception program that creates a trap for an intruder by letting him establish port connections and then drop half open port scan attempts.
- ◆ **Deception system**. Honeypots used as deception systems are smarter than honeypots used as port monitors. This is because a deception system not only allows an intruder to connect to a system but also simulates an environment where an intruder can interact with the system.
- ◆ **Multi-protocol deception system**. This system contains several protocols that simulate environments of different operating systems. The objective is to create environments that seem tempting enough for an intruder to attack. When an intruder attacks the deception system, it responds based on the type of attack and in a manner in which the simulated operating system should behave. For example, a honeypot installed on a Windows NT operating system also has the capability to simulate a UNIX environment. When an intruder sends a message for all computers that have a UNIX operating system, the honeypot responds just as any other vulnerable UNIX system would have responded. This way the attack patterns used by the intruder are known. In addition, the intruder can also be tracked.

◆ **Full system**. A full system is an IDS working with a honeypot. This implies that this system not only acts as a honeypot, but it also sends alerts when an intruder attack is detected.

Advantages of Honeypots

The following are the advantages of honeypots:

◆ **A better detection rate**. The main advantage is that all traffic to a honeypot system is from outside the network and is, therefore, considered as an intrusion. Because there is not much traffic on the system, the chances of missing out on intrusion attempts are bleak and, therefore, there are no false-positive or false-negative errors.

◆ **Misleads the intruders**. A honeypot is deployed at vulnerable points on the network to tempt intruders to attack the systems. Intruders, thinking that it's an opportunity to break into a network, get trapped during the intrusion attempt.

Disadvantages of Honeypots

The following are the disadvantages of honeypots:

◆ **Extra cost**. Like any other security system on a network, honeypots also need to be monitored on a regular basis. This implies that organizations incur extra costs in terms of the resources required for monitoring honeypots and their maintenance. In addition, if the intruder does not attack the resources on a honeypot system then it remains idle and, therefore, proves a futile effort for the organization.

◆ **System exposure**. Once an intruder gains entry into a honeypot system, not only the system but also the network of the organization is completely exposed. An intruder can use the compromised honeypot and the network to launch attacks on other organizations' networks. This may result in legal action because the attacked organization will trace the attack back to the original organization rather than the original intruder, who is using the compromised honeypots as intruders.

Summary

This chapter was a discussion on how to secure a network from attacks that may go undetected, even after security technologies are installed on the network. The chapter began by defining an intrusion-detection system. Next, it clarified confusion related to the need for intrusion-detection systems. Then, the chapter discussed the models on which intrusion-detection systems are based. The next section of the chapter identified the types of intrusion-detection systems available. It covered, in detail, the architecture and working of network-based, host-based, and hybrid intrusion-detection systems. The chapter also discussed various tips to keep in mind while selecting an intrusion-detection system. Finally, the last section of the chapter discussed honeypots, a tool complementing the IDS.

Check Your Understanding

Multiple Choice Questions

1. Consider the following statement:

   An IDS is used to detect network intrusion at the time it is being performed.

   Identify the operational mode and the type of IDS.

   a. Tip-off

   b. Surveillance

   c. Damage assessment

   d. Compliance

2. In case of a network-based intrusion-detection system, which one of the following is used to sniff information from the network?

   a. Command console

   b. Sensor

   c. Network tap

   d. Response subsystem

3. Consider the following two statements:

Statement A: The network-based intrusion-detection system processes TCP/IP packets.

Statement B: The host-based intrusion-detection system processes event logs generated from operating systems and applications.

Which one is TRUE about the statements written above?

a. Statement A is TRUE but statement B is FALSE.

b. Statement B is TRUE but statement A is FALSE.

c. Both the statements are TRUE.

d. Both the statements are FALSE.

4 State whether the following statement is TRUE or FALSE:

The misuse-detection technique operates by comparing the baseline status of activities before and after the intrusion has occurred.

5 Consider the following situation and identify the type of detection architecture being used:

A sensor is used to sniff packets off the network. Once off the network, data is fed into a detection engine to assess its sanctity. If predefined patterns match the pattern of the data packets, an alert is generated and forwarded to the central console. Through the central console, the security officer is notified. In addition, a response is generated and the alert information is stored in a database.

a. Traditional sensor architecture

b. Distributed network-node architecture

c. Centralized host-based architecture

d. Distributed real-time architecture

Short Questions

1. In the network-node architecture, the network sensor is installed on the host computer only. Then, what is the difference between network-node architecture and host-based architecture?

2. Briefly explain the two intrusion-detection techniques, anomaly and misuse detection?

3. How do production honeypots provide support to intrusion-detection systems?

4. Briefly list the steps involved in event logs traveling through a host-based architecture.

5. Briefly explain the process of data packets traveling through a distributed network-node architecture.

Answers

Multiple Choice Answers

1. a. In the tip-off operational mode of the network-based IDS, the detection of network intrusion is done at the time when the intrusion is being performed.

2. c.

3. c

4. FALSE. The misuse-detection technique does not operate by comparing the baseline of activities. Rather, it operates by matching attack signatures with the signatures stored in a database in the IDS.

5. a.

Short Answers

1. The basic difference between network- and host-based intrusion-detection is that network intrusion-detection systems process TCP/IP packets, whereas host-based intrusion detection processes event logs generated from operating systems and applications.

2. The anomaly-detection technique creates a baseline of normal activities on a network. This baseline is generally established on the basis of the statistics recorded from the behavior of I/O operations, CPU usage, memory, user activity, and number of attempted logins. The IDS monitors activities on the network by comparing the behavior of components on the network with the baseline generated. If even a slight deviation is observed (that is, deviation from the normal behavior defined on the baseline), an anomaly-based IDS raises an alarm.

The misuse-detection technique represents attacks in the form of a pattern or signature. In this model, the IDS maintains a database of all the known signatures of attacks. An alarm is raised whenever the attack signature matches the one that the IDS has in its database.

3. Production honeypots provide support by detecting intrusions that go undetected by an intrusion-detection system. Many times, systems on which intrusion-detection systems are installed generate large amounts of data, which makes it difficult for an IDS to detect intrusion and, as a result, false-negative errors occur. Now, here comes the role of the honeypots. Organizations deploy production honeypots on separate servers on the network that have no extra resource or applications installed on them. Their main role is to detect intrusions that may occur from outside the network. Because no extra applications are installed, the server generates event logs of only those activities that are occurring from outside the organization. It is also easy to analyze such data because there is no need to separate normal network usage log data from the log data that is generated by intrusive activities. In this manner, any intrusive activity is easily detectable by production honeypots.

4. The following are the steps involved in event logs traveling through a host-based architecture:

   1. When an action takes place in the system, such as a file being accessed or a program being executed such as Microsoft Word, an event record is created. The record is written to a file that is usually confined by the operating system trusted computing base.

   2. The target agent sends the file to the centralized command console at predetermined time intervals and over a secure communication channel.

   3. The detection engine (on the console), matches the behavior patterns of this file with predefined behavior patterns. The data records are matched in their raw format, which is the original format.

   4. Simultaneously, an event log is created. This log acts as a data archive for the organization in case of legal prosecution.

   5. If the pattern in the file matches the predefined pattern, an alert is generated and forwarded to various subsystems for notification, response, and storage.

6. The security officer is notified through audible or visual methods, such as a pager, e-mail, SNMP trap, or various other methods.

7. A response is generated. The response subsystem matches alerts to predefined responses or takes direction from the security officer to execute a response.

8. The alert is stored in a relational database. The database may also store statistical data in addition to alerts.

9. The raw data is transferred to a raw data archive. The backup of this archive is taken periodically to reduce the amount of disk space used.

10. Reports are generated, summarizing the alert and the event logs. The report also has details of the involved target system and the attack method.

11. Data forensics are used for evaluating long-term trends. Behavior is analyzed using both the stored data in the database and the raw event log archive.

5. The following steps explain the process of data packets traveling through the distributed network-node architecture:

1. When one computer communicates with another computer, network packets are exchanged.

2. Packets are then sniffed from the network through a sensor that is placed on the destination computer.

3. A sensor-detection engine is used to match predefined patterns with the current pattern of data packets. If the pattern matches, an alert is generated and forwarded to the central console.

4. Through the console, the security officer is notified.

5. A response is generated by the response subsystem automatically or as per the directions of the security officer.

6. The alert (containing details of misuse and behavioral patterns) is stored for review, correlation, and assessment at a later stage.

7. Reports are generated summarizing alert activity.

Chapter 10

*Disaster Recovery
and Backups*

In the previous chapters, I have discussed the security aspects of networks and the measures that assist in maintaining confidentiality and data integrity. Implementations of these security measures help in strengthening networks by preventing unauthorized access and data pilferages. However, despite implementation of all possible security measures, it is impossible to make network security totally infallible. Every now and then, you hear of sites being hacked or bank data being accessed and manipulated, and all this happens despite implementation of security measures. Let me check myself. Why talk of networks only. Take any situation in life, be it a party, a conference, an examination. Can anyone guarantee 100 percent success of these events? No, because there is always a possibility of something or the other going wrong.

Let me take an example of an unprecedented adversity or an uncalled for disaster. I was invited to a party the other day, and it seemed like the party was heading for disaster right from the start. First, Jenny (the hostess) had invited people in a hurry by word of mouth. What happened was that there was no count of the number of invitees. That's disaster number one. This led to chaos—space shortage, food shortage, beverage shortage—and to put it in a nutshell, Jenny's party was the ultimate disaster.

Despite all precautionary measures, networks do remain vulnerable to threats of various kinds as discussed in Chapter 1, "Security: An Overview" and Chapter 2, "Common Threats on the Web." This chapter discusses the techniques adopted for identifying and countering loss of data due to threats and disruptions. The chapter begins by discussing disaster scenarios and the need for recovery. Next, the chapter identifies the planning methods implemented to counter disasters. Then it covers, in detail, the RAID and backup technologies that are used to recover lost data.

Defining a Disaster

Businesses all over the world depend heavily on data that contains all organizational information. In the context of networks, disasters are catastrophes that lead to destruction or corruption of valuable data, causing losses and disruption of business operations. Disasters occur because no system or network can be completely shielded from all possible threats. Therefore, disasters have to be countered with advance preparedness to contain possible damage and to effect quick recovery. This is done by using techniques for strengthening the infrastructure and providing for alternative methods for recovering the lost data.

The September 11 strikes caused extensive damage to both property and lives. The loss to organizational data was enormous because the Twin Towers housed numerous business enterprises. Telecom cables went down leaving 9,000 to 14,000 small or mid-size businesses without phones and/or dial-up Internet service. Companies such as SunGard Business Continuity Services and Comdisco supported 22 to 90 disaster declarations, while IBM Global Services worked on recovery efforts for more than 1,200 customers. The disaster recovery plans of most organizations were thereby put to the test over the next few months. With the implementation of disaster recovery strategies, lost data was recovered and most of the organizations were back into business. All this was possible simply because each of these businesses had planned for disasters and had their recovery plans in place.

Disaster Recovery Planning

The disaster recovery plan can be looked at as a roadmap to recover and resume key services in an organization in the event of a disaster. In our context, it is basically a comprehensive set of steps that are to be executed in order to recover lost data. Let me cite an example to highlight the importance of disaster recovery planning. During presentations to clients, don't you always carry extra copies of the reference documents? You probably also carry a backup of the presentation in case of unforeseen situations that may hamper the slide show.

Before drawing up a disaster recovery plan, you need to list its objectives. Some of these objectives could be

- ◆ Ensuring the safety of organizational information and records
- ◆ Availability of materials and equipment required for the recovery of organizational information and records
- ◆ Advance preparation for recovery in case of natural catastrophe
- ◆ Continuity of business in the event of a disaster
- ◆ Reducing effort and complexities of the recovery process
- ◆ Coordination of recovery tasks

The objectives listed above express the intent of the disaster recovery plan. Many more such objectives can be added to the list based on the needs and nature of the organization. What should be borne in mind is that the plan must emphasize procedures and steps to be executed for faster and better recovery of lost data as well as restore and restart processes that are stalled due to the disaster. The planning for disaster recovery begins by identifying possible disaster situations and assessing their impact on business activities, also called business impact analysis. Business impact analysis includes visualizing the following scenarios and their impacts:

◆ **Identifying critical business activities**. An organization needs to continue some critical activities regardless of disasters. Critical activities are those that keep the organization operational, albeit at a lower level, after a disaster has struck. They are also the core activities that help to resume many other dependent activities. Disrupted critical business activities results in the disruption of all associated activities. It is important that critical business activities are conscientiously identified while planning for disasters.

◆ **Identifying the resources required to support critical business activities**. A number of resources are required to support the resumption and sustenance of critical business activities in the event of a disaster. These types of resources include skilled personnel, hardware and software applications, documentation, communication links, and essential support services such as an uninterrupted power supply.

◆ **Identifying possible disaster situations**. Bracing an organization to withstand disasters calls for anticipating potential disaster scenarios. Disasters can strike in the form of natural calamities (fire, earthquakes, and floods), hardware and software failures, hacking and virus attacks, acts of terrorism, or disruptions due to power and processing failures.

◆ **Identifying the controls currently in place**. A control is a mechanism used as a safeguard or countermeasure to reduce the vulnerability of the systems in an organization. An organization is, by default, accessible to controls that are designed to overcome eventualities resulting from disasters. For example, hardware can be secured by using controls in the form of bar code identification equipment, authorized access to hardware, or by implementing and training employees for emergency shutdowns. Similarly, software can be secured by prohibiting unauthorized use, preventing unauthorized modifications, or using virus detection software at regular intervals.

Elements of a Disaster Recovery Plan

The contents of a disaster recovery plan vary from one organization to another, but all disaster recovery plans consist of the following elements:

- ◆ **Executive summary.** This is a synopsis of the intent and purpose of the disaster recovery plan for a particular organization and defines its disaster management policy. This, in turn, details the roles and responsibilities of disaster recovery personnel and also specifies the procedures that are to be implemented for the recovery and resumption of critical business activities. In short, the executive summary includes organizational dos and don'ts to be put into operation in the face of a disaster.

- ◆ **Disaster recovery procedures.** These consist of the processes and steps to be implemented in response to a disaster. These procedures include actions to assess a disaster situation, measures undertaken to restore operations, and specific operations such as system shutdowns, evacuations, and warnings to be implemented when a disaster strikes.

 NOTE

Recovery strategies and procedures are discussed in detail in the next section of this chapter.

- ◆ **Support documents.** These include information such as the list of equipment, supplies, and services needed for restoration and recovery, roles and responsibilities of disaster recovery personnel, emergency telephone numbers, and building plans detailing exits, escape routes, and placement of fire extinguishers. In addition, all agreements with subcontractors, associate companies, and government agencies are also included in these documents.

The real test of a recovery plan begins only after the disaster strikes that leads to system disruptions and data loss. The first action expected after a disaster is damage assessment followed by implementation of salvaging procedures to restore critical business activities. The recovery strategies adopted by organizations that rely heavily on computer and network data include the use of alternate recovery sites, implementation of the techniques of RAID, and backup.

Recovery Strategies

Recovery strategies are the plans and procedures implemented by an organization to recover and restore critical business activities. Recovery strategies should be simple, efficient, and serve the purpose of the recovery procedures. The following are some characteristics to be considered when selecting a recovery strategy. Recovery strategies should be

- ◆ **In accordance with the recovery objectives**. Disaster recovery strategies should meet the requirements specified in the recovery objectives. The objectives of the disaster recovery plan, as you know, vary from organization to organization. This implies that recovery strategies will also differ according to each organization's recovery plan objectives.

- ◆ **Flexible**. Disaster recovery strategies should be flexible in order to incorporate future additions corresponding to the growth of the organization and its resources.

- ◆ **Well-planned**. Disaster recovery strategies should be designed to include all available resources and technologies needed to respond and recover from possible disasters.

- ◆ **Comprehensive**. Disaster recovery strategies should attempt to resolve major types of disasters likely to effect an organization as well as the minor ones.

- ◆ **Cost-effective**. The cost of recovery, as always, is a major consideration for the selection of disaster recovery strategies. The one-time cost of recovery support equipment and ongoing costs for the maintenance of alternate sites should be considered. Obviously, the strategy selected would be the one that facilitates implementation of recovery procedures at minimum cost.

The recovery strategies that I'll discuss in this chapter are the procedures of Redundant Array of Independent Disks (RAID), and backing up system data and files. These two procedures are used to maintain duplicate copies of the system data and files that can be recovered in the event of a disaster.

RAID Technology

RAID technology provides mechanisms for online storage of data in computers. It provides a reliable mechanism to make data available from various types of computers, ranging from personal computers to supercomputers. In the late 1980s, Patterson, Gibson, and Katz of the University of California at Berkeley conceptualized the Redundant Array of Inexpensive Disks (RAID) as a revolutionary mechanism for improved availability and serviceability of data. Thereafter, the RAID Advisory Board substituted the term "inexpensive" with "independent" and thereby introduced a disk subsystem composed of multiple, independent, and high-performance disk drives for the storage of online data.

Although RAID consists of multiple disk drives of similar capacity, the entire disk subsystem seems like a singular reliable and high-speed logical disk drive. RAID technology was not developed for data security alone; it is also a means of ensuring data availability and accessibility at all times. As a result, implementation of this technology not only makes data more secure but also promises constant availability of reliable data.

The multiple disks of the RAID subsystem together are known as an *array*. A typical RAID subsystem consists of two to eight disk drives that can cope with problems as adverse as bad sectors or entire disk failures. Even more surprising is that RAID handles all these problems without the user being made aware of the adverse situation resulting from such failures. Therefore, you could be working and wouldn't even notice or know about the recovery tasks undertaken by RAID. A RAID subsystem is supported by strong features that prevent loss of data in the face of disasters. The characteristic features of RAID are

- The same data is stored redundantly on the multiple disks of the subsystem. As a result, the failure of a single disk does not hamper the process of data retrieval nor does it make the data completely inaccessible. The RAID subsystem can therefore be referred to as a highly fault-tolerant and reliable mechanism for the availability and security of data.

- A failed disk of the subsystem can be replaced while the array is operational. As a result, the accessibility and availability of data is further increased.

- Hard disk partitions can be created in a RAID subsystem that is larger than the largest physical disk available in the market.

- The rate of data transfer in RAID is higher due to the parallel accessibility of data across the multiple disks.

The initial structure of a RAID subsystem consisted of multiple disks of similar capacities. However, the advancements in disk technology have given rise to a RAID subsystem with multiple disks of dissimilar capacity. The disadvantage of such a subsystem is that the disk with the smallest capacity is assumed to have the default capacity of all the other disks. As a result, if a RAID subsystem was to include six 9 GB disks, one 2 GB disk, and one 1 GB disk, the default capacity of all the disks would be evaluated to 1 GB, negating the higher capacity of the other seven disks.

RAID is implemented at eight common levels, each of which provides unique benefits. These include level 0, level 1, level 2, level 3, level 4, level 5, level 6, and level 10. It is important to note that the level of RAID has no connection whatsoever with the superiority in performance. In fact, each level of raid has its own set of advantages and disadvantages. The RAID levels need to be studied in depth so that an appropriate level of RAID is implemented to suit an organization's requirements.

RAID Level 0

RAID level 0 does not implement redundancy while storing data on the disks. As a result, the term *RAID level 0* comes across as a misnomer, justified only by the fact that this level provides a mechanism for data storage on the multiple disks of a RAID subsystem. RAID level 0 uses the method of *spanning* or *data stripping* that splits the data of a file across the multiple disk drives of the RAID array. Although RAID level 0 is a nonredundant disk array, it provides a high I/O performance and can be implemented at a low cost. The high performance of this level is attributable to the following reasons:

◆ The nonredundant storage of data does not require replications or updates of the changed data at multiple locations.

◆ The process of spanning splits the contents of a single file across multiple disks of an array. As a result, the data can be read from or written to all the disks of the array in parallel.

Despite its high performance and low-cost implementation, RAID level 0 is the least reliable and fault-tolerant as compared to the other levels. This is because of the nonredundant feature that leads to data loss in the event of the failure of a single disk in the array. Therefore, Raid level 0 is best suited for environments that depend heavily on the performance and capacity of the storage disks rather than on reliability and constant accessibility of data. A likely environment for the implementation of RAID level 0 is that of supercomputing, where the performance spotlight is on maximized rate of data transfers and file sizes.

NOTE

The initial motive of RAID was to have higher data-transfer rates on large data accesses and higher input-output rates on small data access. In addition, RAID level 0 is still used in supercomputers.

RAID Level 1

As the oldest and the most commonly implemented level of RAID, level 1, when compared to all the other levels, offers a simple, reliable, and maximized mode to make data available and accessible at all times. RAID level 1 uses the *mirroring* or *shadowing* method to duplicate the data in one or more disks of the array. As a result, data shadowing or replication is performed on the primary disk and simultaneously on one or more redundant disks. Therefore, at any given time, there are always two or more copies of the same data available to the user. The high performance of RAID level 1 is attributable to the following reasons:

◆ The data that is retrieved from the disk has the shortest queue, seek, and rotational delays.

◆ The data can be accessed from multiple disks in parallel to the read operations.

The redundancy feature of RAID level 1 makes it the most reliable and fault-tolerant setup for data recovery in case of the failure of a disk. In such a situation, data can be retrieved from other operational disks, a process that is transparent to the end user. On the other hand, the high level of data redundancy makes RAID level 1 the most expensive implementation for data recovery after disasters. The most suitable environment for the implementation of RAID level 1 is database applications that emphasize data accessibility and reliability.

RAID Level 2

RAID level 2 requires special disk features and is, therefore, an expensive and rarely implemented level for data recovery. In this level of RAID, the data from a file or database is infused across multiple disks of the array. The parity information and error-detecting code needed for the identification of a disk failure or the part of the disk with an error is stored in extra disks. The parity information and error-detection code are both created by using a *hamming* code. A hamming code is a binary code that adds three check bits at the end of every four data bits. The check bits serve as identifiers to detect and correct single- and double-bit transmission errors at the receiver end.

RAID level 2 is also a reliable and high-performance implementation but is regarded as an unfeasible solution for data recovery. This is because the storage of parity information and error detection code require an additional three disks for the four disks of the array, which increases the costs of implementation. In addition to this, the external error-control mechanism implemented in RAID level 2 solutions is obsolete and impractical compared to the in-built and internal error-control mechanism incorporated in disk drives today.

RAID Level 3

RAID level 3 was developed to overcome the disadvantages of RAID level 2 implementations. RAID level 3 uses a single parity disk to identify and recover data from failed array disks in contrast to the extra parity disks used in level 2. In this implementation, the data from files and databases are first interleaved byte by byte across multiple disk drives. Then the disk controller generates the parity byte from all the disks containing the data. The parity information is finally written and stored on a single but additional disk. The performance of RAID level 3 is lower than that of the other levels, which is attributable to the following reasons:

◆ RAID level 3 allows processing of a single request (either a read or write) at a time. This is due to the fact that a read request requires access to all the data disks of the array. However, a write request requires support from both the data disks of the array and the parity disk. As a result, at a given time only one request can be processed. The parity disk is not involved with any writing procedures because it does not contain any data.

◆ During error detection, RAID level 3 does not have access to information regarding the exact disk containing the error. As a result, although RAID level 3 facilitates the detection of disk errors, it is unable to correct these errors.

Despite these disadvantages, RAID level 3 is a popular choice for implementation in applications that demand high bandwidth and large volumes of data transfers and not on high data transfer rates. RAID level 3 offers high redundancy in case of data failures and is easier to implement. The cost for implementation is also lower than that for the mirroring or interleaving methods used in levels 1 and 2. RAID level 3 is, therefore, best suited for the transfer of large graphics and image files.

RAID Level 4

RAID level 4 is very similar to level 3, except for the following:

◆ RAID level 4 interleaves data in the form of blocks in contrast to the method of byte interleaving that is employed for RAID level 3 implementations. The interleaved blocks, called *stripping units*, are interleaved across multiple disks of the array.

◆ RAID level 4 also permits independent access of the member disks arrays, a feature that is unavailable in RAID level 3.

Small read requests in RAID level 4 are restricted to a single disk of the array. The read operations are, therefore, very fast. Even the minutest of write requests, however, requires a minimum number of four disks and are referred to as *read-modify-write* procedures. The four operations executed during a read-modify-write procedure are

◆ Reading old data

◆ Reading old parity information

◆ Writing new data to the destination disk(s)

◆ Writing new parity information to the parity disk

NOTE

Read requests whose size is smaller than stripping units are known as *small read requests.*

Despite providing higher performance and redundancy than what is offered by RAID level 3, level 4 has a few disadvantages. The parity disk needs to be updated at the end of every write operation, which at times causes performance bottleneck situations in write-intensive applications. As a result, RAID level 4 is mostly implemented in combination with other complementary technologies such as write back cache.

RAID Level 5

The implementation of RAID level 5 offers improved performance over RAID level 4. The data in RAID level 5 is interleaved as blocks across some or all the disks of the array. There is no parity disk in the RAID level 5 setup. The parity information in RAID level 4 is written on to an extra disk. However, in the case of level 5, the parity information is written on to the next available disk. The advantages of using RAID level 5 are as follows:

◆ The read and write operations run concurrently in RAID level 5. This results in the enhanced performance that is better than any other RAID level.

◆ The parity information is stored in one of the multiple disks of the array. The need for an additional disk is thus eliminated, which reduces the cost of implementation.

◆ The performance bottleneck situations are also tackled by distributing the parity information across multiple disks.

The advantages of RAID level 5 provide excellent read and write performances. The small requests, however, demonstrate slower performance. This is because the read-modify-write procedures need to be performed before updating the parity information in the array disk. The update cycles are long and result in longer write operations. RAID level 5 is, therefore, implemented in combination with other augmenting technologies, such as parallel processing and caching.

RAID Level 6

RAID level 6 includes all the features of RAID level 5 but includes many more enhancements. Like RAID level 5, level 6 also strips blocks of data and parity across an array of drives. But in addition to this, RAID level 6 evaluates two sets of parity information for each block of data. The replication of data in this manner helps to improve fault tolerance. This level can manage the failure of any two drives in the array, as compared to other single RAID levels that can handle, at most, one.

RAID level 6 is slightly worse when compared to level 5 in terms of writing data due to the added overheads of more parity evaluations. However, it is faster in random reads because it spreads data over one more disk.

Theoretically speaking, RAID level 6 is suitable for the same kinds of applications as level 5 but under conditions in which more fault tolerance is required. Practically, level 6 is not popular among organizations because they are not ready to pay the extra cost for a benefit that may be reaped only in a rare event—it is a rare event for two drives to fail at the same time. In addition, the advanced features of level 5, such as hot swapping and automatic rebuild, have made the existence of level 6 less relevant.

RAID Level 10

RAID level 10 includes all features of RAID level 1 and RAID level 0.

Table 10.1 offers a glimpse of the six RAID levels that can be used as a quick comparative guide for studying this technology.

Table 10.1 Features of the Six RAID Levels

RAID Level	Method Used	Capacity	Advantages	Disadvantages
0	Stripping	NxC	High data transfer rates and file sizes	Nonredundant mechanism
1	Mirroring	(N/2)xC	High performance and faster write operations	Implementation is costly
2	Hamming and code parity	(N-1)xC	High redundancy and data availability	Unfeasible
3	Byte-level parity	(N-1)xC	Simple implementation with high error recover-ability	Low performance
4	Block-level parity	(N-1)xC	High redundancy and better performance	Write-related performance bottlenecks
5	Interleave parity	(N-1)xC	High performance, cost-effective, reduces write-related bottleneck situations	Low performance in the case of small-sized write operations
6	Two-level interleave parity	(N-2)/N	Fault tolerant, degradation and rebuilding, random read performance, random write performance	

Another commonly used mechanism for parallel storage of data is called *backups*. Backups can be looked at as a utility used to increase the reliability and availability of system data.

Backup Technology

Disk failures, power outages, and virus attacks are some of the most common causes of data loss and damage. Storage of up-to-date copies of system data in the form of regular backups of servers and local hard disks ensures availability of data at all times. Backup operations require careful planning and support equipment to ensure that data is easily and economically recovered after a disaster. Backups can be of the following types:

◆ **Normal backup**. All selected files are copied and marked for identification so that you know the exact status of the backups at any time. The most recent copy of the backup file is sufficient to restore all the files.

◆ **Incremental backup**. Only files created or modified since the last normal or incremental backups are copied. The files are marked for identification. A combination of normal and incremental backups require the last normal and incremental backup set to restore the data.

◆ **Differential backup**. Only files created or modified since the last normal or incremental backups are copied. However, these files are not marked for identification. A combination of normal and incremental backups require the last normal and differential backup set to restore the data.

◆ **Copy backup**. All selected files are copied but not marked for identification. This type of backup does not affect other backup operations and is, therefore, used between normal and incremental backups.

◆ **Daily backup**. In a daily backup, all selected files modified on the day of the daily backup are copied. As with the previous backup files, daily backup files are not marked for identification.

 NOTE

Regular backups are preferred when only a few people are using the network. The backup is not reflected accurately if many files are in use.

Selecting the Backup Type

The following factors should be considered while choosing the appropriate type of backup:

◆ Normal backups should be chosen when the volume of the data modifications between backups is large. Normal backups can also be used to provide baselines for other types of backups.

◆ Incremental backups are best suited for recording the progression of frequently changing data.

◆ Differential backups can be used to simplify the process of file restoration.

◆ A combination of normal and incremental or differential backups can provide long-term data storage in a small number of media.

Most of the backups provide markings for the identification of previous backups. Backup markers are also known as *archive attributes* and are used to track the last date of a file backup. Any modifications made to a file leads to its marking for a re-backup. Table 10.2 lists the advantages and disadvantages of various types of backups.

Table 10.2 Advantages and Disadvantages of Various Backup Types

Backup Type	Advantages	Disadvantages
Normal	(i) Files are always present on a current backup of the system or media and are, therefore, easy to find. (ii) Recovery of files requires only one set of storage media.	(i) Backups are redundant if files do not change frequently. (ii) Normal backups are time-consuming.
Incremental	(i) Space required for data storage is much less. (ii) Least time-consuming	(i) Files are stored on several media and are, therefore, difficult to find.
Differential	(i) Only the last normal and differential backup media are required for data recovery. (ii) Less time-consuming compared to normal backups.	(i) If the files are on a single medium, recovery takes a long time. (ii) Backups are time-consuming if large amounts of data change daily.

Selecting the Storage Device and Medium

Files can be copied onto a variety of storage devices, such as tape drives and disk drives. Data can also be copied to a logical drive, a removable disk, a disk library, or a network share. Files copied to tape drives are organized into a media pool and controlled by a robotic changer. In the absence of a separate storage device, files can be copied to another hard disk or a floppy disk.

An ideal storage device should have the capacity to backup your largest server. It should provide error detection and correction during backup and restoration operations. Technology is changing with the passage of time, and storage technology is no exception. As a result, it is important to constantly monitor the merits of various storage devices available in the market before deciding on the appropriate device.

The most commonly used storage medium is the magnetic tape. The primary tape drives used for backups include a quarter-inch cartridge (QIC), a digital audio tape (DAT), an 8mm cassette, and a digital linear tape (DLT). All high-capacity and high-performance tape drives use SCSI controllers. Magnetic disks, CD-ROMs (both CD-R and CD-RW), and optical disks can also be used as storage media for file backups.

Remote Storage Considerations

A single media drive can be shared across a network. As a result, you can also copy data onto a remote computer. Remote backup facilitates migration of infrequently used data and should not be confused with or used as a substitute for primary backup media. Crucial, busy, and frequently changing data should not be stored in remote locations.

Remote storage can be looked at as a mechanism to enhance system usability by ensuring a steady supply of free space on the file servers. The segregation of less frequently used data also reduces the load on backup procedures.

Administrators prefer to maintain copies of the remote storage medium to ensure availability of data in the event of storage media failures. Additional copies of the remote storage can also be used to rotate media to off-site storages so that it is available to multiple administrators. The Remote Storage Snap-In is used to identify the status of a media copy. The status detail can be used to process requests for new copies. Media copies should always be a part of normal backup procedures.

Backup Scheduling

The frequency of backups is directly dependant on how frequently data changes and the value of that data. As a result, a setup with frequently changing data will require frequent backups. Similarly, data for all critical business activities will need backups more often. Depending on organizational requirements, backups can be scheduled weekly, monthly, or be just a simple archival of all data files.

12-Week Backup Schedule

The 12-week backup schedule uses a different tape each day for a period of two weeks. The first tape is used again at the beginning of the third week. The cycle continues and data crucial to organizational operations is copied at weekly intervals.

Incremental backups are performed from Monday to Thursday, while normal backups are performed on Fridays. The most recent normal backup is stored on site, while the normal backup of the previous week is stored off site. The cycle is reinitiated at the end of 12 weeks with a new set of tapes.

12-Month Backup Schedule

The 12-month backup schedule uses 19 tapes over a period of a year to copy and store data files. Of these tapes, four are used from Monday to Thursday for incremental backups, and three tapes are used for normal backups on Fridays. The remaining 12 tapes are used for monthly normal backups and are stored off site.

Backup Strategies

Data recovery is guaranteed if proper backup strategies are implemented. A good backup strategy assures data recovery and is the best defense against loss of crucial data. There are three common backup strategies implemented for any computer system. Each of these strategies are determined by the following considerations:

- ◆ **Network or server backup only**. This strategy is implemented if you need to back up your entire network or have storage devices attached to certain servers where users copy their important files.
- ◆ **Individual or local computer backup**. This strategy is implemented if each computer needs a storage device or when each user is responsible for backups of his or her data.

◆ **Server and computer backup.** This strategy is implemented if each department of an organization has a storage device and one of the department's personnel is designated for taking backups of the entire department's data.

Table 10.3 lists the advantages and disadvantages of server-only and local computer backups.

Table 10.3 Advantages and Disadvantages of Server-Only and Local Computer Backups

Backup Type	Advantages	Disadvantages
Server-only	(i) Need for fewer storage devices (ii) The shared media stores multiple backups due to which there is less media to manage. (iii) The cost of server-only backup is less than that of individual computers only if each server has more than one client computer.	(i) There is no backup of registries and event logs of remote computers (ii) The network throughput leads to slow restorations and backups. (iii) Backups and restorations need to be scheduled so that they are performed when network traffic is low or when critical data can be backed up quickly.
Local computer	(i) Fewer network resources are dedicated to lengthy backup procedures. (ii) File recovery is quicker.	(i) Use of more storage devices adds to the costs.

 NOTE

Backups protect data from virus attacks. However, considering that some viruses take weeks to become visible, it is advisable to maintain backup tapes for at least a month. This will help you to restore a system to its uninfected state in the face of a virus attack.

Backup Scenarios

Backup strategies need to consider system configurations before implementation. System configurations range from a simple, small network requiring backups for small amounts of data to a network that extends to a large area requiring backups for huge volumes of data. Let's consider the backup strategies for each of these network scenarios.

Small and Medium LAN Backups

The following four steps illustrate an approach that can be adopted for working out a backup solution for a small LAN:

1. Select a reliable, fast, high-capacity, cost-effective, and compatible tape drive for system backups. The capacity of the tape cartridges should be enough to backup the entire server.

2. Install the tape controller card in the server. When using SCSI, you'll need to install the tape drive on its own controller.

3. To ensure efficient backups of the system state data, connect the tape drive to the server. You can also backup user files from the server to remote computers.

4. Maintain a tape circulation schedule to conserve tapes that back up less frequently used data. Encourage users to get into the habit of copying critical data to the server at the end of the day.

Large or 24-Hour Operation Backups

Backing up large volumes of data, such as databases or graphics files, is a time-consuming process. As a result, the approach used for small and medium backups proves inadequate and inefficient for larger backups. It is, therefore, a good practice to use a backup utility to copy data while the application is available to the clients.

Backups of critical data can use the host-based or hardware-based redundancy arrays of RAID. A software mirror of two independent hardware-controlled RAID arrays can be used for backing up extremely critical data. The implementation of this technique ensures that there is no operational failure in the event of a disk or array failure. A failure in network components such as an adapter, video device, IDE adapter, or power failures can be easily replaced without affecting any operations. The two terms that are frequently used with backups are *Data* and *Target*. Data represents a computer containing the data to be backed up. Target represents the computer that runs the backup. The following three methods are used for backing up large volumes of data:

- ◆ Method one: backup Data locally to disk
- ◆ Method two: backup Data over the network to Target

◆ Method three: backup Data by using hardware mirroring and third-party utilities

Method One

Network backups of Xcopy can be used to move the resulting backup file to the Target. The backup contents of the Target and Data should be compared regularly to verify consistency of their contents. The transfer time for a backup can be estimated by using the data transfer rate and the total amount of transferred data.

Method Two

Backup data can be copied to another disk or disks on Data. To do this, bring the Data online and copy it using a backup device connected to Data. Data can also be copied over the network to Target. The use of Data or Target for the backup depends on the following factors:

◆ The availability of the target computer.

◆ The presence of backup policies that require backups to be performed on predetermined computers.

◆ The time and cost of a backup from Data as compared to the transfer of files to Target.

Method Three

Backup data can be mirrored across the network to another computer while the files are being used on Data. This method is best used when you cannot afford to lose data due to disk or array failures. The process of transferring data from the mirror computer to Data after a failure on Data is time-consuming, but it is preferable to losing all created and modified data since the last backup.

The previous sections have discussed in depth the various mechanisms for ensuring data accessibility in the wake of disasters. I'll now discuss the various factors that go into designing and formulating the backup and restoration procedures.

Backup and Restoration Procedures

The choice of backup and restoration procedures varies from organization to organization. At the end of developing appropriate backup and restoration procedures, you'll need to test, document, and verify their impact in the face of a disaster. The following considerations (in the form of checklists, questions, and suggestions) can help to derive an appropriate backup and restoration procedure for an organization:

- Delegation of tasks
- Formulating time-sensitive backups
- Tasks to be undertaken in the event of a backup problem
- Security considerations
- Policy considerations
- Technical considerations
- Testing backup and restoration procedures
- Documenting backup and restoration procedures
- Verification operations

Delegation of Tasks

It is advisable to entrust responsible personnel with backup and restoration procedures in the organization. The following questions can help in delegating these tasks:

- Who drafts the policies to decide which files and computers are backed up? How is the policy made available to others within an organization?
- Who is responsible for the backups?
- If backups are automated, who handles disruptions to the backups?
- Who is responsible for backups in the absence of designated personnel?
- Who is the reporting authority for backup success or failure? Who notifies users about a backup failure?

Formulating Time-Sensitive Backups

The time required for the retrieval and restoration of data after a disaster is as important as determining backup duration and frequency. The following questions can help in determining the duration of restoration procedures:

- Do total and partial backups occur at the end of business hours?
- When should the backups be undertaken? Should they be before or after business hours?

- What is the frequency of full and incremental backups?
- What is the duration of backups and retrievals from a local storage area? Are remote storage copies accessible at any time during normal business hours?
- What is the duration of a full restoration process in the face of computer failures?

Tasks to Be Undertaken in the Event of a Backup Problem

The following issues should be considered before the occurrence of a backup failure:

- Determine the reporting authority and the deployed process in the event of a failure.
- Take into consideration the availability of standby hardware sites or the loaning of such sites from a vendor in the case of hardware failures. Determine the time needed for replacement of failed hardware.
- Determine the availability of technical support to tide over software and hardware failures.
- Determine if computer configuration information is available to the technical support staff. If not, ensure information availability to eliminate chaos in the event of disasters.
- Determine the effect of software and hardware vendor support on the time taken for failure fixes.
- How are shifts maintained for backup personnel if the organization has overnight duty? Are overnight personnel expected to work the next day after overnight duty? Determine the personnel to take the place of trained staff during troubleshooting or restoration procedures.

Security Considerations

The following questions should be considered to ensure the security of backup operations and locations:

- Where are the backup tapes stored?
- How is the backup location made secure from natural disasters?

- What are the methods used to monitor the activities of the backup location?
- Are the on-site backup tapes accessible to the concerned personnel?
- Where are copies of the backup media stored?
- Is the backup location bonded?

Policy Considerations

The following issues should be kept in mind while developing the backup and restoration procedures:

- What is the organization's backup policy? Does the backup plan comply with the policies defined by the organization?
- Does the company policy call for the backup of all modified files or does it require backups of only critical files of certain users, groups, departments, or divisions?
- Are there any disks or volumes on computers that do not need backups?
- Are the end users responsible for the backups of their own systems?
- Does the amount of storage work have a charge-back system?
- What are the validations performed on the backup process?

Technical Considerations

The following questions can help in determining the mode of backups for your organization:

- What are the conditions that need to be satisfied before starting backups?
- Is the backup initiated from the command prompt, icon, or by batch?
- Are the created logs in the appropriate format?
- Does the backup work in situations such as long paths, odd file names, large file sizes, or large number of files? Can files with these characteristics be restored without any problems?
- Is the backup taken on a local tape drive, done remotely over the network, or done remotely over the WAN?
- Do backups take place per schedules?
- Are any verifications done to ensure that the backed up data is correct?

Testing Backup and Restoration Procedures

It is important to check and verify backup and restoration procedures to estimate the time needed for data recovery. Testing also verifies the dependability of the plan and the resources used for backup and restoration. Any fallout during testing can be addressed and eliminated to ensure implementation of the right procedures for data backup and restoration.

Periodic trials of backups and restorations can uncover hardware problems that do not show up during software verifications. Organizations can also use simulations to test the designed procedures. For example, in the case of backups implemented by mirroring, disk failures can be simulated to check for the infallibility of operations. Simulations in this context can be implemented by removing or powering down one of the mirrors.

Documenting Backup and Restoration Procedures

Backup records should be stored systematically to eliminate the chance of lost information and also facilitate faster data retrieval and restoration. The following are a few methods used to document backup and restoration procedures:

◆ **Media labels**. Labels should contain information such as the date, type of backup, and list of contents that help locate specific backups.

◆ **Catalogs**. Backup files can be cataloged on the backup media and also stored temporarily for future reference.

◆ **Log files**. These consist of information about the names of the files and directories of the backup and restored files. Printed logs help to locate specific files for backup and restoration.

Verification Operations

During verification, the files on the disk are compared with the files on the backup media. This process is initiated at the end of the backup or restoration procedures. The duration of the verification is the same as that for the backup or restoration procedure. It is a good practice to verify the contents of the disk and backup or restored files after each procedure.

Summary

This chapter discussed the security countermeasures implemented for data recovery in the face of disasters. The chapter began by defining disasters and the importance of planning data recovery after a disaster. Next, the chapter discussed RAID as the mechanism to facilitate storage of redundant data on additional disks that can be used to restore and recover critical business activities in the face of a disaster. RAID, in a way, is a setup initiated by an organization to counter disaster. It works along the lines of the famous proverb, "An ounce of prevention is worth a pound of cure," more apt in the case of the ever-vulnerable networking and computing systems. Virus attacks and other disaster agents cannot be totally eradicated. However, an organization can prepare for adverse eventualities by using technologies such as RAID and backups. The chapter then moved on to discussing the backup mechanism implemented to regularly copy data on additional storage disks and media.

The need for planning data recovery in the event of disasters is a very important organizational decision. Entire business operations depend on data that is stored on the network. It is, therefore, important to secure and make the data available to an organization at all times.

Index

A

access control
  in Apache, 210–212
  for IIS (Internet Information Server),
    204, 208–209
  ITSEC (Information Technology
    Security Evaluation Criteria) stan-
    dards, 165
  in Linux, 195–196
  in Microsoft Windows 2000, 170–172
  for operating systems, 162
  threats, 38–39
access control list (ACL). *See also*
    Microsoft Windows 2000
  in Linux, 195
accidental threats, 26
account lockout policy for Microsoft
    Windows 2000, 183–184
accountability
  ITSEC (Information Technology
    Security Evaluation Criteria) stan-
    dards, 165
  of operating system, 162
accuracy standards, ITSEC (Information
    Technology Security Evaluation
    Criteria), 165
Active Directory service. *See* Microsoft
    Windows 2000
active spoofing, 98
ActiveX controls, 121, 147
  Authenticode protecting, 149–150

  digital signatures on files, 148–149
  ensuring security in, 148–154
  indirect commands in, 151
  Internet zone security level settings,
    changing, 154
  malicious code in, 151
  with medium security level, 118
  posing as secure control, 151
  proxy firewalls and, 304
  script viruses on, 49
  setting security policies, 151–154
  threats in, 150–151
  types of, 147–148
Address Resolution Protocol (ARP), 82, 83
Adelman, (inits), 246
Adobe Acrobat, 147
advertising in Reverse Social Engineering
    (RSE), 30
AFS (Andrew File System), 253
alert() method in JavaScript, 134
alert notification in IDS, 336
algorithm scanning, polymorphic viruses
    and, 51
algorithms. *See also* encryption algorithms
  Digital Signature Algorithm (DSA), 263
  message digest algorithms, 261
  in public key encryption, 239
AMANDA (Advanced Maryland
    Automatic Network Disk
    Archiver), 198
anomaly-detection technique, 330, 333–334
AntiSniff program, 344